Family Values

and the Rise of the Christian Right

POLITICS AND CULTURE IN MODERN AMERICA

Series Editors:
Margot Canaday, Glenda Gilmore, Michael Kazin,
Stephen Pitti, Thomas J. Sugrue

Volumes in the series narrate and analyze political and social change
in the broadest dimensions from 1865 to the present, including ideas
about the ways people have sought and wielded power in the public
sphere and the language and institutions of politics at all levels—local,
national, and transnational. The series is motivated by a desire to
reverse the fragmentation of modern U.S. history and to encourage
synthetic perspectives on social movements and the state, on gender,
race, and labor, and on intellectual history and popular culture.

Family Values

and the Rise of the Christian Right

Seth Dowland

PENN

UNIVERSITY OF PENNSYLVANIA PRESS

PHILADELPHIA

Published by
University of Pennsylvania Press
Philadelphia, Pennsylvania 19104-4112
www.upenn.edu/pennpress

Printed in the United States of America on acid-free paper
1 3 5 7 9 10 8 6 4 2

Library of Congress Cataloging-in-Publication Data
Dowland, Seth, 1979– author.
Family values and the rise of the Christian right / Seth
Dowland.
    pages   cm. — (Politics and culture in modern America)
Includes bibliographical references and index.
ISBN 978-0-8122-4760-2
1. Christian conservatism—United States—History—20th
century. 2. Christian conservatism—United States—Political
aspects—History—20th century. 3. United States—Politics and
government—20th century. 4. Sex role—Religious aspects—
Christianity. I. Title. II. Series: Politics and culture in modern
America.
BR526.D69   2015
261.70973'09045—dc23   2015007476

For Ami

CONTENTS

Introduction

On October 4, 1997, hundreds of thousands of people—mostly men—crowded the National Mall in Washington, D.C., to sing, pray, and make promises to change their lives. Beginning around noon, a series of evangelical Christian speakers took the podium on the steps in front of the Capitol. The speakers at the rally, sponsored by the evangelical men's organization Promise Keepers, encouraged men to confess their failures. These calls for repentance emerged from the group's insistence that "men have been irresponsible. Men have not stood strong for their convictions. Men have not been men of their word." According to Promise Keepers founder Bill McCartney, "The reason we see a downward spiral in morality in this nation is because the men of God have not stood together."[1] In response, these men pledged to "Stand in the Gap" between God and the world. Recalling a passage from the book of Ezekiel in which God calls for a man who would "stand in the gap before me for the land,"[2] Promise Keepers vowed that they would assume their biblical responsibilities to lead their families, honor their wives, and restore morality to the nation.

Critics cried foul. "The Promise Keepers speak about 'taking back America' for Christ, but they also mean to take back the rights of women," said Patricia Ireland, president of the National Organization for Women, "Their call for 'submission' of women is one that doesn't have a place in either the pulpit or the public sphere in the 1990s."[3] *The Nation* called the group "the third wave of the religious right."[4] Liberals charged that the "Stand in the Gap" march signaled Promise Keepers' unspoken theocratic agenda and viewed the rally as a recruiting platform for the Republican Party. It was not difficult to make that connection. Promise Keepers endorsed the "family values" rhetoric that had characterized evangelical conservatism for a couple decades. This rhetoric reflected a political agenda that ministers and conservative politicians deployed to attract conservative evangelicals. The gathering of nearly a million men on the National Mall recalled smaller rallies during the 1970s and 1980s in which evangelical Christian ministers urged their listeners to vote Republican.

Yet Promise Keepers insisted they had no political agenda, unspoken or otherwise. "Promise Keepers wants to make one thing perfectly clear," declared the organization magazine *New Man*. "The massive October gathering in Washington is not for politics or protest. It's a God thing."[5] Later in the same issue, Promise Keepers founder Bill McCartney said, "We don't have a political motive."[6] The Promise Keepers' disavowal of politics was telling. It reflected evangelicals' growing discomfort with the partisan tone of evangelical political action groups like the Moral Majority and Christian Coalition. "If this turns into the Christian Coalition," vowed one evangelical radio host, "I'm out of here." While Promise Keepers' decision to hold its largest rally on the National Mall created an unavoidable political veneer, leaders and members of the group did not embrace the partisan invective of earlier conservative evangelicals.

By 1997, they did not have to. At that point, "family values" rhetoric had pervaded white evangelical Christianity, drawing on theological resources to animate a vision for social renewal. This vision included opposition to abortion, gay rights, and major feminist objectives. It supported private Christian schools, home schooling, and a strong military. Conservative evangelicals believed these positions would sponsor the creation of strong families, which were essential to national greatness. The positions encompassed in "family values" coincided frequently with the agenda of the Republican Party, which increasingly saw white conservative evangelicals as a crucial bloc of support. The GOP accommodated the language of family values in its platforms and campaigns. To be sure, not all family values initiatives were explicitly partisan. Evangelicals campaigned for family values by creating private Christian academies, by establishing home schools, and by rallying men to return to the faith. But these initiatives existed alongside other movements—opposing abortion, feminism, and gay rights—that won endorsement from the Republican Party. The vision of family values created a bond between evangelicalism and political conservatism. The phrase was capacious enough to accommodate a variety of initiatives but specific enough to mark boundaries between conservative evangelicalism and broader society. The Promise Keepers' disavowal of political motives belied the deep connections between evangelicals and political conservatives. While not every evangelical (or even every Promise Keeper) voted

Republican, focusing on family values had become a hallmark of both evangelicalism and political conservatism.

These connections developed over time and depended on a sense that secular forces threatened the family. Evangelical leaders envisioned the family as the central unit of American society, and they framed their political activities throughout the 1970s, 1980s, and 1990s as a defense of the "traditional" family. In 1963, evangelist Billy Graham noted, "there are many stresses on family life and family life is the basic unit of society."[7] In strikingly similar language, Southern Baptist leader Morris Chapman echoed Graham's comments thirty-five years later. "There's such a rapid unraveling of family in society," said Chapman. "If the family is in fact destroyed we'll absolutely lose all hope in America. The fabric of America is the family unit."[8] By the end of the twentieth century, conservative evangelicals conceived of family values as central to the faith.

This book examines the history of how and why family values came to play such a prominent role in evangelical worldviews—and how these conservative Christians deployed the language of family values to transform American political culture. The social movements of the 1960s, including the sexual revolution, the civil rights movement, feminism, and gay rights, shattered conservatives' perception of a national consensus. The partial success of these social movements caused conservative white Americans to feel both disempowered and disillusioned. Liberals had won notable gains from the 1930s to the 1960s, including the enlargement of the welfare state, the advance of civil rights, almost unbroken control of the White House, and a series of Supreme Court decision that struck against both segregation and Protestant Christian moral control. In the early 1970s, white conservatives surveyed the American landscape and saw economic crises, spiraling crime, urban riots, and endless wars—both hot and cold. They determined that the nation had gone off the track. In particular, conservatives sensed that liberals had undermined traditional values. This climate was ripe for a politics that celebrated a nostalgic ideal of the home.[9] As a result, politicians on both sides of the aisle increased their calls for a return to family values. Though liberals agitated for broader conceptions of family life, conservatives succeeded in defining the ideal family in American political discourse. This ideal family featured a breadwinning father, stay-at-home mother, and well-tended children. Such an ideal resonated with evangelicals, as it spoke to two key beliefs: gender roles are God-given destinies, and lines of authority matter. In a rapidly fragmenting culture, evangelicals gravitated to the family values ideal and made it the most potent force in late-twentieth century American politics.

A History of Family Values Politics

Family values rhetoric achieved its greatest prominence in the 1970s, 1980s, and 1990s, but the roots of this development stretched back several decades. During the 1910s and 1920s, conservative Protestants campaigned for Prohibition and against the perils of evolution and Catholicism. They tied these campaigns together by articulating how "the family was the key to saving the republic."[10] Families shielded children from "antireligious" ideas like evolution. Alcohol undermined the family by causing husbands to squander their paychecks on drink and bring boorishness home. Catholicism upended Protestant familial norms with its celibacy requirements for priests and nuns. Early twentieth-century evangelicals took aim at different targets from the late twentieth-century evangelicals discussed in this book, but the conservative evangelicals of the 1910s and 1920s laid the groundwork for the family values coalitions of the 1970s and 1980s.

Concern for family values intensified in the 1950s. The baby boom in 1946–1964 saw a dramatic increase in marriage rates and childbearing, accompanied by a temporary dip in the divorce rate. These demographic trends caused an increasing proportion of Americans to care about family life. Furthermore, the Cold War—and the threat posed to Americans by Soviet communism—forced Americans to craft a more coherent articulation of the "American way of life." The American way of life emphasized the triumph of capitalism but was best epitomized by the nuclear family, which lived amid abundance in rapidly growing suburbs. These families showed that American capitalism offered the best standard of living on the globe. They also provided a sense of security and containment in a world wracked by anxiety and insecurity.[11] During the early Cold War, conservative evangelicals contributed to the growing consensus that American strength lay in its commitment to families. In the fifteen years following World War II, millions of American joined churches and started families. Many sensed that these activities went hand in hand with preserving the American way of life.

The social revolutions of the 1960s shattered the illusion that Americans were united behind Cold War family values. Parents of baby boomers saw procreation as a "defense—an impregnable bulwark" against the growth of the Communist menace.[12] When the Food and Drug Administration approved an oral contraceptive in 1960, then, not all Americans perceived the decision as a simple matter of giving women access to birth control. While Protestants mostly endorsed "the Pill," they worried about its use among unmarried women and deplored the sexual revolution the Pill helped launch.[13] Similarly, gays and lesbians came in for censure not only because of their "immorality," but also because they "selfishly" removed themselves from the duty of creating families. When the gay rights movement took off after 1969, conservatives who defended family values decried what they perceived as an assault on American values.

The civil rights movement posed a different sort of challenge. Although many African American activists shared the "family values" of white conservatives—the civil rights movement drew leaders and supporters from socially conservative black churches—almost no African Americans lived in the booming suburbs. Blacks owned a paltry amount of land and property in comparison to whites, and relatively few could afford the luxury of living on a single income. White suburbanites erected barriers that prevented African Americans from accessing the suburbs, including housing covenants, antibusing initiatives, and occasional literal roadblocks preventing transit between cities and their suburbs.[14] The civil rights movement came about in part because African Americans demanded equal access to the nation's growing wealth, much of it concentrated in the suburbs. The nonviolent activism of the civil rights movement spurred passage of major civil rights legislation in the mid-1960s, but for years afterward, suburban whites used "colorblind" measures to preserve the racial homogeneity of their enclaves. As civil rights activists grew frustrated with the slow pace of chance, more radical leaders emerged. The growth of the Black Panthers and the summer riots of the late 1960s demonstrated the depth of America's racial divide. The increasing violence and radicalism of the civil rights movement in the late 1960s exacerbated white fears about the movement's assault on decency and order.

Campus uprisings and increasing drug use further signaled a society in decline. Evangelicals perceived the unrest that rocked American colleges and universities in the late 1960s as proof that the nation had abandoned the values of earlier generations. Some conservative evangelicals blamed campus turmoil on excessive permissiveness. In particular, they blamed the prevalence of a gentle parenting philosophy championed by Benjamin Spock in his

1946 bestseller, *The Common Sense Book of Baby and Child Care*. These evangelicals found their champion in USC Medical School professor James Dobson, whose 1970 book *Dare to Discipline* rejected Spock's parenting advice and advocated for firmer discipline in traditional families. Other evangelicals blamed social mayhem on lack of moral regulation. "We're in the process of committing moral suicide," wrote *Christianity Today* editor Harold Lindsell. "We have fornication, adultery and lesbianism, homosexuality, wife-swapping, rape, sodomy, incest. . . . One out of every two marriages will end up in divorce. . . . The world is on fire."[15] Lindsell called for Christians to "occupy until He comes," meaning for evangelicals to combat the lawlessness and anarchy that was rocking American society. Like many other evangelicals, Lindsell thought a better future demanded returning to the values of the past. He asked evangelicals to stand up for traditional morality in political and social life.

The social revolutions of the 1960s, then, caused many white Americans to feel as though the nation had lost its moorings. Increasingly, politicians from both parties laid the blame for societal chaos on the failures of the American family. In 1965, Assistant Secretary of Labor Daniel Patrick Moynihan wrote *The Negro Family: The Case for National Action*. The report's most famous line declared that African American men were caught in a "tangle of pathology." Moynihan ascribed the breakdown of urban centers to the decline in responsibility among African American men. Though he lamented racial prejudice and outlined the historical reasons for black poverty, Moynihan believed African Americans needed to reverse the trend of black women assuming the economic responsibilities for raising children. Commentators drew on Moynihan's problematic logic—which omitted factors that were causing women of all races to assume more economic burdens in the 1960s—to describe the breakdown in black families. When riots broke out in Los Angeles a few short weeks after Moynihan's report appeared, columnists had an easy explanation for what had happened: black youth who did not know their fathers and spent little time with their mothers had embraced violence over values.[16]

The 1960s also caused white evangelicals to fret about increasing degeneracy in their own ranks. Baptist minister Jerry Falwell's 1965 sermon "Ministers and Marches" infamously condemned civil rights activism as incompatible with the gospel. But it also revealed the types of concerns typical of many white evangelicals at the time. "Very little is said about alcoholism," wrote Falwell. After also censuring tobacco use, gambling, theological liberalism, and dancing among Christians, Falwell asked, "Why is there not a display of concern about the lowering of moral standards among our young people?"[17] Conservative evangelicals like Falwell looked around their churches and communities in the late 1960s and saw a grim picture. Traditional authority structures had come under attack. In 1962 and 1963, the U.S. Supreme Court had ruled devotional bible reading and mandatory prayer in schools unconstitutional. The hippie movement and sexual revolution challenged moral norms. These transformations illustrated to evangelicals just how fragile the 1950s consensus was. "No one would deny that our world is undergoing a time of unusual turmoil," wrote one. "Rising crime rates, increasing use of narcotics and hallucinogenic agents, pornography and lawlessness are all evidences of a moral breakdown which is frightening in its extent."[18] Where liberals saw social movements of the 1960s as catalysts of social justice, conservatives saw them as incubators of societal breakdown. Increasingly, they blamed growing immorality on liberal changes to society that undermined traditional families. Over the course of the 1970s, evangelical leaders and conservative politicians increased their call for the nation to return to family values.

This call for family values both emanated from racial fears and set in motion a shift within white evangelicalism that would eventually reshape not only conservative Protestantism but also politics in the U.S. and abroad. As the civil rights coalition fractured and radicalized in the late 1960s, Republican politicians—most notably Richard Nixon—concocted a "politics of decency" that called for law and order and made coded appeals to white voters.[19] Family values, at least initially, operated similarly. It hearkened for a past where racial lines were clear. More insidious, it imagined a family structure that excluded most racial minorities, who rarely had the luxury of living on a single income. The stay-at-home mother became one of the most prominent tropes of family values, and women who embodied that ideal—Phyllis Schlafly, Beverly LaHaye, and Vicki Frost, among others—were celebrated, even if they ventured far outside the home in defense of their right to stay within it. African Americans who heard white conservatives celebrating stay-at-home moms and denigrating welfare queens had little doubt about the implicit meaning of family values.

While family values politics had significant racial implications, family values rhetoric became such an important part of American political discourse that nonwhites did not reject the phrase. In the 2008 presidential campaign, Barack and Michelle Obama promoted their commendable family and talked about family values in terms that would have made Jerry Falwell smile. New Latino immigrants celebrated their commitment to family and collaborated with white conservatives on anti-homosexual ballot measures. Family values went interfaith and international: in 2013, the president of Kazakhstan said that family values were central to Islam.[20] The popularity of family values appears unlikely to wane in the near future, even as its meaning becomes increasingly contested. Because conservative white evangelicals talked loudest and earliest about family values, they won the right to define the concept in the 1970s, 1980s, and 1990s. The following chapters illustrate the ways evangelicals won those battles.

What Family Values Meant to Evangelicals

Evangelicals have long held substantive concerns about the state of American society, and they felt a mandate to guard against declining morality. In the 1970s, conservative white evangelicals worried that the turmoil of the 1960s had eroded traditional sexual norms, weakened America's defense against communism, and promoted a humanist ideology that demeaned Christianity. Near the end of the decade, conservative evangelical leaders increasingly blamed these developments on the demise of the "traditional family." Without strong families, the reasoning went, America was slowly losing its moral compass. These leaders determined to protect the family at all costs.

But evangelical Christians were not the only Americans concerned about the family in the 1970s. Scores of politicians on both sides of the aisle wondered about the role of families in the success of the nation. After decades of building a national welfare state, Americans wondered how the promise of the "Great Society" might be achieved. Increasingly, politicians suggested that the answer to the nation's ills lay in strengthening its families. Moynihan's 1965 report became something Moynihan himself never intended, as conservative writers like James Kilpatrick and Robert Novak cited the report to blame urban violence solely on the "pathology" of black families. Using the report this way ignored Moynihan's focus on the history of slavery and segregation that had caused economic inequality. But one of Moynihan's central assumptions caused relatively little controversy: few commentators on either side doubted that the national policy-makers should support the strengthening of the family.

This agreement—that the family was an appropriate concern of legislators—belied disagreements about the proper structure of the family it-self. The United States has never featured uniform family structures. Histo-rian Stephanie Coontz has called our vision of a breadwinning father, stay-at-home mother, and children who enjoyed a lengthy and protected childhood "the elusive traditional family," highlighting the relative scarcity of this particular family structure in American history. Over the last four centu-ries, Americans have lived in single-parent homes, multigenerational homes, homes with two working parents, orphanages, and countless other familial arrangements. Colonial Americans endorsed patriarchy, while nineteenth-century Victorians encouraged mothers to invest their energies in children. "Traditional" families often relied on domestic help, and for much of Ameri-can history the relationship between husband and wife was stilted and for-mal. Many of the assumptions modern Americans make about the traditional family contain a mixture of ingredients that have not existed as ideals simul-taneously at any point until the very recent past.[21]

Yet ideology trumped reality in the realm of family values. From the late 1960s to the late 1990s, conservatives succeeded in defining traditional fami-lies in national political discourse. The encouragement of families with a breadwinning father, stay-at-home mother, and well-tended children became a major goal of national policymakers. According to historian Robert Self, family values displaced equal rights as the "driving force of American poli-tics" during this period. Politicians on both sides of the aisle promoted legis-lation by using the rhetoric of breadwinner conservatism, which called for a "return" to idealized family life. Whereas the breadwinner liberalism that had dominated American politics in 1932–1965 focused on carving out equal rights for all Americans, breadwinner conservatism subtly shifted the em-phasis from "rights" to "liberty." For instance, conservative politicians de-fended the traditional family against the regulatory apparatus that would strip families of their rightful authority.[22] Prominent liberal campaigns of the 1970s, including feminism, gay rights, and abortion rights, came under at-tack from conservatives, who defined each movement as an attack on liberty and family.

Protecting the family rose to the top of policymakers' agenda at the same time as a postindustrial economy was reshaping patterns of work and home life. American manufacturing jobs began their long decline in the late 1970s. After the postwar boom of the 1950s and 1960s, income growth weakened in the 1970s. These economic realities meant that more and more families de-pended on two incomes, and more and more of those incomes derived from service sector jobs. The ideology of family values ostensibly resisted these trends, as it called for a breadwinning husband to provide for his wife, who stayed home with her children. But looking closely at the rhetoric of family values crusaders shows how they accommodated the new shape of American economic life. Family values enjoined men to invest themselves in their wives and children, ensuring that they contributed to the emotional life of their families at a time when more and more wives were working. At the same time, family values stressed men's "headship," giving them titular authority in a world where the jobs that had once validated their masculinity were disappearing. Millions of conservative women applauded family values, as it encouraged their husbands to invest in home life and told them doing so showed true manliness.[23]

Women were the driving force of many family values campaigns discussed in this book, from crusades against textbooks to rallies against abortion rights to campaigns against the Equal Rights Amendment. Feminist leaders like Gloria Steinem and Bella Abzug could not fathom why women would support family values. To them, the conservative ideology seemed to demean women and deny them equality. But, as historians have shown us, "housewife populists" saw threats in different places than did feminists. Where feminists worried about income inequality and sexism, conservative women decried educational experts and psychologists who threatened their authority as mothers.[24] These "suburban warriors" emerged in places like Orange County, California, and Cobb County, Georgia, determined to roll back state-mandated reforms that would undermine family values.[25] For instance, Texan Norma Gabler launched a years-long crusade to rid school textbooks of liberal values, particularly those that challenged her understanding of morality and traditional values. In 1977, Southern Baptist singer Anita Bryant led a successful campaign against a referendum that would allow gays and lesbians to become teachers in Dade County, Florida. These and other family values women strayed far outside the home, but always on the premise of defending their homes. They used the rhetoric of family values to fight for their rights as wives and mothers.

Evangelicals played a key role in shifting the political battleground from "equal rights" to "family values." Rhetorically, the phrase family values appealed to a wide cross-section of voters (including many non-evangelicals). It portrayed a partisan agenda as a commonsensical response to liberals' "attack" on the family. It also resisted easy definition. Conservative politicians and ministers couched their criticism of almost everything they opposed—abortion, feminism, gay rights, nuclear disarmament, and high taxes—in the language of family values. The rhetorical link among these disparate initiatives was a focus on how specific policy measures would promote the traditional family.[26] If the family was key to national survival—something both Republicans and Democrats believed—then campaigns identified as "anti-family" faced an uphill climb. While Christian right was never the "disciplined, charging army" of liberal fears (the phrase comes from a 1981 *New Yorker* article about the Christian right), the emphasis on family values resonated throughout this loosely connected network.[27] It provided coherence for the Christian right.

The prominence of family values in the rhetoric and political activities of conservative Christians reveals two primary beliefs at the core of conservative evangelicalism. First, evangelicals believe that gender is a biological category—not a social construction, as feminists argued—and as such, gender provides identity and should stand at the center of social organization. Evangelicals rooted this belief in their reading of the biblical creation story, in which God created humans "male and female." Although the roles evangelicals assigned to men and women had more to do with nineteenth-century Victorian ideals than with the world of the ancient Mediterranean, evangelicals commonly described the gender norms they promoted as biblical. In evangelicals' perception, both popular culture and the government seemed determined to upset these "biblical" gender roles. Most notably, many evangelicals feared that feminists threatened to demean women's roles as mothers and homemakers. (There were, of course, a large number of evangelical feminists who celebrated the women's movement.) For the large subset of conservative Christian women who did not endorse feminist goals, campaigns against the Equal Rights Amendment and, later, legalized abortion became powerful ways to signal their disapproval. Likewise, the disproportionate attention evangelicals paid to gay rights suggested the centrality of proper gendered behavior in evangelicals' understanding of social order. The Promise Keepers movement, with its focus on strong men taking the lead in families and churches, signaled the importance evangelicals attached to masculinity. Because they understood gender as a fundamental marker of human identity, evangelicals focused much attention on how humans should embody their gendered roles.

Second, the evangelicals who formulated the family values vision insisted that lines of authority matter and must be observed in order for society to function well. The gendered order evangelicals prized emerged from deeper assumptions about authority. Just as God held power over creation, evangelicals believed a rightly ordered society featured clear lines of authority. They worried that liberals threatened to do away with authority structures that had provided stability for generations. Of course, these authority structures were often racial: white evangelicals long supported the status quo that put them in power over blacks. Few white evangelicals supported the civil rights movement, a failure that numerous historians have documented. What is less clear is how evangelicals' belief in authority animated their post-Civil Rights politics. As theological defenses of racial segregation became taboo, evangelicals increasingly focused on the ways liberals threatened the gendered order and authority structure of traditional families.[28] They worried that schools threatened to empower children at the expense of parental authority, and that feminists intended to demean motherhood in order to place women in men's natural roles. A robust sense of masculinity's importance led them to celebrate strong fathers. The traditional family became the exemplar of authority because of its gendered order. And evangelicals believed that what was good for the family was good for the nation. As such, they championed institutions and agendas that promised to check liberals' assaults on family values and return men and women to their God-given roles.

These two beliefs—in the centrality of gender and in the importance of authority—animated the concept of family values for conservative Christians and enabled them to effect significant political change in a variety of institutions. The conservative evangelicals who supplied most of the support for the Christian right believed that the family was one of two institutions "ordained by God." (The other was the church.) During the 1970s, leaders of the Christian right centered their critique of post-1960s American society on the disintegration of the traditional family. Jerry Falwell's 1980 polemic *Listen, America!* articulated this social critique. "The strength and stability of families," he wrote, "determine the vitality and moral life of society."[29] It followed that any organization or ideology opposing the family threatened society. Over time, Christian right activists identified a wide range of issues—from schooling and marriage to abortion, gay rights, and the military—through which to articulate a positive vision of traditional gender roles. Families with a breadwinning father, stay-at-home mother, and well-scrubbed children became the antidote to nearly all America's ills. By privileging the gender roles and authority structures of the traditional family, conservative evangelicals believed they could arrest the liberal drift of the nation and stop its demise.

Family Values, Evangelical History, and Political Activism

Evangelicals' focus on family values has become such an integral part of Republican politics that journalists frequently equate evangelicalism with political conservatism, but careful study of evangelical history demands a more nuanced appraisal. Evangelicalism emerged as the dominant form of American Protestantism in the early nineteenth century, when widespread revivals, democratizing pressures, and the growth of Methodists and Baptists transformed the religious landscape of the United States. Evangelicals believed in the importance of individual conversion and in the ability of individuals to accept the offer of salvation and to read the Bible for themselves. This emphasis marked a shift from earlier Puritans and Anglicans, who stressed the authority of God and viewed believers as part of a community rather than as autonomous individuals. The philosophical and geographical characteristics of the new nation encouraged evangelical theology. Enlightenment ideas about individual rights, alongside the wide geographic dispersal of the new nation, created a situation where evangelicalism could thrive.

Evangelicals, however, retained Puritans and Anglicans' mandate for ensuring morality prevailed in society. Although they championed religious liberty, evangelicals never envisioned the United States as a secular society. Rather, they believed that religion (by which they meant Protestant Christianity) played an essential role in forming moral citizens essential to the survival of democracy. Furthermore, they saw religious institutions as critical safeguards against the amorality of the state and other nonreligious institutions. Nineteenth-century evangelicals thereby promoted both revival and social reform, seeking to save the lost and working to reform society. Reform movements championed by evangelicals included abolition, temperance, and the mission to convert slaves. Evangelicals also spearheaded the creation of a "Christian" defense of slavery as a way of saving lost (African) souls and "caring" for the less fortunate. Though evangelical leaders of these movements disagreed with one another about the proper ends of Christian social action, they shared an assumption that their faith commanded them to work for the improvement of society. They possessed a "custodial impulse" that compelled them to support social reforms throughout American history.[30]

This custodial impulse meant that evangelicals were always engaged with American politics. Popular narratives of twentieth-century evangelicalism have suggested that evangelicals retreated from politics after suffering humiliation during the 1925 Scopes trial, in which conservative evangelicals challenged the teaching of evolution in Tennessee public schools. News accounts of the trial, particularly those by acerbic *Baltimore Sun* columnist H. L. Mencken, portrayed evangelicals as backward and anti-intellectual. Midcentury Protestant liberals treated evangelicalism as a backwater, while political liberals saw conservatism as a discredited philosophy.[31] As a result, early accounts documenting evangelicals' "political awakening" in the 1980s typically exaggerated evangelicals' political quiescence after Scopes. Evangelicals never stopped working to enact their vision of a moral society. In fact, evangelicals passed more anti-evolution laws in the five years after the Scopes trial than they had in the decade prior to it.[32] Evangelicals provided some of the most popular attacks on communism during the 1950s; Oklahoma minister Billy James Hargis actually lost his license for religious broadcasting when the FCC deemed his anti-communist radio show too political. An emerging scholarly consensus suggests that while conservative evangelical politics reached a crescendo on the national level with the 1980 election of Ronald Reagan, the roots of evangelical political activism stretched back decades.[33]

Even so, evangelicals' theology predisposed them to be wary about political entanglements. Evangelical theology drew from at least three streams of American Christianity: a Baptist tradition that emphasized an individual's autonomy to claim salvation, a Wesleyan tradition that longed for the perfection of humanity, and a Reformed tradition that focused on God's authority over all creation. The belief that religion and politics should not mix emerged in part from a Baptist theological tradition steeped in notions of religious liberty and "soul competency." In the American colonies, Baptists often felt persecuted by the established churches: Puritans, Presbyterians, and Congregationalists. As a result, they united with surprising allies to advocate for religious liberty. The deist Thomas Jefferson wrote his famous line advocating a "wall of separation" between church and state in a letter to the Danbury (Massachusetts) Baptist Association, which, like Jefferson, worried about the power of established churches. Though Jefferson shared virtually no theological commitments with the Baptists, both believed religion needed to be separated from government. Moreover, Baptist theology tended toward an individualism that militated against political activism. According to Baptist theologian E. Y. Mullins, "All men have an equal right to direct access to God. . . . The [primary] religious relation is one between God and the individual person." As a result, Mullins declared that any "hindrances" that came in the way of that relationship—including "a system of political government or an authoritative church"—were systems of "spiritual or political tyranny."[34] Mullins' writings crystallized impulses that had colored Baptist theology for centuries. Baptists believed that the most important relationship was between an individual and God. Therefore, all social institutions (including the church and the government) were secondary. Mullins and other Baptists advocated religious liberty (a "free church in a free state," as he put it), which allowed believers to worship freely but did not encourage them to bend government to their whims. Owing to both pragmatic concerns about persecution and an individualistic theological tradition, Baptists denounced religious involvement in politics.

This posture put Baptists at odds with some Wesleyans and with the Reformed tradition. Though it is generally helpful to view evangelicalism as a coherent theological tradition, doing so obscures some tensions in the movement. Baptists, Wesleyans (like the Methodists), and Reformed churches (like the Presbyterians) vied for supremacy within evangelicalism. These were not wholly compatible traditions. Presbyterians did not share Baptists' individualism, nor were they as reticent to become involved in politics. The broader Reformed tradition to which Presbyterians belonged taught that the gospel should shape law, education, and government. Reformed thinkers have insisted that Christians redeem not only individual souls but the larger culture as well. As a result, evangelicals from the Reformed tradition tended to view Christians' involvement in politics more positively than did their Baptist counterparts—at least for most of the twentieth century.[35]

Masking some of these theological and denominational differences was essential to evangelicals' political success in the second half of the twentieth century. As they did with the phrase family values, conservative Protestants used the term evangelical (or, often, simply "Christian") to portray a narrow theological vision as a widely held belief. For instance, conservative evangelicals who schooled their children at home often purchased curricula informed by a particular strand of hyper-Reformed theology known as Christian Reconstructionism. Reconstructionists held a theocratic agenda that clashed with Baptist beliefs about separation of church and state. But their homeschool curricula muted the particularities of Reconstructionist theology and—more important to most homeschool parents—provided a "Christian" understanding of history, science, and literature that resonated with evangelicals concerned about the secularism of public education. Unlike the theological disputes that divided conservative Protestants in the early

twentieth century, the political collaboration of late twentieth-century evangelicals depended on eliding theological and denominational boundaries
that had once separated them.

As a result, some treatments of evangelical politics have assumed evangelicalism consisted of a monolithic bloc of believers, conservative in both
theology and politics. That understanding will not suffice. Instead, I propose
using a definition of evangelicals that attends to theological impulses and to
historical developments. As I use it in this book, evangelical denotes Protestant Christians who emphasized the importance of individual conversion,
the authority of the Bible, and the divine command to regulate morality in
society. These theological impulses characterized evangelicals throughout
the twentieth century. As evangelicalism evolved over the twentieth century,
however, it became sharper in its engagement with culture, using family values politics to soften theological divides and attract additional supporters. As
a result, late twentieth century evangelicals had become more prominent
players in partisan politics than their early twentieth-century predecessors. A
"trans-denominational populism" increasingly characterized American
evangelicalism, contributing over time to the erosion of theological, denominational, and regional boundaries that used to divide American
Protestants.[36]

While evangelicals shared theological impulses, they were not uniformly
conservative. For instance, some evangelicals believed their understanding of
Jesus and their reading of the Bible commanded them to champion liberal
causes such as civil rights, the war on poverty, the antiwar movement, and
feminism. These evangelicals voiced their view of Christian political engagement in the 1973 "Chicago Declaration of Evangelical Social Concern."
Drafted at a conference over Thanksgiving weekend, the declaration spoke
out against racism, hunger, militarism, and materialism. It argued that Christians ought to focus their political energies against these evils, and it explicitly connected evangelicalism to liberal politics.[37] The group Evangelicals for
Social Action emerged from the Chicago meeting, joining the group Sojourners as a home for theologically conservative Protestants who championed liberal political campaigns. Since 2005, when liberal evangelical leader
Jim Wallis published God's Politics, liberal evangelicals have won increasing
amounts attention from the national media. Journalists long accustomed to
reflexively associating evangelicalism with conservative Republicans have
treated this other side of evangelicalism with fascination and curiosity.

The curiosity comes naturally, because a majority of white evangelicals have supported the Christian right. The Christian right encompasses leaders, institutions, and lay Christians who supported conservative social and political campaigns. The conservative politicians and ministers who led the Christian right—men and women like Jerry Falwell, Phyllis Schlafly, Tim LaHaye, James Dobson, Anita Bryant, Richard Viguerie, and Francis Schaeffer—believed God and scripture endorsed an essentially conservative politics. During the cultural revolutions of the 1960s, the urgency of holding onto—conserving—traditional values took on increased importance. Believing themselves custodians of morality, evangelicals worried that the sexual revolution, civil rights movement, second-wave feminism, and gay rights movement signaled a society in collapse. In the late 1970s, Christian right leaders crafted a message that spoke to rank-and-file evangelicals' concerns about America. The message placed emphasis on preserving family values. It resonated in part because evangelicals had been involved in conservative politics for decades and in part because it connected ongoing grassroots movements—Christian schools, homeschooling, opposition to the ERA, and anti-abortion activism—to a broader family values agenda. The Christian right, then, is best understood as national coalition of conservative Christians (mostly evangelicals along with some Catholics and Mormons) who had participated in conservative social and political initiatives for decades before winning widespread attention during the 1980 presidential election. The family values agenda was a key factor in connecting the Christian right to the Republican Party and thereby elevating its national profile. Evangelicals flocked to the banner of the Christian right—not unanimously or uncritically—but in large enough numbers that journalists and scholars have rightly identified evangelicalism as a conservative movement. The custodial impulse and conservative values have predominated in American evangelicalism. The Christian right of the late twentieth century attracted broad evangelical support because it forwarded a vision of social and political action that resonated with the dominant strains of evangelical belief.

The most notable exception to this characterization of evangelicalism is African American Protestants. Attempting to understand evangelicalism without incorporating African Americans is a fool's errand. Scholars have shown how black Christians have deployed evangelical tendencies to read themselves into the scriptural narrative and to argue for political reforms redressing racial inequality. These scholars have also demonstrated the influence African Americans have had on the evolution of white evangelicalism, by calling out white evangelicals on the emptiness of their rhetoric about

Christian freedom.[38] Power structures that placed whites over blacks have encouraged the development of segregated religious congregations and have largely precluded interracial political collaboration. Accustomed to discrimination from white Christians, black Christians have typically opposed the dominant political party among white southern evangelicals, which has changed over time from Democrats to the GOP. As a result, African American Christians in the United States are frequently evangelical in theology and on the opposite side of the political divide from their white co-religionists.

And yet, the same socially conservative impulses that attracted white evangelicals to the family values agenda found a foothold among African American Christians. Notable black evangelicals like E. V. Hill left the Democratic Party in the late 1960s and 1970s, as they grew disillusioned with liberalism.[39] Leaders of the civil rights movement like Fannie Lou Hamer opposed abortion—or, as they put it, championed the civil rights of the unborn. Black congregations tended to regard homosexuality with greater skepticism than did white congregations. African American evangelicals voted Democratic, but they were not social liberals. The family values agenda spoke to deeply held beliefs among black evangelicals.[40]

They did not, however, join the Christian right in significant numbers. The Christian right was overwhelmingly white. The whiteness of the movement derived from several related factors. First, the racial homogeneity of evangelical churches encouraged networks to form within (rather than across) racial boundaries. Second, some key planks of the family values agenda assumed middle-class economic status. Sending a child to a Christian school required money; homeschooling required mothers to forsake paid labor. In a nation where racial oppression had created huge economic inequalities favoring whites, these economic choices were unavailable to most African Americans. Third, the white southern evangelicals who supported Christian right initiatives frequently had opposed civil rights activism as well. Jerry Falwell typified white southern Christians when he preached against the civil rights movement in 1965, arguing that the gospel was about saving souls rather than effecting political transformation. Fifteen years later, however, Falwell had become the most visible leader of an explicitly politicized evangelicalism. His "political awakening" struck many black Christians as insincere, and they viewed the Christian right as a thinly disguised white response to the civil rights movement.

This book examines the factors that led to the Christian right's racial homogeneity, even as it stresses the importance of family values. The rhetorical prominence of "family values" in the movement testifies to the difficulty of assessing the racial politics of the Christian right. "Family values" resists easy definition. Liberal critics of the Christian right have complained for years that caring for poor children and single mothers should be seen as championing family values. But the conservative evangelicals at the center of this story defined family values differently. By "family" evangelicals meant two heterosexual parents and their children, preferably with the husband as breadwinner and the wife as stay-at-home mother. The racial salience of this definition is implicit. White evangelicals could read it as a "colorblind" defense of traditional values even as African Americans saw it as a product of white privilege. While some black evangelicals championed family values, many more saw that rhetoric as yet another means of reifying white power structures.

Children, Mothers, Fathers

The malleability of "family values" facilitated its rise to prominence among conservative evangelicals. This book tells the story of that rise. To do so, I aim to make sense of how the Christian right responded to the liberal reforms of the 1960s and 1970s with a family values agenda that was grounded in and resonated with evangelical theology. I also show how family values became central to evangelical rhetoric in the 1980s and 1990s. This book, in short, narrates the theological origins and political evolution of the family values agenda.

I have organized this book into three sections: children, mothers, and fathers—a structure that both follows a rough chronology and underlines how the "traditional family" animated the Christian right's political strategy. The earliest campaigns of the Christian right came in the area of education, where some evangelicals fostered the rapid growth of private Christian academies and others battled to retake control of public schools. I look at these educational issues in Part I, where the first three chapters examine Christian schools, battles over public school textbooks, and spread of homeschooling. These stories illuminate early uses of rhetoric and social networks that later animated the Christian right. In Part II, which comprises Chapters 4 and 5, I examine battles against the Equal Rights Amendment and legalized abortion. These fights appealed to evangelicals concerned about protecting motherhood and homemaking as the proper province of women. Subsequent campaigns for a strong military and against gay rights illustrate evangelicals' commitment to masculinity, which is the subject of Part III. Chapters 6, 7, and 8 detail political campaigns, theological arguments, and social movements devoted to promoting Christian masculinity. A commitment to family values threaded through all these campaigns and provided cohesiveness to an otherwise disparate group of evangelical activists.

Placing family values at the center of the Christian right upsets other narratives, including those that view the search for a "Christian America" as the central theme of the movement and those that see the Christian right as a politically opportunistic movement pursuing a series of loosely connected policy goals. Understanding the centrality of the family in evangelical identity helps make sense of the trajectory of the Christian right.[41] Specifically, focusing on the family demonstrates how the growth of Christian schools and campaigns against the public education establishment in the early 1970s—all done in the name of protecting children—created both institutions and language that fueled evangelical politicization in the late 1970s and 1980s. Grassroots campaigns against abortion and the ERA featured housewives who thought feminists threatened the family. The Christian right's strident defense of military might and castigation of gay men emanated from a normative masculinity that privileged strength, discipline, and fatherhood. Conservative evangelicals came together in the name of the family, an institution most of them saw as under attack by a hostile federal government.

The Promise Keepers testified to the importance of the family values agenda. National in scope and committed to racial reconciliation, Promise Keepers belied characterizations of evangelicals as provincial or racially homogenous. By the end of the twentieth century, a new generation of white evangelicals had made peace with the civil rights movement and had asserted themselves on a national stage. Promise Keepers suggested ways evangelicals had changed, yet the group also showed continuities. Evangelicals retained a thoroughgoing conservatism on issues of gender and authority. They had preached a platform of family values for two decades, linking evangelical Christianity with conservative politics even as Promise Keepers pledged non-partisanship. The rhetorical power and theological resonance of family values put that agenda at the center of American evangelicalism. When Promise Keepers pledged to "Stand in the Gap," they meant they would fight for their families.

PART I

Children

CHAPTER 1

Christian Schools

The September 1962 issue of *Christian School Guide* sounded warning bells about the recent Supreme Court decision in *Engel v. Vitale*, which prohibited public schools in New York from opening the school day with a mandatory prayer. "With the removal of God from the classroom," blared the magazine's front-page story, "They have taken away My Lord." The magazine's editor, Chicago-based school administrator Mark Fakkema, reported that an investigation had "revealed that at the beginning of our nation (1776) study materials used in schools were 100% Christian. In 1850 they were 50% Christian." In 1962, however, "government schools" were almost devoid of Christian influence. To be sure, thousands of public schools ignored the *Engel* decision for years. But the die was cast. God had been kicked out of the public school classroom. Evangelical Christians could not afford to leave their kids in it.[1]

Fakkema's decision to spotlight the *Engel* decision presaged five decades of evangelicals' anxiety over the fate of religion in public schools. In 1962, when the Court handed down the decision, a vast majority of conservative Protestants enrolled their children in public schools. Private religious schools in the United States were overwhelmingly parochial schools, most of them Catholic or Lutheran. The *Engel* decision, coupled with the court's decision to outlaw devotional Bible reading in public schools via the 1963 case *Abingdon v. Schempp*, helped change that. Those two decisions convinced increasing numbers of conservative Protestants that public schools had forsaken their religious roots and now aimed to indoctrinate children with humanism.

In response, evangelicals began building private schools at a breathtaking pace. Between 1970 and 1980, enrollment in non-Catholic, church-related schools increased 137 percent, from 561,000 to 1,329,000.[2] The fast growth continued into the 1980s: the Association of Christian Schools, International reported nearly 1,000 new member schools between 1980 and 1985 (a 66%

increase).[3] While older private schools (mainly parochial schools and college preparatory academies) experienced moderate expansion during this two-decade explosion of private school growth, most of the increase occurred in new academies launched by conservative evangelicals. In fact, Catholic schools were closing at alarming rates during the late 1960s and early 1970s. Catholic schools educated over 10% of school-aged children in the mid-1960s, but as white Catholics fled cities for the suburbs, hundreds of parochial schools closed. Since Catholic schools had become so integral to American education, state and federal officials worried about their decline and experimented with voucher systems that provided funds to parents who sent their children to private schools. But the shuttering of Catholic schools continued. Evangelicals, meanwhile, built up their educational empires—both K-12 schools and colleges—in the growing suburbs. By the early 1980s, preachers like Jerry Falwell and Tim LaHaye claimed that evangelicals were opening three new private schools every day.[4]

Examining the dramatic growth of Christian schools provides a compelling place to study the origins of the family values movement. Other studies of the Christian right begin with the mid-century evangelism of Billy Graham, the 1970s campaign against the Equal Rights Amendment, or evangelicals' loud protests against abortion and gay rights in the 1980s and 1990s.[5] All those stories are important. But Christian academies stand out for a couple reasons. First, leaders of these schools disseminated a vision of social order that spotlighted the role of the family and the importance of authority. Conservative Protestants rejected the 1960s mantra "question authority." They believed that external authority was essential to social order. Specifically, conservative Christians argued that God—the ultimate authority—had ordained only two human institutions: the family and the church. Christian school proponents felt that public schools denigrated the family and ignored the church. Conversely, Christian academies viewed themselves as both "a reinforcement of the Christian home" and as an extension of the local church; they were often literal extensions of the church's building.[6] Private academies thereby served as visible manifestations of the social order conservatives thought essential. These schools provided a refuge for family values.

Second, the rapid growth of Christian schools encouraged the building of national networks of conservative evangelical ministers, school administrators, and parents. Parents who pulled their kids out of public schools did not necessarily know how to run schools themselves. They relied on literature and periodicals from groups like the Association of Christian Schools,

International (ACSI), American Association of Christian Schools (AACS), and National Association of Christian Schools (NACS) to set up and sustain their fledgling academies. The National Association of Evangelicals launched the NACS in 1947, and it published materials designed to help Protestants launch Christian academies from its headquarters in Wheaton, Illinois. In the 1970s, the AACS, based in Tennessee, and ACSI, based first in California and later in Colorado, emerged and quickly became the two largest Christian school organizations in the country. By the mid-1980s, AACS and ACSI claimed 2,808 member schools.[7] Though that number reflected only a fraction of the myriad Christian schools dotting the American landscape, AACS and ACSI membership became increasingly important to schools whose student body drew from constituencies beyond the congregation of the sponsoring church. These organizations began by filling an immediate need: helping ministers and parents figure out how to open and operate a Christian school. They published pamphlets listing curricular resources and local contacts for Christian school administrators.

While these national organizations provided basic instructions for launching Christian academies, AACS and ACSI newsletters and curricula also disseminated a political vision that gave Christian school devotees a common language for addressing the plight of the nation. Recall Fakkema's description of public schools: what had once been "100% Christian," in the minds of evangelicals, had become the province of humanism. Private Christian academies became the first line of defense against the secularization of the next generation. Christian school organizations helped connect men and women concerned about the plight of education and set the table for future battles over the soul of America.

Christian Schools and Desegregation

The expansion of Christian schools coincided with desegregation of public schools in the South, and although scores of Christian academies cropped up in the Midwest and in the Southwest, the rate of expansion among Christian schools was highest in the South.[8] Two Supreme Court decisions—*Green v. County School Board of New Kent County* (1968) and *Swann v. Charlotte-Mecklenburg Board of Education* (1971)—built on the 1954 *Brown v. Board of Education* decision mandating desegregation of public schools. In *Green*, the Court ruled that southern school systems could no longer justify segregation by pointing to difficulties in implementing full integration plans. The Court ordered school systems to take necessary measures in order to desegregate immediately. Three years later, *Swann* affirmed cross-town busing as a legitimate means to ensure desegregation in the public schools. The latter decision, especially, struck a nerve with parents, many of whom resented busing even if they were generally amenable to school desegregation. Christian schools found themselves the beneficiaries of parents' frustration. "I am revolting against busing," said one when asked why she enrolled her child in private school. A school administrator admitted, "the busing order gave us five to ten years of growth compressed into one year."[9] These comments revealed the ways the Supreme Court inadvertently spurred Christian school growth.[10]

Moreover, while many Christian academies allowed for token integration in the early 1970s, whites constituted the vast majority of students. Paul F. Parsons, a journalist who studied Christian schools in the mid-1980s, estimated that minorities constituted less than 3 percent of the student population in the vast majority of Christian schools. Only about 10 percent of Christian schools featured student bodies with 10 percent or more minority enrollment. Although some administrators told Parsons, "we want blacks in the school," African Americans showed little inclination to send their children to Christian schools. Some black parents cited financial obstacles to enrolling their children; others perceived the schools as white flight academies.[11] Furthermore, private Christian schools rejected some public school reforms that appealed to African Americans. For instance, public school emphasis on multiculturalism found little favor in the Christian academy movement, which privileged older textbooks filled with "traditional values"—and few minority authors.

The makeup of Christian school leadership also demonstrated whites' control over the movement. In 1987, the executive board for the Association of Christian Schools International included 28 white males, one white female—and no minorities.[12] As one historian put it, "Academy supporters wanted to create a world where racial tensions did not exist, so they built schools where racial differences had no place."[13] In other words, the schools' professed desire for increasing diversity did not mean they went the extra mile to recruit black students or make their academies friendly to skeptical African Americans.

Yet to say the schools benefited from resistance to public school desegregation does not exclude other rationales for Christian education—nor does it account for schools that emerged in regions where desegregation was not seen as threatening. One historian has suggested that we divide private institutions into "segregation academies," which were public in all but name and existed solely to perpetuate segregation during the late 1960s, and "church schools," which emerged in the 1970s to combat perceived secularism in the public schools. These categories prevent historians from lumping all private schools into a single category.[14] Plenty of Christian schools emerged during the 1970s for a complex assortment of reasons, which included avoiding desegregation and combating secularism.

Take, for instance, Lynchburg Christian Academy (LCA), a private school launched by the Reverend Jerry Falwell, who would later become the most visible member of the Christian right. Opened in 1967, the same year Lynchburg public schools desegregated, LCA immediately faced the wrath of a group of liberal clergy, who charged the school with racism. They published an ad saying, "We [who are] sensitive to Our Lord's inclusiveness . . . deplore the use of the term 'Christian' in connection with private schools which exclude Negroes and other non-whites."[15] Falwell later maintained that the school never had a "whites only" policy, but the *Lynchburg News* described the school as "a private school for white students," a designation neither Falwell nor the school challenged at the time.[16] Falwell himself had preached at least two sermons against the civil rights movement in 1964 and 1965. Demonstrators from the Congress on Racial Equality had protested at Falwell's church, and black members were not permitted until 1968.[17] In the context of Falwell's record on civil rights during the 1960s—and given the timing of the school's opening—it is difficult to see Lynchburg Christian Academy as anything but a segregation academy.

Yet LCA would need to find new ways to maintain its existence after the first few years of public school desegregation. In the late 1960s African Americans made up only 19.5 percent of Lynchburg's population, the second-lowest proportion among Virginia cities.[18] By the late 1960s white southerners in most communities had learned how to desegregate in ways that did not threaten their control over the schools.[19] In cities like Lynchburg, white control over public schools meant that desegregation proceeded in ways that guaranteed minimal disruption to white communities and schools. (Busing, of course, would have changed this reality, but Lynchburg did not have a court-mandated busing program in 1967.) In cities where whites could not achieve numerical dominance in public schools, private schools—segregation academies—proliferated. A study of school desegregation in Mississippi, for instance, found that the emergence of all-white private schools "was more closely related to the black percentage of population within the school district's boundaries than to any other factor."[20] Lynchburg, with its relatively low proportion of African Americans was, if nothing else, demographically atypical among cities featuring segregation academies. The timing of LCA's emergence was not coincidental; school founders knew public school desegregation would cause some white parents to send their children to private schools. But as desegregation proceeded, and whites maintained majority control over public schools, LCA would need other rationales to sustain its enrollment.

LCA's early promotional materials provided a glimpse of how the school would market itself. A pamphlet called "Five Things We Think You Will Like About Lynchburg Christian Academy" ticked off the main advantages of religious schooling: quality education, no drug problem, legal Bible reading and prayer, no hippies, and the teaching of patriotism. The pamphlet featured an energetic fife and drum corps comprised of patriotic-looking young men and contrasted it with a sullen group of hippie protesters. A smiling teacher, backed by religious messages on a bulletin board, presided over a class of attentive students. The message was obvious: LCA provided a haven from the degeneracy that marked the hippie generation. It promoted a love of country and a respect for authority.[21]

LCA also promoted family values. Thomas Road Baptist Church (TRBC), which sponsored the school, asked all faculty and staff to attend a "Family Seminar" at the church. The director of the Family Services Department at TRBC, Al Kinchen, spoke at a parent-teacher fellowship meeting in 1972. Topics covered included "overcoming a condemning attitude, gaining victory over impure thoughts, qualities for developing a successful marriage, how to follow God's chain of command in marriage, [and] how to teach a child to stand alone on the side of right."[22] The school responded to the threat of a culture that questioned authority by underlining both the importance of the family and the lines of authority within it.

LCA concern for family values demands attention to the ways academy leaders and parents depicted the role of Christian academies. The school benefited from backlash toward public school desegregation, and it did not admit even a single minority student in its first two years. But looking at it solely as a segregation academy obscures the complex factors that fueled its success. By the mid-1970s, LCA enrolled a small proportion of minority students, lessening the difference between its racial composition and that of the

1 QUALITY EDUCATION. Students who graduate from Lynchburg Christian Academy receive a diploma from a fully accredited high school. Not only is Lynchburg Christian Academy accredited, but we feel that the curriculum is advanced significantly beyond the average public school in America.

2 NO DRUG PROBLEM. The drug abuse problem in our American schools is at epidemic stage today. Because our total faculty and administrative staff is composed of Christian people with high morals and standards, we are able to prevent such a drug problem at Lynchburg Christian Academy. This is not to say that no LCA student has ever used drugs. No school could make that statement in total honesty. However, we can say, to the best of our knowledge, we have no drug abuse problem.

3 BIBLE READING AND PRAYER ARE LEGAL AT LYNCHBURG CHRISTIAN ACADEMY. We have regular chapels in which we teach young people how to live by Biblical principles. Every day, young people are taught how to develop a personal relationship with Christ. The school is totally non-denominational and young people from all faiths attend. Over 700 are presently enrolled.

4 WE HAVE NO HIPPIES. Neatness of appearance, proper length of hair for boys, and right attitudes towards elders are all a part of our curriculum. We teach our young people to say "yes sir" and "no sir." Our students are taught the importance of dressing neatly and acceptably. They are also taught the "sacredness of hard work." Young people are no worse today than 25 years ago. They simply come from worse homes and schools. Proverbs 22:6 says "Train up a child in the way he should go; and when he is old, he will not depart from it."

5 OUR STUDENTS ARE TAUGHT TO LOVE AMERICA. Patriotism is a part of our program. Our students are taught to love this great nation and to respect her. We have never had an anti-American demonstration.

Figure 1. This 1975 advertisement for Lynchburg Christian Academy listed "five things we think you will like" about the school. Image courtesy of Liberty Christian Academy.

city's public schools. Parents who sent their children there responded to the school's nostalgic appeal to an "old-fashioned" environment and curriculum. This appeal worked brilliantly. In the early 1970s LCA moved from cramped Sunday school rooms to a new facility and earned accreditation. By 1972 an initial enrollment of 105 students had swelled to 684. And in 1971 Falwell opened a liberal arts college—now known as Liberty University—to augment his educational empire. At the end of the twentieth century, Liberty enrolled a higher proportion of African American students than any other Virginia university, save for historically black colleges. If the school's origins lay in the fallout from public school desegregation, its subsequent development depended on other factors.

The segregationist origins of countless private Christian academies have obscured a commitment among school proponents to proper order. The ministers and parents who enrolled their children in Christian schools had an ugly record on civil rights, which they camouflaged in the 1970s and apologized for in the 1980s and 1990s. It would be easy, then, to dismiss these schools as bastions of racism. But a better understanding of the underlying commitment of conservative evangelicals to proper order helps make sense of the schools' mission in the 1970s and beyond. Academies discovered a winning strategy in pitching family values to parents concerned about public education. Christian school periodicals and recruiting materials portrayed "government schools" as places of disorder and chaos, and this depiction resonated with conservative evangelicals across the country. They sent their children to these schools for a variety of reasons—including both avoidance of desegregation and attraction to the academies' promises to defend family values.

The Creation of "Secular Humanism"

Where critics of Christian schools cited the academies' attempts to undermine Supreme Court decisions such as *Green* and *Swann*, the schools' defenders fixated on a different pair of high court rulings: *Engel v. Vitale* (1962) and *Abingdon School District v. Schempp* (1963). In the former case, the Supreme Court ruled that New York public school teachers could not open the school day by reciting the "Regents' Prayer," a twenty-two-word petition that read: "Almighty God, we acknowledge our dependence upon Thee, and we beg Thy blessing upon us, our parents, our teachers and our Country."

Writing for the majority, Justice Hugo Black held that "constitutional prohibition against laws respecting an establishment of religion must at least mean that in this country it is no part of the business of government to compose official prayers for any group of the American people to recite as a part of a religious program carried on by government."[23] The Court found that the Regents' Prayer violated the establishment clause, even though the prayer was nonsectarian and, for teachers, voluntary. In *Abingdon*, the Court ruled against devotional Bible reading in public schools. The lone dissenter, Justice Potter Stewart, sounded a note of concern that would be repeated endlessly by Christian school advocates. "A refusal to permit religious exercises," he wrote, is "not the realization of state neutrality, but rather the establishment of a religion of secularism."[24] The Court disagreed and, in the minds of Christian school leaders, established secularism as the religion of the public schools.[25]

By the 1970s, Christian school advocates saw the decline of public schools as the inevitable byproduct of a lengthy campaign by secularists to wrest control over education from churches. Paul Kienel, California-based executive director of the Association of Christian Schools International, repeatedly outlined his version of the history of American schooling in his weekly newsletter, *Christian School Comment*. Beginning in 1837 with the exploits of Horace Mann, a Unitarian, government agencies had systematically encroached on educational terrain formerly controlled by evangelical Christians. Mann had urged the state of Massachusetts to provide for the education of its children, a task previously shouldered by the church. Though Kienel conceded that nineteenth-century public education remained largely under the control of evangelical Christians, deeper problems for conservative Christians emerged in the early twentieth century, when the philosopher John Dewey assumed control of Columbia University Teachers College. By graduating hundreds of educators and launching satellite institutions, Dewey and Columbia spearheaded a movement to reshape American education. According to Kienel, Dewey's "'progressive education' ideas divested America's public schools of their evangelical Protestant character and made them insensitive to the evangelical Christian community."[26] Moreover, the secularization of public education had not come about by accident. According to another California pastor, Tim LaHaye, "atheistic humanists took over the school system."[27] In Christian school advocates' version of history, humanists had planned to eliminate the church's influence on the schools. By the middle of the twentieth century, evangelical leaders argued, aggressive secularists had won control of public education after a century-long struggle to drive Christians away.

Secular control of education boded ill for Christians not merely because public schools could not teach religion, but because they actively persecuted it. Christian educators contended that a new "religion" now governed public education: secular humanism. According to a history textbook popular among Christian schools, "Humanism . . . tries to build man up by playing down or ignoring God."[28] Secular humanists promoted a worldview that rejected original sin and located authority within individuals rather than God. The curriculum championed by humanist educators invited children to discover the good within themselves by fostering creativity and experimentation. Whereas traditional education had relied on authoritative instruction and strict discipline, secular humanist education encouraged teachers to relax standards and embrace tolerance. Such ideas appalled conservative Christians. A. A. Baker, founder of Pensacola Christian School (by 1974 the largest Christian school in the nation), minced no words in his evaluation of progressive education: "I believe that the strength and greatness of America today are being sapped by a godless liberal theology and a God-denying progressive philosophy of education."[29] In a similar vein, a 1972 brochure for Lynchburg Christian Academy proclaimed public schools "a major threat to the Christian church" because their refusal to acknowledge God as the ultimate reality was "to deny the Creator and to misinterpret the creature."[30] Christian school leaders argued that secular humanists not only avoided religion but also denied its legitimacy—and Christian parents needed to remove their children from public schools at once.[31]

This bleak picture of progressive education earned credibility because it resonated with many Americans' perceptions of public schools. When asked about popular opinion of public schools in 1970, a public school administrator replied, "the very people who normally are public schools' strongest supporters have lost faith. Ten years ago . . . no one would have dreamed that a school bond issue would ever be voted down."[32] But by the dawn of the 1970s, suspicious voters wondered about the return they were getting on their tax dollars. According to a 1972 handbook for a Christian school, parents were realizing that "the permissive pragmatic philosophy of progressive education" has led to a "de-emphasis on many academic subjects, [resulting] in the fact that the student thus receives neither intellectual training nor factual knowledge."[33] Americans questioned the efficacy of public schools, as it appeared that the United States was falling behind all other industrialized nations in academic performance. Christian school advocates provided a plausible explanation for the demise of public schools: secular humanist educators in the mid-twentieth century had loosed education from its traditional moorings. As a result, parents could not trust public schools to educate their children effectively.

Christian school leaders contended that secular humanism not only sapped the academic value of education, but also that it threatened the moral development of American students. By denying the existence of a Creator and locating authority within the individual, humanists removed the possibility of judgment. According to Christian school advocates, teachers could no longer label student behavior right or wrong because they could not appeal to an external moral standard, like the Ten Commandments. In countless newsletters and marketing pamphlets, Christian school leaders depicted the public school classroom as a place where sin went unchecked and teachers commanded little respect. A 1968 newsletter from a Baptist church proclaimed, "Grotesque misbehavior, individual and organized . . . now characterizes many public schools."[34] Likewise, a 1975 marketing brochure for Lynchburg Christian Academy claimed, "the drug abuse problem in our American schools is at epidemic stage today" and attributed the rise of hippies to "worse homes and schools" than had existed in the 1940s and 1950s.[35] Conservative Christians held little doubt that public schools had hastened the decline of American culture by encouraging the anti-Christian principles of progressive education.

Because secular humanism did not offer a standard of right and wrong, said Christian school advocates, public schools could no longer practice effective discipline. "Traditional education," wrote Baker, "is God centered . . . [and] authoritarian in its approach."[36] But progressive education had encouraged students to experiment with morality and to question authority. In pamphlets and newsletters, Christian school leaders depicted public school classrooms as places where disobedience reigned. One brochure declared, "many of today's students are misguided, un-disciplined, and rebellious toward authority."[37] Handcuffed by restraints placed on them by progressive education theories, teachers could do little to combat the chaos of public school classrooms. In their book *Schools on Fire*, evangelical leaders Jon Barton and John W. Whitehead contended that public schools had shown "constant deterioration since 1963—the same year that the Supreme Court ruled both prayer and devotional Bible reading unconstitutional in our public schools." Barton and Whitehead cited rising rates of teen crime, educators' admission that discipline was non-existent in some public school classrooms, and the pervasiveness of "secular humanism" in public school curricula and instruction in order to portray a "moral crisis in the blackboard jungle."[38]

Secular humanism also seemed to foster tolerance for Communism. Pensacola Christian School President Baker made this fear explicit in a discussion about the school's curriculum: "We don't have textbooks that teach a humanistic, socialistic, communistic philosophy."[39] Baker's easy association of humanism, socialism, and communism reflected an understanding common to many Christian school proponents. According to the 1937 Humanist Manifesto, which Christian school leaders saw as the philosophical basis for progressive education, "the existing acquisitive and profit-motivated society has shown itself to be inadequate . . . [and] a socialized and cooperative economic order must be established."[40] This line exposed to evangelicals the sinister agenda of secular humanists. Secular humanism encouraged progressive educators to foster a seemingly benign tolerance, but that tolerance diminished the competitive spirit that fueled the free market system. Weakness in the face of the hard realities of life led humanists to advocate socialism, which most conservatives equated with communism. Thus, Christian school leaders expressed dismay—if not surprise—that a prominent public high school textbook "reveals a very clear support of Marxism."[41] The Cold War context of the mid-twentieth century demanded that people choose between capitalism and communism, and according to conservative Christians, humanists had chosen the latter.[42]

Kienel aptly summarized the feelings of many Christians when he wrote, "The moral and academic devastation" that followed implementation of progressive education "has placed our nation at risk."[43] By embracing progressive education, public schools had forfeited their educational prerogative. America's problems had reached epic stage. And Christian academies presented themselves as the necessary solution. "Private Christian schools," argued one supporter, "are our nation's greatest need."[44]

Gender Roles and Family Values

If progressive education had bankrupted America's public schools by preaching tolerance, Christian schools responded by emphasizing their commitment to order. Christian academy leaders believed God still had a plan for the proper ordering of society, and Christian education could not shrink from teaching children about the realities of social order. Public schools' seeming insistence on erasing all social divisions contradicted divinely ordained divisions and hierarchies in human society, and to deny them was to deny scriptural teaching. For instance, a literal reading of Ephesians 5—"wives, submit to your husbands"—showed that the Bible gave husbands authority over their wives. Likewise, Romans 13—"Let everyone be subject to the governing authorities . . . whoever rebels against that authority is rebelling against God"—sanctioned governmental authority and condemned protest. Evangelicals frequently quoted passages like these to argue that liberal notions of egalitarianism and civil disobedience went against the Bible's insistence on proper order. According to conservative evangelicals, God did not intend societies to be undifferentiated masses. Rather, God had ordained certain people—by gender, calling, or election—to govern others. Christian schools understood their task to involve teaching students how to assume their God-given roles and responsibilities in society.

Christian schools' teaching of divine order began with delineating differences between men and women—differences public schools seemed eager to erase. According to Christian school advocates, secular humanists encouraged people to think of gender as socially constructed, a product of history and culture that bespoke sexism and patriarchy. A public school psychology textbook contended, "we are trained gradually in the ways of behavior as a male or female . . . we learn how to be a man or a woman sexually—as if we were in a play." Mel and Norma Gabler, parents who embarked on a well-publicized crusade against public school texts like this one, found that statement both blasphemous and ridiculous. "This theory rejects God who stated that He made us male and female," they wrote. "You are either a male or a female and there is just no way to get around it."[45] Evangelicals saw gender as a God-given difference, with the particular roles of men and women spelled out in scripture. Their schools, then, would inculcate gender-specific behaviors in students in response to God's commands.

The first task in establishing a gendered order involved making visible the differences between boys and girls. Christian school leaders repudiated the counterculture movement of the 1960s, in which men grew their hair long and women ditched prim dresses for bellbottoms. Almost all Christian schools featured strict dress codes and hair policies. The final rule of Lynchburg Christian Academy's dress code was a direct rejoinder to gender-benders in the counterculture: "FADS OR PECULIAR DRESS AND HAIRCUTS ARE NOT PERMITTED." In case students seemed mystified

about what constituted fads or peculiar dress and haircuts, the student handbook laid out extensive guidelines for girls and boys. For instance, girls had
to wear dresses, and this meant no "shorts, slacks, culottes, scooter skirts,
pantsuits, or tennis shoes." Boys had to wear slacks and collared shirts, and
their hair "must be neat and may not be over any part of the ears, back of
collar, or in the region of the eyes."[46] Dress and hair codes like these were not
exclusive to Christian schools, nor did every Christian school share the
strictness of LCA.[47] But most Christian schools saw dress codes as a critical
venue for differentiating themselves from gender ambiguity in the secular
world. As an LCA promotional leaflet proclaimed, "You can tell our boys
from the girls without a medical examination."[48]

Beyond physical appearance, Christian schools mandated practices that
would help students learn what it meant to be male or female. Bruce Jackson,
education director for the American Association of Christian Schools, instructed member academies to teach boys "craft skills, work habits, garden-
ing, manners, economics, leadership, music, and rhetoric." Girls, on the other
hand, ought to learn "cooking, housekeeping, household management, manners, sewing, growing and arranging flowers, interior decoration, literary
skills, and child care."[49] Again, these gender stereotypes were not the exclusive province of Christian schools. Yet they were ubiquitous in the world of
Christian schools, and they communicated important realities academy supporters saw in the world: men and women were fundamentally different.
Gender was not a malleable category. And Christian schools would emphasize the proper roles of men and women.

Believing the Bible taught that men were to lead families, conservative
evangelicals made sure their schools' reinforced "male headship." In a book
on the philosophy of Christian school education, Long Beach, California,
pastor David Hocking explained, "the order in the family established the husband first, then the wife and finally the children."[50] Students at Christian
schools, said Hocking, must understand this ordering as a biblical principle.
As part of their training, boys had to learn the leadership qualities they would
need in adulthood. Christian schools sanctioned masculine prerogative in
both explicit and implicit ways. For example, Lynchburg Baptist College,
which initially shared facilities with LCA, expected "a married male student,
as the head of his household, to see to it that his wife dresses with appropriate
Christian modesty."[51] More implicit clues signaling Christian schools' pre-
sumption of male leadership also appeared in academy literature. In his man-
ual on running a Christian school, for instance, A. A. Baker used pronouns

that assumed headmasters were men and receptionists were women (teachers could be either male or female).[52]

Though similar assumptions persisted in other arenas of society, Christian schools' rejection of gender ambiguity stemmed from their interpretation of the Bible. Dress codes referenced biblical commands to justify their regulations on hair length and appropriate attire. According to the student handbook for Wake Christian Academy in Raleigh, the school dress code adhered to scriptural standards such as, " 'It is a shame for a man to have long hair,' 'Let women adorn themselves in modest apparel,' [and] avoid 'anything whereby the brother stumbleth.' "[53] The schools believed creating an atmosphere where boys learned to become men and girls learned to become women was essential to their overall mission of following the Bible. "Most [Christian school] leaders," wrote Paul Kienel, "agree that there are scriptural guidelines that call for boys to appear masculine and for girls to dress and wear their hair in a feminine manner."[54] Scripture also instructed believers on the appropriate ways for men and women to interact. Thus, schools like LCA promised to teach "what the proper respect between mother, father, child, husband or wife, and God should be."[55] Because Christian academies believed themselves to be extensions of the family—and because the family was "one of the institutions God has ordained to carry out His plan for a Christian's life"[56]—Christian schools repudiated public schools' "attack" on the family. Conservative Christians read in the Creation story that God intended men and women to play distinctive roles within the family. Their schools would reinforce that principle.

Academies asserted the biblical basis for inculcating gender roles in their students, but the schools' emphasis on masculinity and femininity clearly reflected a reaction to contemporary political movements. The burgeoning women's rights movement threatened traditional mores and called into question conventional social arrangements. One of the major complaints a Christian school administrator made regarding a public school textbook was, "Nowhere was it suggested that being a mother or homemaker was a worthy and important role for a woman."[57] This statement reflected conservatives' deep misgivings about the changes that had wracked American society in the 1960s and 1970s. By removing their children from public schools seemingly committed to the elimination of traditional gender roles, evangelicals maintained a sliver of the rapidly disintegrating status quo. Conservatives' rejection of gender ambiguity went beyond fidelity to the Bible. The conservative Christians who sent their children to Christian schools hearkened for an idealized society where men and women lived in harmony because they recognized their proper roles. The Bible certainly seemed to legitimate conservatives' assumptions about gender. But Christian schools also benefited by enabling conservative Christians to reject, in a tangible way, progressive stereotypes about "modern" men and women that threatened the gender-specific world they once knew.

The irony was that Christian schools felt the need to teach a gendered order they saw as part of God's creation. If men and women were created to fulfill certain roles, why did academies have to show boys and girls how to assume those roles? Two assumptions among Christian school advocates dictated the need to teach gender norms. First, conservative evangelicals stressed the doctrine of original sin, or the belief that all humans are born with corrupted natures. According to this doctrine, boys and girls needed discipline and instruction to tame their natural sinfulness. Second, all Christian school advocates assumed the decline of American society and pervasiveness of liberalism had poisoned the cultural assumptions that used to govern society. Where proper order had once existed, gender confusion now reigned. Academies saw themselves as restorers of a previous golden age. Ignoring the racial discrimination that had characterized their golden past cost Christian schools the support of conservative black Christians and earned them the ire of liberal critics. But their focus on teaching students gender roles appealed to a wide cohort of white conservatives who saw restoration of proper order as essential.

By encouraging students to see the misbegotten aims of secular humanism in its teachings about gender, Christian schools put a fine point on the unease many parents felt not only about public education, but also about the liberal drift that had pushed American society away from traditional mores. Conservatives believed that secular humanists—along with their feminist allies—ignored both the teachings of scripture and humans' inherent tendencies to gravitate toward gender-specific roles. Christian schools restored godly teachings to the classroom by focusing on the ways boys became men and girls became women. To conservative Christian parents, such teaching seemed appropriate, not discriminatory. By emphasizing their fidelity to teaching God-given gender roles, Christian schools offered conservatives a clear and attractive alternative to misguided public schools.

Christian America

Christian schools also celebrated America as God's chosen land. Progressive education, wrote A. A. Baker, said "nationalism is a dirty word, [and] the American way is not the best way."[58] Christian schools, on the other hand, assumed patriotism and faithfulness went hand in hand. This assumption stemmed from conservatives' belief that true faith required fidelity to God and country. Whereas public schools could only acknowledge government by the people, Christian schools recognized government as a God-given mechanism for the ordering of human societies. Thus, Christian schools— not public schools—represented the best hope for restoring patriotic fervor among the nation's youth. A 1968 editorial in *Free Will Baptist* captured well conservatives' feelings about America: "We are the greatest nation in the world. . . . Yet, there is something missing in the soul of this great nation in which we live." The answer was not to give up on this country. Rather, by "dedicating [themselves] to the task of . . . Christian education,"[59] evangelicals could right the ship. Christian schools would restore Godly principles to America by teaching its children that their government demanded respect and submission.

In order to assert that students must respect the government, Christian schools needed to establish that America possessed religious foundations. Jerry Falwell wrote, "I believe God has blessed this nation because in its early days she sought to honor God and the Bible. . . . Our Founding Fathers were not all Christians, but they were guided by biblical principles. They developed a nation predicated on Holy Writ."[60] He believed the forms of government and economy put in place by the founding fathers reflected humans' best attempt at installing a godly government. America's free enterprise system provided an outlet for people's innate competitiveness, and the separation of powers checked humans' sinful inclinations. Public schools, with their emphasis on individuality and experimentation, tried to suppress natural human tendencies by eliminating "competition in any form."[61] Christian schools, on the other hand, thought they taught the American way. LCA thereby promised to teach "the sacredness of hard work."[62] Similar statements appeared in countless Christian school publications, as Christian schools portrayed their educational priorities as consistent with the ethos of the nation's founders.

The dualistic worldview promoted by the Cold War shaped Christian schools' understanding of America's Christian past. Christian schools feared that public schools were verging on teaching communism. One academy supporter charged that communism was the "one religion taught in [public] school," and thought only private church schools could teach "traditional American principles of loyalty to God, country and home."[63] Few Christian school leaders made statements as bald as that one, but most suggested that public schools encouraged a perilous drift toward communism. Christian schools, on the other hand, forbade any teaching that might shed a positive light on Communists. One academy told parents, "the school opposes all efforts to foster in children socialistic and communistic ideals which result in a 'one world' philosophy that weakens our national sovereignty."[64] Communists lurked as a major threat, and public schools' embrace of humanism cracked open a door for the red menace. Christian schools slammed that door shut.

Nostalgia also played a significant role in Christian schools' patriotism. Evangelicals in the 1960s and 1970s longed for an era when young people loved their country and submitted to authority. A wistful editorial in the March 1973 LCA newsletter reflected the sense that Christian schools offered students a return to their parents' America. "Remember the tears that flowed gently and warmly down your cheeks as you were reminded of how God has blessed America?" asked the author. Such sentiments were in short supply near the end of the Vietnam War, and Christian schools celebrated those brave few who persisted in patriotism. And patriotism meant more than simple love of country. The editorial linked Americanism with more specific moral demands: "Remember the days when people dressed reasonable and decent? Remember the days when parents ruled the home and children obeyed? Remember the days when teachers controlled the classrooms?" The editorial identified patriotism with a vision of life in Christian schools. Students embodied a nostalgic view of America that stood counter to prevailing trends in popular culture. These children, the editorial implied, would be the ones to restore America's greatness.[65]

Christian schools communicated that they represented the true spirit of America. In their eyes, America had once been great because of its Christian principles, and evangelicals determined to return the nation to greatness by restoring those principles. Christian schools appealed to many conservatives who had tired of seeing college students protest the war and hippies glorify the counterculture. Promotional materials like LCA's "Five Things We Think You Will Like About Lynchburg Christian Academy" capitalized on conservatives' disillusionment with anti-Americanism. "We have no hippies," the brochure declared, and "Our Students Are Taught to Love America."[66]

Loving America entailed specific political positions. According to ASCI President Paul Kienel, "Secular education is so completely peopled and supported by the liberal community, only the wildest dreamer could predict a return to 'normalcy.' . . . The Christian school system is God's school system."[67] Christian academies connected conservative politics with patriotism, and patriotism with holiness. Evangelicals argued that liberals had knocked America off its moorings by attempting to remove the religious aspects from American politics. Christian school leaders therefore saw no conflict in promoting patriotism at the same time they denigrated the liberal-controlled government. "We wave the flag . . . as a reminder not of our allegiance to America right or wrong, but to the principles on which America was founded," said one school administrator.[68] In other words, evangelicals believed liberals violated America's Christian past.

In 1976 Falwell provided students with opportunities to demonstrate their commitment to Christian America—and political conservatism—by leading a group of Lynchburg Baptist College students on a tour of 141 cities, including 44 state capitals, where the program typically took place on the capital building steps. The group performed a program called "I Love America!" Falwell followed the performances with a stump speech on the degeneracy of American culture, a trend he linked to liberals' control of courts and schools. Falwell missed the irony of celebrating America at the same rally in which he railed against it. But he could hold these two positions simultaneously because he meant two different things by "America." On one hand, America represented ideals Falwell celebrated: freedom, discipline, order, and pride. On the other hand, the federal government of the late twentieth century seemed determined to destroy Falwell's idealized vision of the country. He attacked American government even as he longed for a nostalgic American ideal.[69]

Only one institution survived Falwell's critique of modern America: the military. In the minds of Christian school leaders, the military represented the only American institution that had neither obliterated gendered order nor ignored the importance of authority. Though few schools undertook a campaign as ambitious as Falwell's bicentennial tour, nearly all Christian schools trumpeted their patriotism by honoring military heroes and encouraging students to celebrate their country. A description of a school ceremony at Wake Christian Academy typified the patriotic assemblies most Christian

Figure 2. Baptist minister Jerry Falwell led college students on a tour
of 141 U.S. cities in 1976. Photograph by Mark Foley, courtesy of the
State Archives of Florida.

schools hosted. "The student body and teachers gathered around the flag pole
to the music of John Phillip Sousa's marches," reported the Academy newsletter. "The ceremony consisted of the presentation, the acceptance, the raising
of the new flag, pledge of allegiance, and a challenge by Rev. Jim Aycock on
patriotism."[70] Ceremonies like these cemented Christian schools' support of
the military—an unpopular stance among many young people in the waning
years of the Vietnam War. Christian schools supported the military because
it championed virtues like duty and honor, and many encouraged their male
students to enlist. Conservative Christians believed God had sanctioned the
military as a necessary defense against the spread of "godless Communism."

Christian schools' celebration of the American military resonated with
their teachings about gendered order. Whereas hippies combined the twin
sins of unfaithfulness to America and rebellion against their God-given gender roles, "real men" fought for their country and cropped their hair short. By
inculcating practices that marked boys as masculine and girls as feminine,
Christian schools prepared students for service to a country that desperately
needed them. Without clear teaching about God's plans for men and women,

public schools had encouraged a drift away from values that had made the nation great. While evangelicals allowed that frustration with the war accelerated young people's disillusionment with their country, they maintained that widespread anti-Americanism among teenagers reflected systemic flaws in the ways America educated her young. Christian schools determined to instill a clear sense of gender roles in students as a way of restoring the "golden age" of the nation. Christian schools' promotion of patriotism, then, stood alongside academies' instruction on gender roles as a fundamental component of God's plan for society.

Authority, Family Values, and Politics

By emphasizing biblical gender roles, Christian schools revealed their underlying commitment to proper lines of authority. Academy advocates believed public schools mistakenly tried to empower children at the expense of teachers' authority. James Dobson, a professor of pediatrics at the University of Southern California who launched Focus on the Family in 1977 and later became one of the most influential conservative evangelical leaders in the country, aptly characterized evangelicals' views of public schools in his 1970 bestseller, *Dare to Discipline*: "Despite the will of the majority, the anti-disciplinarians have had their way. The rules governing student conduct have been cut down, and in their place have come a myriad of restrictions on educators."[71] As a result, he argued, students were running amok in public school classrooms. Christian school advocates saw instilling a little fear in their charges as a good thing in a society becoming overly enamored of positive reinforcement.

Yet Christian academies were determined not to become yet another institution taking authority away from the family; academies claimed to derive their authority from their partnership with the family. Schools went out of their way to trumpet their ancillary role to the family. A 1971 Lynchburg Christian Academy mailer, for instance, advertised 90 percent attendance at Parent-Teacher Fellowship meetings, signaling the integration of family and school that the academy idealized. The LCA student handbook claimed, "It is . . . the school's desire to be a reinforcement of the Christian home."[72] This connection between the school and the family legitimated academies' educational endeavors. Because God had put parents in charge of children, conservative evangelicals could only sanction those institutions that recognized the family's primacy. A 1967 booklet produced by the National Association of Christian Schools illustrated this belief. "Parents are accountable to God for the training of their children," it read. "The Christian school does not remove responsibility, but it will work with your home and your church to fulfill the obligation."[73]

Christian schools emphasized their support for "parents' rights." Connie Marshner, a conservative activist who wrote a 1978 book about public schools called *Blackboard Tyranny*, contended that "Parents' rights come from God by way of the natural law; the existence of the family unit presupposes parental rights; continuation of civilized society presupposes the existence of the family unit."[74] This view typified Christian school advocates' view of parental authority. Because families were essential to the continuation of civilization, society had to grant parents ultimate authority over their children. Leaders of Christian academies took a dim view of liberals' attempts to empower children. They referred to the UN declaration of 1979 as the International Year of the Child as a manifestation of "kiddie lib," which would "further undermine the American family."[75] Christian schools promised parents that mom and dad would maintain (or regain) authority over their children.

Christian schools' support for families and parents' rights further discredited public schools. Progressive educators, in the minds of Christian school advocates, had done everything possible to alienate parents. As a result, these schools had wrongly excluded families from their children's education. If the authority to educate "belongs exclusively to parents and the church," as the Christian Legal Association claimed, public schools were "usurpers," and Christian parents needed to wage "a spiritual conflict" to regain control of education.[76] Private Christian academies, in declaring solidarity with families, signaled their willingness to fight against public schools.

The fight against public schools became one of the earliest venues for the politicization of family values. The bleak view of secular education disseminated by Christian school advocates in the 1960s and 1970s created a subset of evangelicals who felt that public education was neither positive nor benign. These evangelicals worried public education intruded on the domain of families. As Marshner argued, "children, victims of several generations of progressive education in its various incarnations, are illiterate, ignorant, uncultured, undisciplined, immoral, and irreligious—in short, uncivilized." Those who managed to escape such a dire fate were those who grew up "in a family environment."[77] In this view, conservative Christians could no longer afford to tolerate public schools that threatened to destroy America's foundations by undermining its families. In short, supporters of Christian schools viewed their academies as defenders of family values.

At the same time, opponents of the Christian school movement saw it as a bastion of segregation and a hindrance to the proper education of children. As the Christian school movement continued to grow throughout the 1970s, media watchdogs and governmental agencies began to take a closer look at the new schools. The Lamar Society, a group of liberal southerners concerned about desegregation, funded a two-year study of private academies that resulted in the 1976 publication of *The Schools That Fear Built*, written by a journalist and an education professor.[78] Throughout the book, authors David Nevin and Robert Bills referred to private schools as "segregation academies" and concluded, "these are schools for whites," which clearly violated the Supreme Court's desegregation mandate.[79] For many observers, Christian schools' segregated origins (and still largely segregated student bodies) trumped all other facets of the movement.

By the mid-1970s, Christian schools' phenomenal growth rate compelled the Internal Revenue Service to launch a review of its guidelines for offering tax exemptions to private religious schools. According to the 1970 *Green v. Connally* decision, nonprofit organizations that discriminated on the basis of race could no longer receive tax exemptions. Few schools lost their exemption, however, and in 1976 the plaintiffs, a group of Mississippians who believed private schools in their state continued to discriminate, reopened their case against the IRS. The IRS had collected enough other evidence to suggest that segregated schools were violating the *Green* ruling, and the organization agreed to revise the protocols for schools receiving tax exemption. Ultimately, the IRS decided that "reviewable" schools (most of those formed after the 1954 *Brown* decision) had to feature a "significant" proportion of minority students (defined as 20 percent of the percentage of the minority school-age population of the community served by the school). In plain language, the new guidelines meant that the majority of new Christian schools had to enroll a quota of minority students or face the loss of their tax-exempt status, a potentially fatal blow.[80]

The decision touched off a firestorm among Christian school supporters. One declared that all Christian schools started after 1957 would "be automatically assumed to be racially discriminatory" and "guilty until proven innocent."[81] Another called the IRS "arrogant" and "highly secretive," and urged Christian school advocates to write letters to their Congressmen every week.[82] Followers heeded the advice. Over 400,000 protest letters flooded the Capitol; another 120,000 found their way to the offices of the IRS.[83] The grassroots response forced the IRS to hold four days of hearings on the issue and led the Republican Party to condemn the new guidelines in its 1980 platform. The Reagan administration did away with the guidelines in 1982, only to see that decision overruled by the Supreme Court a year later in *Bob Jones University v. U.S.* Although the 1983 *Bob Jones* decision upheld the policy originally mandated by 1970's *Green* decision—private schools that discriminated according to race could not receive tax exemption—few academies actually lost tax exemption.

Moreover, the real lesson of Christian school advocates' battles against the IRS from 1978 to 1983 seemed to be the willingness of evangelicals to engage in politics. Indeed, conservative activist Paul Weyrich dated the emergence of the Christian right to battle over tax exemptions for private schools. "What changed," he said, "was not the school-prayer issue, and it was not the abortion issue. . . . What caused the movement to surface was the federal government's moves against Christian schools. This absolutely shattered the Christian community's notion that Christians could isolate themselves inside their own institutions and teach was they pleased."[84] Alongside grassroots movements designed to stop ratification of the Equal Rights Amendment and to agitate against legalized abortion, the fight to preserve Christian schools' tax exemptions became one of the most important issues in the political mobilization of conservative evangelicals during the late 1970s. Over the 1960s and 1970s, Christian academies evolved into places where evangelicals spread the word about secular humanism and the fight against feminism. They became bastions of a gendered order and developed the beginnings of a family values agenda. In evangelicals' eyes, Christian schools stood as beacons of a gendered order that they hoped to reestablish across America.[85]

Networks Emerging

From the perspective of Christian school advocates, the family values they championed—including both fidelity to biblical gender norms and respect for authority—appeared out of favor among the public education establishment. Indeed, the IRS battle confirmed to some evangelicals that the government had sinister plans for their children and would brook no attempts to remove students from public schools. The notion of government as enemy helped evangelicals align themselves with the conservative wing of the Republican Party, a marriage many contemporary observers found mystifying.

Notably, 1964 presidential nominee Barry Goldwater blasted evangelicals' ascent in the GOP, referring to "special-issue religious groups" as "divisive element[s] that could tear apart the very spirit of our representative system."[86] He believed evangelicals held views antithetical to traditional conservatism, which wanted a smaller government less intrusive on people's private lives. His criticism focused on the ways the Christian right wanted to expand government control over people's sexual lives and personal decisions.

Conservative evangelicals, on the other hand, saw themselves as fighting alongside political conservatives to check the expansion of a growing—and increasingly liberal—federal government. And Christian schools provided a perfect forum in which to wage this battle. Christian school leaders argued that public schools had foisted a liberal agenda on unsuspecting parents. These leaders constructed a narrative that cast evangelicals as embattled Christians trying to stave off the advances of secular humanism. "The gradual secularization of public schools has caught most Protestants asleep," said a National Association of Christian Schools pamphlet. "The faith of [Christian] children is being undermined in public schools."[87] The sense that the federal government was attacking the family's educational prerogative was critical to Christian schools' success. School founders trumpeted the ways the government intruded on the rightful domain of families.

As Christian school organizations—especially AACS and ASCI—matured in the late 1970s, they served two crucial functions in the politicization of evangelicals. First, they offered conservative Christians a common language for describing the ways the government demeaned the family. Newsletter after newsletter decried the rise of secular humanism in public schools and described the reasons Christians needed to remove their children from humanism's baleful influence. Christian school advocates repeatedly insisted on the importance of discipline. They hammered relentlessly against government attempts to empower children at the expense of parental authority. The words of *Christian School Comment*, *Christian School Alert*, *Christian School Communicator*, and *The Christian Teacher*—not to mention the numerous "how to start a Christian school" books that emerged in the late 1960s and early 1970s—seeped into Christian school handbooks and textbooks. As a result, Christian school students, parents, teachers, and administrators developed a similar (though not monolithic) view of the problems facing American society. A Christian school in Alabama was as likely as one in California to decry the rise of humanism and loss of discipline in public schools. This shared language led to a shared politics.[88]

Second, Christian school organizations helped mobilize conservative Christians politically. The fight against the IRS in 1978 provided one example; another came five years later. When state authorities closed a Christian school in Nebraska in 1983, supporters rallied across the country. For seven years, Faith Baptist Church in Louisville, Nebraska, had refused to submit to mandatory state accreditation procedures. The school argued that the state had no right to require teacher certification or inspect the school's curriculum. A series of state courts, however, affirmed Nebraska's requirements for private schools. After appealing its case all the way to the U.S. Supreme Court (which refused to hear it and thereby ratified the Nebraska court decisions), Faith Baptist Pastor Everett Sileven refused to abide by the courts' decision. The state found him and parents who enrolled children in the 28-person school in contempt of court, and in December Nebraska authorities imprisoned seven parents, while Sileven went into hiding. More than 150 ministers trekked to Louisville to defend Sileven and his academy and to report on the plight of the school. Ed Nelson, an AACS board member from Denver, said he felt "an awful sense of emptiness and horror" at the thought of the pastor's imprisonment, while Jerry Falwell promised to feature the "religious persecution" of the tiny school on his radio and television programs.[89] Even President Reagan chimed in, telling the National Religious Broadcasters that "the jailing of a minister, the padlocking of a church, and the continuing imprisonment of fathers of students" showed that Nebraska's government officials had lost their way.[90]

Reagan's willingness to comment on the plight of a 28-person Christian school in Nebraska testified both to the political power evangelicals wielded by the mid-1980s and to the ways Christian school networks had facilitated the political rise of conservative evangelicals. Christian academies, along with the organizations that formed around them, served as one of the key institutions in the politicization of conservative evangelicals during the 1960s and 1970s. Believing public schools intended to pull children away from their families, conservative Christians founded scores of new academies that popularized some key pieces of the family values agenda. They taught children their roles as young men and women and instilled the importance of authority. Furthermore, the school newsletters popularized the notion that a liberal education establishment had subtly but completely eliminated the traditional values that had once characterized public schools across the country. Launching Christian schools was one logical response to this problem. Another involved taking on the public school establishment itself.

CHAPTER 2

Textbook Politics

In November 1974, as private Christian academies boomed, rural public schools in Kanawha County, West Virginia, stood virtually empty, victims of a two-month-old boycott that led to absenteeism rates of 90 percent or more. Incensed about the introduction of a new language arts curriculum, conservative Christians in the hills around Charleston had promised to keep their children out of the schools as long as the controversial books remained in them. In late September, their actions had forced the school board to impose a thirty-day moratorium on the use of the new curriculum. Five weeks later, the board reinstated the books. Boycotters were unbowed. They vowed to keep their children out of school. On 9 November, the Reverend Avis Hill told a crowd of 2,000 "flag-waving" supporters, "I would rather see my daughter in the funeral home, in God's hands, than five years from now have my daughter stab me in the back because of the books." He then warned the authorities: "We have just begun to fight."[1]

Hill's words captured the intensity of emotion that colored the West Virginia controversy and signaled the main concern of the boycotters: public schools were attempting to undermine the values that had provided stability in rural communities for generations. Observers of the controversy, noting that few protesters claimed to have read the books, said the textbooks were emblematic of larger cultural battles between rural and urban communities or between Christian and secular constituencies.[2] For instance, *Charleston Gazette* city editor Don Marsh wrote, "the books were only a symbol. . . . Many of the protesters are demonstrating against a changing world."[3] According to conservative school board member Alice Moore, the county's new language arts curriculum featured a systematic effort to eradicate conservative values from the next generation. The conservative school protesters in West Virginia believed new textbooks aimed to alienate children from their parents' values.

Figure 3. A protester in the Kanawha County, West Virginia, textbook protest made clear which book she wanted taught in school. Image courtesy of Bill Tiernan.

Alice Moore's frustration with the textbooks highlighted the importance conservative Christians placed on "parental rights," an important part of the family values movement. In a 1974 article, Howard Phillips, a leader of conservative Republicans, offered a clear statement of the importance of parental rights. "There is," he wrote, "no more natural relationship than that between parent and child. When it becomes too easy or common for bureaucracy to interfere with that relationship, America will never be the same."[4] As the government institutions most likely to threaten that relationship, public schools became battlegrounds where conservatives fought to defend their children from the specter of liberalism. Textbook protesters pointed out that their tax dollars paid for the schools and argued that they should exert control over what went on inside. Public educators bristled at the interference. But parents like Moore insisted that they, as the moral and spiritual custodians of their children, deserved primacy of place when it came to education.

Evangelical protests against public education happened all over the country during the 1970s,[5] yet two textbook controversies stand out from this time period—one long and patient, the other brief and fiery. In Texas, retirees Mel and Norma Gabler began systematically reviewing public school textbooks in the early 1960s, looking for evidence of "anti-God" and "anti-American" material. The Gablers made an annual pilgrimage to Austin in order to testify at the statewide textbook adoption hearings, where publishers who violated the Gablers' conservative viewpoints found themselves on the receiving end of harsh critiques. By 1980 the Gablers' relentlessness had caused several textbook publishers to revise curricula so that it met with the Texas couple's approval. The Gablers' efforts to reinstate "traditional" values represented one strategy evangelicals adopted in textbook protests. The Gablers believed publishers had stripped textbooks of the stories and standards that had molded generations of Americans. They determined to recast public school curricula via painstaking attention to detail and requests for revision. In short, the Gablers focused on incremental changes to textbooks as part of a decades-long effort to insert conservative values in public education.

A different approach characterized the short-lived but intense conflict over English textbooks in Kanawha County. While Moore followed the Gablers' focus on textbook minutiae, the West Virginia protest's chief legacy was its populist character. Fed up with the educational establishment, parents spread word of the boycott via phone. Fed up with the coal companies, miners joined these parents by striking. As a result, some rural schools in Kanawha County reported near-zero attendance in September, and "wildcat" strikes were costing coal producers over \$250,000 per day by mid-October. The link between English textbooks and the school boycott was tenuous, and that between public school curricula and coal mining was nonexistent. Reporters suggested that the coal miners striking on behalf of textbook protesters were engaged in a duplicitous effort to reduce coal stockpiles in advance of a looming contract negotiation. The miners' choice to strike alongside the textbook protesters signaled a cultural rebellion against outsiders. This rebellion drew on an odd mixture of conservative longing for a nostalgic ideal and labor activism against management. The protesters did not even share religious commitments: a local businessman launched the "Non-Christian American Parents" as a secular wing of the textbook protest. In short, a slew of mixed motives and disparate groups fueled the West Virginia protest. They shared only a widespread resentment of elites and outsiders. This populist protest fit perfectly in the nascent family values movement, which emphasized commitment to the nurture of families against whatever entities encroached on their turf.

These two textbook protests featured different modes of activism in the family values movement. In Texas, conservative parent-activists led a patient, thorough attack on textbooks, based on rigorous reviews of curricula and a strategy of working within the system. In West Virginia, protesters eschewed the political process in favor of strikes, boycotts, and demonstrations. These two movements depended on each other. The West Virginia protesters drew on the Gablers' systemic critique to articulate their otherwise inchoate anger, while the Gablers pointed to the protesters' rage as evidence that their views resonated widely. And though the protests in Texas and West Virginia took different forms, evangelicals in both places shared the sense that outsiders were trying to corrupt their children. Though relatively few politicians were talking about "family values" during the mid-1970s, these movements illustrated the symbolic power of parents—especially mothers—fighting for their children.

Evangelicals and Public Education

Evangelicals' frustration with public schools in the 1970s belied a long history of support for public education among conservative Protestants. New England Puritans launched the earliest compulsory schooling campaigns in North America. Throughout the colonial period, conservative Christians launched schools to combat the "savagery" of American life. These schools privileged moral education as a way of inculcating Christian virtue among citizens. In the early nineteenth century, democratizing influences encouraged American Christians to read the Bible for themselves so they would not have to depend on the interpretations of ministers. Evangelicals published millions of Bibles and tracts, all of which encouraged the broadening of literacy. Primary schools often used these Bibles and tracts, alongside readers heavy with scriptural passages, to instruct their students. While secondary education in the nineteenth century became increasingly secular and vocational, public schools around the country retained a strongly Protestant character. They hardly seemed threatening to evangelicals, since evangelicals largely dominated them.[6]

At the dawn of the twentieth century, debates over the teaching of evolution in public schools changed the relationship between evangelicals and public schools. Charles Darwin's theory of natural selection threatened Christians who believed in a literal interpretation of the biblical creation story. Increasing numbers of biologists accepted Darwinian evolution, and public school textbooks began to reflect this growing scientific consensus. Conservative Christians fought back in the early 1920s, passing laws in five southern states forbidding the teaching of evolution in public high schools. The American Civil Liberties Union (ACLU) challenged Tennessee's law in the 1925 Scopes trial, which charged biology teacher John Scopes with illegally teaching Darwinism to high school students and pitted atheist trial lawyer Clarence Darrow against William Jennings Bryan, a three-time presidential nominee who championed the anti-evolution cause. Bryan represented a faction of conservative Christians called fundamentalists, who took their name from a series of pamphlets called *The Fundamentals*, published from 1910 to 1915. Fundamentalists argued that "modernists" threatened the foundations of Christian civilization. Though fundamentalism had not emerged as a response to the teaching of evolution, fundamentalists increasingly became identified with the anti-evolution cause in the 1920s. Bryan successfully represented them in the Scopes trial, as the judge upheld the Tennessee statute and fined Scopes $100 ($50 higher than Tennessee law permitted—a technicality that allowed Scopes to win his appeal). In the five years after the trial, fundamentalists worked with other Americans concerned about the teaching of evolution, and they succeeded in pushing through a host of anti-evolution statutes across the nation.[7]

In spite of these victories—and in spite of fundamentalism's internal concerns with theological issues unrelated to evolution—popular media portrayed the Scopes trial as a fatal blow to fundamentalism. While several scholars have shown that fundamentalism hardly suffered a mortal wound in 1925, the perception of defeat shaped both fundamentalists and non-fundamentalists alike. Fundamentalists believed their values had lost sway in public schools, and over time they crafted a narrative of embattlement that pitted true Christian believers against a the powerful forces of secularism. They believed these secular forces controlled American government, and they saw public schools as agents of indoctrination. Yet fundamentalists and evangelicals never ceased fighting for the return of "Christian" (i.e., evangelical) education in the public schools. They contended that a minority of noisy and aggressive secularists had hijacked the school system against the unstated but strong wishes of a Christian majority.

Fighting Textbooks in Texas

Among evangelical activists who agitated for public school reform, Mel and Norma Gabler stand as the most important. In 1961, according to the Gablers, their son Jim came home complaining about his high school history class. Jim told his parents that his textbooks taught him a history different from what had learned at home. Whereas Mel and Norma had extolled the leadership and faith of George Washington, Jim's textbook offered "only a brief sentence . . . about the loyalty of [Washington's] army at Valley Forge and nothing about his deep religious faith." Moreover, "there was nothing about any restrictions on the federal government and nothing about rights or freedoms retained by the people and the states." This portrait of American history and government struck the Gablers as revisionist and liberal, and, in the words of their authorized biographer, "set Mel on fire."[8] Jim's role in this story was key: the Gablers predicated their activism on an attempt to shield their son from liberal education.

The Gablers determined to exert some control over their son's curriculum. According to Texas policy, the State Department of Education had to solicit public comment on all proposed textbooks for Texas public schools in an annual public hearing, offering the Gablers a forum for airing their complaints. Norma agreed to attend the 1962 adoption hearings in Austin alone. "I had never traveled anywhere in my life by myself," she said. "I was just going to do it that one year, but it was just something that went on and on."[9]

In fact, she appeared in Austin every autumn for the next two decades. She faced what she described as humiliating treatment in the earliest years, when state board members and textbook publishers dismissed her as a shrill, out-of-touch reactionary. But she returned each year with increasingly detailed "bills of particulars" (lists of objectionable material) for textbooks under consideration. She was never quite as reticent one might imagine from the authorized biographies, and her status as mother of an aggrieved son lent her important rhetorical standing. In the family values movement, the mother carried symbolic power. The ideology of family values suggested that women's highest calling lay in the home, where she reared and taught her children. Threats to this idyllic vision of home sanctioned mothers like Gabler to leave the domestic sphere and agitate against "anti-family" forces. The Gablers predicated their activism on their son Jim's frustration with the public schools. Justified by the schools' violation of parental rights, Norma could range far outside the home in defense of her family. The Texas Board of Education understood this symbolic power, and though they chafed at Gabler's tedious critiques of school textbooks, the adoption board allotted her more and more time at the hearings.

Though writing "bills of particulars" was a new political strategy, Norma Gabler's rhetorical and symbolic power as a mother echoed the California "housewife populists" of the 1950s. During that decade, conservative women across Los Angeles and Orange County banded together in conservative bookstores, lectures, and political rallies. They campaigned against social scientists and educational bureaucrats, arguing that southern California's public schools were attempting to undermine parental authority and to inculcate liberal values in their children. These women embedded "powerfully localistic, antiexpert, home-rule dimensions" in conservative politics—themes Gabler exemplified in her crusade against liberal textbooks.[10] Gabler used her status as an aggrieved mother to claim political authority. As policymakers became more inclined to promote the traditional family, that status gave Gabler power.

Still, a decade passed before Gabler began to see measureable success. In 1973, she brought two proposed offerings in sociology and psychology to the hearings wrapped in brown paper bags. She claimed the ploy helped her avoid arrest. "These [books] are so dirty I was afraid I might get picked up and charged with possessing pornography," she said. And it was not dirty pictures or depictions of sexual acts that raised her ire. Rather, Gabler bemoaned the books' support for gay rights. "Read this chapter," she challenged

the board, "and see if you don't think it makes an all-out play for the homosexual."[11] Coming on the heels of a horrific crime spree in which three gay
men killed twenty-seven teenage boys in Houston, Norma Gabler's accusa-
tion resonated in an atmosphere of heightened fear.[12] The state adoption
board rejected six of the eight books the Gablers had marked objectionable
(by far their highest rate of success in protesting textbooks), and sent the
other two books back to their publishers for revision. Gabler had leveraged
dogged research, rhetorical power as a mother, and a clever public relations
ploy in acquiring a measure of power over Texas public school curricula.

This power was not trivial. Whereas other states allowed local school districts to determine which curricula they would adopt, Texas districts could
purchase only books on the statewide approved list. That list typically included only five series in a given discipline. The five publishers whose books
made the cut in a given field were assured of high volume sales for a six-year
period. (Textbooks in two or three disciplines came up for adoption each
year; those chosen won a term of six years on the approved books list.) As
one of the largest states with a statewide adoption procedure, the Texas hearings often became a make-or-break event for a textbook series. "Partly because they wield their influence in Texas," said a 1984 *Christianity Today*
article, "the Gablers are regarded as two of the most powerful people in education today."[13] A 1980 *Baltimore Evening Sun* article put it in starker terms:
"the Gablers make grown men and women in the $700 million textbook pub-
lishing business quake with fear."[14] Because of Texas's adoption procedures,
which provided virtually limitless time to object to books line-by-line, the
couple became the most significant force in the revision of textbooks for public schools.[15] Books the Gablers barred from Texas schools faced an uphill
battle in the multimillion-dollar textbook industry.

As their fame spread in conservative circles, the Gablers' reviews of books
became the basis for conservative protests in other states. In the late 1960s
the Gablers founded Educational Research Analysts, a nonprofit organization that institutionalized the work they had begun. Educational Research
Analysts hired a staff of reviewers and became a national clearinghouse for
conservative reviews of textbooks.[16] Its website flatly stated, "Other states
should always demand the Texas edition of a book if there is one; and if there
is no Texas edition it is probably an inferior book. . . . Publishers submit their
least offensive books in Texas, because Texas has 'watchdogs.' "[17] Losers in the
Texas adoption process thereby lost not only Texas's huge market, but also
struggled in other states. And when textbook controversies cropped up

elsewhere, local leaders often phoned the Gablers for advice and support. Alice Moore, the West Virginia school board conservative, contacted the Gablers early in her 1974 campaign against liberal textbooks, and soon afterward the Texas couple visited the region for a speaking tour. When the Christian right became a national political force in the late 1970s, leaders such as Jerry Falwell, Phyllis Schlafly, and Richard Viguerie publicly commended the Gablers' work. Conservatives around the nation cheered the Gablers as exemplary of what could happen when decent parents stood up for family values.

Their opponents, not surprisingly, chafed at the Gablers' power. Critic Edward Jenkinson said that the Gablers "search for anything that does not coincide perfectly with their particular view of reality or with their perception of any subject matter."[18] Likewise, in a 1981 article for *Texas Monthly*, scholar William Martin blasted the Gablers. "Norma Gabler's difficulty with unanticipated questions is a communicable disease, and she is working to spread it," wrote Martin. "The Gablers seem incapable of considering the possibility that a textbook might meet their criteria of fairness, objectivity, and patriotism and still be critical of any aspect of American life."[19] Martin's frustration with the Gablers' conservatism mirrored that of many people associated with education. Teachers, publishers, and textbook writers had spent two generations shaping a public school system that valued critical thinking and embraced American pluralism. The Gablers threatened to dismantle that system. According to them, public schools that valued critical thinking skills and pushed students to explore questions rather than memorize pat answers undermined family values. If parents taught children about the faith and courage of George Washington, why did schoolteachers think they had a right to undermine the message?

The Gablers' rhetorical strategy, which made liberals out of former centrists, became a fixture of Christian right politics. In Texas, the Gablers could count on support from archconservatives, but more important, they could assume most Texans wanted to be included in the rhetorical categories they constructed. Their authorized biographer described them as "the cream of self-reliant Middle America. They lived by the old landmarks, took child-rearing seriously, supported community institutions, sang 'God Bless America' with a lump in their throats, and believed that the American system of limited and divided governmental power was the best under the sun."[20] That description portrayed the Gablers as "centrist" conservatives. That is, the Gablers—not their opponents—stood for the values and assumptions of the

majority. Assertive liberals provided a necessary foil. Madalyn Murray
O'Hair, founder of American Atheists, lived in Austin and regularly provided
Texas Christians with a rhetorical target as she dismissed religious faith. The
publishers and board members the Gablers fought against hardly hewed to
O'Hair's atheism—many were Christians themselves—yet the Gablers successfully painted them into a corner. They could choose one side or the other:
either they agreed with the Gablers and supported the values of right-
thinking people, or they chose the secularism of people like O'Hair.

This "us against them" model mirrored developments in postwar American religion that had increasingly polarized liberals and conservatives, especially in the southwest.[21] Historian Andrew Manis has located a "distinctively
contentious mode of religious interaction on America's Southwestern frontier," specifically in Texas.[22] Drawing on the legacy of Texan fundamentalists
like J. Frank Norris, late twentieth-century conservatives in that state rose to
the forefront of the American right by displaying a muscular conservatism
that gave no quarter to liberalism. Norma Gabler may have played up her
innocence, but she was no shrinking violet. The Gablers drew on a wellspring
of hard-edged conservatism that had wide appeal in east Texas. Their success
depended on their ability to make a "distinctively contentious" religious
mood normative for a wide swath of conservative Texans. For if textbooks
threatened people who "lived by the old landmarks" and sang "God Bless
America" "with a lump in their throats," it was high time to take on
textbooks.

Righteous Certainty

The Gablers frustrated opponents who failed to understand the couple's gen-
erous estimation of textbooks' power. Whereas publishers and adoption
boards saw teaching tolerance as a necessary piece of pluralistic education,
the Gablers feared too much tolerance in textbooks would fundamentally
alter the national landscape. They frequently quoted publishing magnate
D. C. Heath, who said, "Let me publish the textbooks of a nation and I care not
who writes its songs or makes its laws."[23] Because they, like Christian school
advocates, believed curricula played a significant role in the moral education
of students, the Gablers raised the stakes of textbook debates. A short story
that dwelled on sexuality threatened not only to take away a child's innocence
but also to push that student away from his parents' values and toward an

ambiguous morality. While progressive educators contended that they were broadening students' horizons, allowing them to engage new ideas and arrive at their own conclusions, the Gablers and their allies argued that such "broadening" foreclosed the possibility of students' choosing their parents' conservatism. And moving away from "traditional" values entailed enormous social costs. One of the Gablers' mimeographed flyers proclaimed, "UNTIL TEXTBOOKS ARE CHANGED, there is no possibility that crime, violence, VD and abortion rates will decrease . . . TEXTBOOKS mold NATIONS because they largely determine HOW a nation votes, WHAT it becomes and WHERE it goes!"[24] Liberal textbooks, in other words, meant a liberal America.

The Gablers' belief in the determinative power of written texts emerged at least in part from their faith in scripture. Their authorized biographer claimed that before they began reviewing curricula, "Mel and Norma Gabler trusted textbooks almost as much as they did the Bible."[25] This faith depended not only on the books' ability to communicate historical facts or mathematical principles, but also on the texts' explicit moral code. For the Gablers, textbooks played a complementary role to the Bible, which, in their reading, "prescribed the only code by which civilizations can effectively remain in existence!" Textbooks were not quite as authoritative as the Bible, but the Gablers clearly expected school curricula to reinforce the "Christian-Judeo morals, values, and standards as given to us by God through His Word." For people who once trusted public school curricula "almost as much as they did the Bible," the permissiveness that pervaded contemporary texts struck the Gablers as an abdication of responsibility. "Too many textbooks," they complained, "leave students to make up their own minds about things." Prescriptive teachings on morality, which progressives had labored to eliminate from public school classrooms, seemed crucial to the Gablers.[26]

The Gablers also approached textbooks as references for facts rather than conduits of critical thinking skills, a perspective that predisposed them against ambiguity in any form. Just as they expected the Bible to present straightforward moral commands, they believed textbooks ought to teach straightforward prescriptive lessons. For instance, they derided the "new math" not only because it hampered children's arithmetic skills, but also because "such abstract teaching to young minds will tend to destroy the students' belief in absolutes." Likewise, they thought that a growing emphasis on social history did not awaken students to new ways of thinking about our nation's past; it threatened the tried-and-true version of history that had inspired generations of patriots. Norma scored points at the 1972 adoption hearing by pointing out that one history book being considered for use in Texas schools gave six and a half pages to Marilyn Monroe and only five lines to George Washington. She asked, "is Texas ready for Marilyn to become mother of our country?"[27] Norma's denunciation of Macmillan Publishing's "sexy" history book grabbed headlines around the country. It also signaled the unshakeable confidence the Gablers felt about American history. "The Gablers seem to believe," wrote William Martin, "that all the essential pertinent facts are well known and should be taught as they were in older textbooks."[28] History had not changed—textbooks had.

Control over the teaching of history occupied a central role in the Gablers' campaign. They championed the teaching of the American Revolution as a golden age where men of faith banded together to throw off the yoke of tyranny, a familiar tale to most American schoolchildren. But the Gablers worried that new social historians muddied the waters by highlighting the Founding Fathers' foibles and celebrating underrepresented people or groups. When Mel compared his son's textbook (published in 1955) to texts published in 1925 and 1885, familiar stories' conspicuous absence in the later text signaled to him a conspiratorial attempt to remove religion and conservatism from the nation's history. "Change does not always spell progress," he said, "nor does newness guarantee improvement."[29] In a society they perceived as poised on the brink of catastrophe, the Gablers felt a need to retain an unambiguous story of national origins, populated by men of unassailable good intentions.

Control over history entailed more than just a familiar retelling of the nation's founding myths, it also made normative the social and cultural conventions of earlier generations. Specifically, the Gablers celebrated the fixity of gender roles. According to Martin, "the Gablers' resistance to cultural variation and social change is seen nowhere more clearly than in their attitude toward sex roles."[30] Whereas eighteenth- and nineteenth-century Americans understood their God-given responsibilities as men and women, twentieth-century feminists wanted to upset the apple cart. According to a 1984 *Christianity Today* article, the Gablers "credit feminists with the greatest success in changing texts over the past ten years." The National Organization for Women, they said, "obtained 1,651 generic alterations in elementary spellers and math books for Texas, alterations such as changing 'mother will bake a cake' to 'father will bake a cake.'"[31] Changes like these, though innocuous in isolation, convinced the Gablers that feminists intended to reshape schoolchildren's conceptions of gender roles. And feminist-inspired modifications displayed a stubborn rejection of obvious realities. "Feminist pressure groups," said Norma, "are trying to depict America in texts not as life has been or is, but as they want it to become—a completely egalitarian society.... They're trying to force women into a role reversal that's against our culture and tradition and in some instances against the Bible."[32]

The Gablers felt threatened by feminist-inspired changes to schoolbooks because the alterations delegitimized family values. Feminists, said Norma, "give the impression that a woman becomes a slave in marriage" and "act as if motherhood is second-class." They shunned taking their husbands' names and avoided bearing children at all costs. Norma, however, "like[d] to be Mrs. G" and considered motherhood "the highest privilege a woman can have."[33] Understanding the importance conservative Christian women placed on their roles as wives and mothers helps explain why textbook changes seemed such a threat. It was not simply that texts did away with traditional gender roles; the Gablers felt that feminists disparaged conservative women's choices. Even a Massachusetts education official recognized that the privileging of feminist-inspired depictions of women in textbooks represented a "distortion" that was "deeply offensive to those women, whether conservative Christians or not, who choose to devote at least some years to the full-time care of their children."[34] Norma and her compatriots stopped short of saying all that women should remain in the home, and Norma's example clearly repudiated the notion that women had no place in public life. But the Gablers felt a woman's glory lay in the home. Textbooks that advanced egalitarian agendas, such as the desire for women to earn pay equal to men, ignored that such agendas could come only if women "abandon their highest profession—as mothers molding young lives."[35]

The Gablers also targeted biology textbooks that endorsed evolution. The Gablers viewed evolution as an assault on the biblical creation story and as "the cornerstone of secular humanism."[36] That is, by conceding that humans descended from animals, evolutionists dismissed the Bible's depiction of humans as created in the image of God. Christians had long used that tenet not only to justify humans' exalted status in the created realm, but also to hold people accountable for their sin. Because humans were created in the image of God, God related to humans in a unique way, offering them a covenant, law, and redemption. For the Gablers and other evangelicals, suggesting that humans had evolved did more than threaten scripture (which was bad enough). It undercut the need for God, threatened humans' place in the created order, and contended that all human behavior and morals had evolved as part of a natural process. Sin became a cultural particularity rather than a universal truth. Secular humanists, thought the Gablers, translated this dismissal of sin into advocacy of experimentation and libertinism in the classroom. The Gablers thereby fought passionately—and successfully—against science books that presented evolution as an established fact. Texts in the 1950s and 1960s, reflecting the consensus among academic scientists, portrayed evolution as the foundation of modern biology. But by the end of the 1970s, owing in part to the Gablers' efforts, one high school biology textbook contained only three references to evolution, while another gave the "scientific" theory of creation the same number of pages as it did evolution. "If there is one battle Mel and Norma Gabler have been winning in the last twenty years," said one reporter, "it is their fight to have creationism taught alongside evolution."[37]

In 1970 the Gablers' concerns about textbooks won official sanction when Texas passed a series of adoption guidelines for all textbook series. These requirements included prohibitions of profanity, obscenity, or "blatantly offensive language."[38] Moreover, they demanded that positive depictions of women include mothers and homemakers alongside truck drivers and executives. Publishers bent under the pressure, revising entire series or offering two versions of the same text: the standard version and a special "Texas version" that omitted potentially offensive words and stories. Yet even for publishers who could afford to publish two sets of the same textbooks, decisions about what to include were fraught with peril. In an interview with *Christianity Today*, Richard Carroll, president of textbook publisher Allyn & Bacon, admitted, "We now consider it an editorial mistake to have a violent episode in a reader."[39] The same could be said for profanity or an overabundance of feminism. That Carroll called inclusion of violent episodes an editorial mistake (rather than a judgment call) indicated the self-censorship publishers had adopted as a result of the Gablers' efforts. Because they knew the Gablers would comb through their books line by line and cause trouble for texts that impugned conservative values, textbook publishers encouraged editors simply to remove potential targets.

With each issue the Gablers addressed—whether it was social history, feminism, or evolution—they displayed a rigorous consistency in their worldview. Their surety contrasted sharply with liberals' desire for questioning and deconstruction of pat narratives. Norma put it simply when she told an interviewer, "What some textbooks are doing, is giving students ideas, and ideas will never do them as much good as facts."[40] The distinction between ideas and facts baffled educators, who had become increasingly skeptical of any hard-and-fast truths. But to conservatives, the Gablers' message communicated an epistemic certainty that emerged from their faith. They inherited a philosophical tradition called common sense realism, which taught that things appeared as they were. Common sense realism held that the Bible and nature corresponded; one could assume that observations of society and nature would confirm the teachings of scripture. Conservatives had long since given up hope that historians, feminists, or scientists would share this belief, but they doggedly maintained that "ordinary people" enjoyed as much right to interpret their surroundings as did experts. Common sense realism was a populist philosophy that devalued the importance of expertise. As one critic noted, anti-textbook leaders "claimed not that they were more expert than the teachers who chose the books but that experts were not be trusted."[41] The experts waffled on important issues, encouraging schoolchildren to find their own values. Conservatives told children what to believe, an activity they considered essential to their proper role as parents. And they could be sure that right-thinking people would endorse their teachings because their common sense epistemology left little room to doubt fundamental assumptions.

Mel and Norma Gabler's conviction that parents ought to control their children's education resonated among evangelicals. Drawing on the same history of public education that Christian school advocates had articulated, the Gablers feared that John Dewey and his secular humanist disciples had taken control of the nation's schools and turned them into "government seminaries."[42] They argued that the schools aimed to erase moral foundations that had provided stability for generations. In response, the Gablers showed up in Austin year after year, arguing for and winning the right to make incremental changes to textbooks destined for Texas public schools.

Their efforts continued to resonate. In 2010, a battle over social studies standards in Texas textbooks garnered national attention, as Don McElroy, a dentist, fundamentalist, and member of the state board of education, spearheaded efforts to revise history books by including a greater emphasis on America's "Christian origins." McElroy told a *New York Times* reporter how he met with textbook publishers over Mexican food and told them, "We want stories with morals, not P.C. stories." After this meeting, a publisher wrote McElroy an email thanking him "for the impact [McElroy has] had on the development of Pearson's Scott Foresman Reading Street series." Watchdog Kathy Miller expressed incredulity at McElroy's dismissal of standards crafted by experts. "Last year," she said, "Don McElroy believed he was smarter than the National Academy of Sciences, and he now believes he's smarter than professors of American history." [43] A similar attitude characterized the Gablers. They might not have believed they were smarter than the experts they battled, but they certainly believed they had just as much right to shape schoolbooks. This conviction in parents' rights to shape their children's education stood as an essential component of family values.

Controversy in West Virginia

While the Gablers' complaints displayed ideological coherence and won them considerable power, many reporters questioned their representativeness. The Gablers portrayed themselves as centrists. Yet neither held an elected office, and the textbook selection process afforded them disproportionate power. Critics charged them with extremism and contended they had a tiny constituency. But the 1974 textbook controversy in Kanawha County, West Virginia, suggested otherwise. The *New York Times* covered the West Virginia story almost daily in September and featured front-page stories on the controversy throughout the fall. The grassroots origins and widespread support for this protest offered the Gablers populist cover. They could point to it as an example of "decent people" becoming fed up with the "educational establishment." Especially in its earliest stages, the West Virginia protest lacked the ideological coherence of the Gablers' campaign. But the Kanawha County controversy displayed grassroots opposition to educational elites.

In the late 1960s, Kanawha County introduced sexual education in all grades, prompting Alice Moore, wife of a Churches of Christ minister, to review the new curriculum. What she found appalled her. Moore felt the curriculum taught "children how to think, feel, and act about morals, a prerogative which she felt should be restricted to home and church." In 1970 she ran for an open spot on the Kanawha County school board, campaigning against the sex ed curriculum. Moore faced an uphill battle: school board members typically claimed educational experience or expertise, and she had none. Moreover, she faced an incumbent who led 2 to 1 in polls just a week before the election. But her opponent's negative ads, which portrayed Moore as a rabid censor, backfired. A local janitor purportedly rescued a stack of Bibles from incineration in one of the county schools. Moore's campaign ran an ad in which she held up a charred Bible and said, "They have the nerve to call *me* a book burner." That ad struck home. Moore won a spot on the board.[44]

Four years later, Moore inaugurated a campaign against textbooks that thrust Kanawha County into the national spotlight. That March, following established protocol, a textbook review committee forwarded their recommendations for a new language arts curriculum to the school board and made the curriculum (which encompassed more than 300 volumes) available for public review. Most people familiar with the adoption process expected the board to rubber stamp the textbook committee's recommendation at its 11 April meeting. But Moore contended that a month was not enough time to review all the volumes, and in April she convinced the board to pass only a temporary approval of the books, conditional on board members' review of the new curriculum.

In May Moore again objected to the language arts textbooks, this time attracting the notice of the local news media and laying the groundwork for a controversy that would roil Kanawha County for the next eight months. At the 23 May 1974 school board meeting, Moore called the proposed English texts "trashy, filthy and too one-sided." She said, "I am on this Board and represent a wide constituency of people who don't want this trash."[45] The board postponed voting on the books' permanent adoption once more, scheduling a June meeting devoted to discussion of the proposed curriculum. Letters to the editor from both pro- and anti-textbook partisans flooded Charleston's two daily newspapers, the *Gazette* and the *Daily Mail*. The local ABC affiliate ran a series of on-air editorials supporting the books during the first week of June. Moore fought back, speaking in the press and at local churches. When the school board reconvened on 27 June, a crowd of 500 packed the school administration building. Those who could not fit inside stood outside in a driving rain, peering through the windows. Several hours of heated testimony ensued, but in the end the board voted 3-2 to adopt all but eight of the most controversial books. (New board member Matthew Kinsolving joined Moore in voting against the books.) Conservatives expressed disappointment, but most felt the June meeting signaled the end of their protest. "Now the issue is mercifully over," opined the Charleston *Gazette*.[46]

It was not. When schools opened in September, protests against the books intensified and moved away from official forums. Over Labor Day weekend, conservative parents spread word of a countywide boycott of schools. Moore sympathized with but did not "discourage, encourage, or participate in the boycott."[47] Marvin Horan, a Free Will Baptist minister from the rural part of the county, assumed leadership of the anti-textbook forces. At a rally the night before schools opened, Horan told the crowd, "We could use a big

book-burning right here"[48]—an activity Moore had explicitly repudiated in
her initial campaign for the school board. When asked about the boycott,
Moore said, "I haven't been involved in this in any way, and I didn't know Mr.
Horan until yesterday."[49] But the protest had moved away from school board
meetings and adoption hearings. Leaders like Horan took the fight to the
people. Schools opened 3 September with 20 percent fewer students than on
opening day in 1973.[50] Many schools in and around Charleston (the county
seat and state capital) reported no major drop-off in attendance, meaning
that high rates of absenteeism prevailed in rural schools. Still, the climate was
tense countywide. One Charleston teacher said, "The chaos initiated on the
opening day of school was awesome."[51]

Protesters lodged a wide variety of complaints against the textbooks.
Alice Moore complained about teachers guides that encouraged open-ended
questions rather than didactic instruction. Moore deemed such methods
wishy-washy and ineffectual. Other leaders of the protest focused on profanity and material that challenged the Bible's authority. The Rev. Lewis Harrah,
for instance, said, "one third-grade textbook that he read would undermine
at least 7 of his church's 15 basic standards" and "our belief that the Bible is
absolute."[52] Still other protest leaders admitted they "wouldn't turn a page of
the filth[y]" textbooks.[53] These men and women relied on multi-page ads in
local newspapers that dutifully transcribed every passage in high school literature anthologies that featured the words bitch, hell, or damn, along with
passages that offered even the most tepid questioning of the Christian God.[54]
Protesters cited the passages in these ads as proof of the curriculum's attack
on conservative values. Some of the ads displayed passages that appeared
only in literature supplements for high school classes as if these passages featured in elementary school readers. Some ads ran passages that appeared in
none of the books under consideration.

Yet if protesters displayed confusion over what the books actually said,
they achieved more solidarity in tactics. Realizing that a school boycott alone
might fizzle, textbook protesters set up pickets at local coal mines, convincing miners, many of whom went to church or worked with textbook protesters, to walk off the job. Wildcat strikes (unsanctioned by the miners' union)
began just two days after the school boycott. At the height of these strikes in
early October, picketing miners closed nearly all the mines in a four-county
area around Charleston. "Whatever kept the miners out of the mines," wrote
one reporter, "provided the anti-textbook movement with enough power to
force concessions."[55] The concessions included a thirty-day moratorium on

use of the new books, which were removed from all Kanawha County schools during the third week of classes. The miners' strike added supporters and financial pressure to the protest, allowing it to stretch from days into weeks.

Union president Arnold Miller displayed frustration with the wildcat strikes. The UMW contract expired on 12 November, and Miller, untested in nationwide contract negotiations, did not want miners striking without union approval. Moreover, the UMW believed picketing miners were preventing colleagues who wanted to work from doing so. Just one day into the wildcat strike, Miller's press secretary Bernard Aronson said, "We are outraged that people who have private concerns which have nothing to do with coal miners would deprive miners of their wage earnings over an issue that has no bearing on coal miners' work. We expect and call on the men to go back to work and ignore this foolishness."[56] While some critics claimed that the UMW leaders secretly rejoiced at the walkout, which depleted coal stockpiles that would have helped coal companies weather the impending nationwide strike, the danger of a rogue group of miners concerned union leadership deeply. They repeatedly called on miners to abort the wildcat strike and fall in line with union decrees.[57]

Miners, however, had other plans. They resisted demands by Miller and mine operators to return to work through the middle of October. On 14 September, the *Charleston Daily Mail* reported that the textbook controversy had metamorphosed into "an outright coal mining strike."[58] Harry Whittington, one of the miners who went on strike, put his opposition in patriotic terms. "We just want people to know that we believe in our flag," he said. "Khrushchev even told Kennedy he could take over this country if he could reach our children."[59] Miners and textbook protesters set up pickets at mines in Kanawha, Boone, and Fayette Counties (neither Boone nor Fayette used any of the controversial textbooks). Violence erupted at some picket lines, and two men were shot (protesters fired on a trucker trying to cross a picket line, and a pro-textbook advocate shot someone he mistakenly identified as an attacker).[60] Not all miners supported the strikes. "We supported the book boycott, but not the present strike," said one. "Those are miners out there for picketing, but not for the UMW."[61] At the height of the protest in early October, miners were losing $220,000 in wages daily. While many supported the school boycott, they could not afford lost wages. Picketers counted on coal miners' respect for picket lines, and miners largely stayed out of mines where protesters had set up pickets. But newspaper reports made it clear that a substantial portion of miners wanted to honor the UMW demands to return to work, even if they sympathized with the school boycott.

While miners fought over whether to participate in the protest, leaders of the school boycott disagreed about how to proceed. Like other populist uprisings, the Kanawha County controversy featured a range of grievances, strategies, and goals. At a rally on the third weekend of the boycott, Rev. Marvin Horan argued that parents should return their children to school and solicited contributions so anti-textbook forces could fight a court battle against the books. The school board, after all, had put a thirty-day moratorium on the new English books. "If the board is still sticking those books in" after the moratorium, said Horan, "we'll get the miners to go out with us and get a new contract from the school board." Horan's fellow pastor Ezra Graley, on the other hand, urged boycotters and striking miners to "hold the battle line" and asked parents and children to "stay home until this thing is over."[62] The various factions of anti-textbook activists vied for attention and competed over strategy, creating a protest that attracted nationwide attention but lacked coordination. Moreover, a powerful array of institutional opponents—from the school board to the UMW—lined up against the protesters. This powerful opposition, alongside the increasing stress of missed school days and lost wages, threatened to derail the protest as the fall wore on.

At the beginning of October, however, political conservatives from across the country flocked to Kanawha County, giving the movement coordination and direction. During the first week of October, the Gablers flew in for a whirlwind speaking tour. James McKenna, a lawyer for the conservative Heritage Foundation, promised his legal services to the anti-textbook cause for as long as necessary. Robert Dornan, a California Republican who would win election to Congress in 1976, began touting the protesters as exemplary Americans, determined to check the advance of a liberal onslaught. These men and women framed the textbook controversy as a family values protest. Dornan, for instance, said that the "thin slice" of West Virginians who supported the textbooks "also support such issues as abortion, legalization of marijuana, forced busing for racial balance and pornography." Dornan's characterization homogenized both the protesters and their opponents. He painted a picture that portrayed the protest as a struggle for "what parents want."[63] That language resonated with the anti-textbook activists but did not capture the multiplicity of forces at work in the controversy.

Even as the protest gained high-profile activists and a more streamlined profile, violence escalated and exacerbated tensions. The school board's thirty-day moratorium on new textbooks expired in the second week of October, when a textbook review committee voted 11–6 to reinstate some of the book series under protest. That night, protesters firebombed two schools and broke windows at a third.[64] Two weeks later, again in the middle of the night, anti-textbook operatives threw a lit stick of dynamite through a window of a rural elementary school.[65] And on the night before Halloween, someone left fifteen sticks of dynamite under the gas meter at the board of education building (they did not explode). No injuries resulted from these incidents, but schools incurred damages amounting to several thousand dollars. In late October attendance dropped to its lowest level of the year. Unbowed—or perhaps hardened—by the escalating violence, the review committee recommended the reinstatement of all the books at its 8 November meeting (only Moore dissented). And while the board hoped this decision would be final, those longing for an end to the controversy would once again be disappointed.

The 8 November vote to reinstate the books triggered a new wave of demonstrations, and the persistence of the boycotts in rural areas of the county finally forced sweeping concessions from the school board. Protesters fired shotguns at two school buses over Veterans Day weekend. No one was hurt, but tension remained high. The mayor of Cedar Grove, a rural community in Kanawha County, unintentionally alleviated some of the stress by issuing an arrest warrant for pro-textbook school board members. The charge was contributing to the delinquency of minors. The board members seemed bemused by the stunt—they beat the charges—but the pressure remained. Superintendent Kenneth Underwood announced his resignation in early December. Despite voting to reinstate the books, the board demanded that two of the most controversial series remain in the school library (thus ensuring that most students would not use them). And at its 23 November meeting, the board adopted a series of guidelines for textbook adoptions that honored most of the anti-textbook forces' demands. Future books could not "intrude into the privacy of students' homes by asking personal questions," and they "must recognize the sanctity of the home and emphasize its importance as the basic unit of American society."[66] Such requirements represented triumphs for the protesters. Meanwhile, national conservative leaders helped anti-textbook West Virginians gain an audience with U.S. secretary of education Terrell Bell. Bell promised an investigation into the West Virginia situation. "Publishers must recognize that we have compulsory attendance laws and that children are the captive audience of the schools," he said. Parents "have a right to expect that the schools . . . will support the values and standards that their children are taught at home."[67] Protesters viewed Bell's statement as a presidential endorsement of their cause.

At the end of September the protest seemed riven by factions; by early December it had forced sweeping concessions from the board and won an audience with the secretary of education. This success depended on two developments: the ability of outside leaders to craft an effective narrative for the protest and the appearance of violence as a reminder of the seething resentment underlying the official narrative. The Gablers, McKenna, and Dornan provided direction, money, and an imprimatur from the family values movement. Their support also created both real and rhetorical foils against which protesters could direct their anger. Prior to mid-October, the school boycott and the miners' strikes seemed to have little in common. But in the weeks after the arrival of national conservatives, the West Virginia controversy became embedded in the family values movement. Protesters talked about protecting parents' rights. Moreover, unsanctioned violence put everyone on edge. Leaders like Alice Moore distanced themselves from the violence, and firebombing elementary schools was hardly good PR for the protesters. But the violence did give anti-textbook leaders power. Pro-textbook advocates lost resolve in the face of attacks.

In the end, the pro-textbook forces "won"—the books remained in the schools—but it was a pyrrhic victory. The most controversial texts had to stay in school libraries, where few students bothered to seek them out. The county split violently over the books, turning neighbors against neighbors. Mike Edds, an early supporter of Alice Moore, lamented the results of the protest. "I've become a realist," he said. "I don't think you can reform the system. I've become polarized too, and it just breaks my heart. . . . I guess my idealism has died."[68] In 1979 the *New York Times* ran a five-year anniversary story that suggested time had brought healing to Charleston. But clearly the battle had left scars, too. Jim Lewis, a pro-textbook Episcopal minister who received death threats throughout the controversy, called Moore's reelection to the school board in 1976 "the hardest pill to swallow." Moore, for her part, acknowledged that turmoil had not ended in 1974. "We've had four superintendents in 10 years," she admitted. Still, anti-textbook forces believed the books had "been cleaned up" in the ensuing five years. "The new textbooks took most of the villains out," said then-superintendent Robert Kittle. "The literature reflects more heroes than villains. More respect has come back for the home, family and country."[69] The 1974 protesters did not win the battle, but by 1979 they seemed to possess the upper hand in an ongoing culture war.

Figuring out what motivated the West Virginia controversy is no easy task. Many members of the national media initially attributed the split between pro- and anti-textbook forces to Kanawha County's rural/urban

Figure 4. Kanawha County protesters advocated for religious values in school textbooks. Image courtesy of Bill Tiernan.

divide. The county encompassed 913 square miles and hosted more than 100 schools, many of them small outposts in mountain "hollows" more than an hour by car from Charleston. But all the public school administrators and board members (including Moore) lived in Charleston or its suburbs. Rural Kanawhans felt city dwellers did not take them seriously. And the media agreed. The *New York Times* declared, "In the hollows outside Charleston, God comes simple and unvarnished. . . . The beliefs of rural people are guaranteed to win disdainful shrugs at cocktail parties from Charleston to New York, and that, apparently, is all they were good for in the power structure of the Kanawha schools." The *Times* reporter noted that in 1973 the county had stopped inviting parents to serve on the textbook advisory committee. Even though most of the parents who had served in earlier years came from the Charleston area, rural parents complained that the county no longer even gave the appearance of caring what they thought.[70]

But the rural/urban divide in Kanawha County only partly explains the passion of the protest. Three months after school opened, the county asked parents whether their children could use the new language arts curriculum. Nearly two-thirds of Kanawha County parents did not grant their students permission to use the books. Even if *all* rural parents—a group that made up about a third of the county's population—opposed the books, nearly half the opposition had to come from Charleston or its suburbs.[71] Clearly many city dwellers, like Alice Moore, felt that the new books were a threat and that the school board showed little inclination to honor their beliefs. They may have kept their children in school (urban and suburban attendance levels remained normal throughout the boycott), but conservative parents in the Charleston area sympathized with the protest. The media's focus on the rural/ urban split probably satisfied liberals who could then imagine the protesters as benighted rural populists. But simple geography did not explain the widespread disapproval of the books in Charleston and its suburbs.

Other reporters focused on the way the protest highlighted racial divides. In his report on causes of the school boycott, *New York Times* reporter Ben Franklin suggested, "Race was perhaps as major a hidden sore point as prudery in general," noting that protesters commonly attacked selections written by black authors.[72] Indeed, anti-textbook forces complained loudly about English books' inclusion of stories by African American authors Eldridge Cleaver and Gwendolyn Brooks. They contended that stories of inner-city slums held little relevance for children of "creekers," rural, white Appalachian residents who faced some of the most grinding poverty in the nation. Moreover, racial homogeneity in Kanawha County (fewer than 6 percent of 1970 residents were African American[73]) meant few black voices were part of the debate over the books. The NAACP did show up in late November to support the books, and the Ku Klux Klan staged a poorly attended rally in January 1975. Outsiders focused more attention on the racial dimensions of the controversy, which were not apparent in the early weeks of the fall. While the controversy mainly pitted white conservatives against white liberals, the protest certainly reflected the American racial divide.

Implicit questioning of Christian theology in some of the textbooks also contributed to the controversy. An advanced high school literature supplement called *Man in Literature*, for instance, opened with a W. H. Auden essay that described humans as "the result of natural selection, sexual reproduction and social conditioning." The reader's third selection, Karl Capek's "The Last Judgment," featured God as a character witness for a serial murderer. "Because I know everything," said God, "I can't possibly judge. That wouldn't do at all." In the story, a jury of religious zealots nonetheless sentenced the killer to eternal damnation.[74] Conservative evangelicals who paged through *Man in Literature* did not have to look far to find selections that repudiated their beliefs.

Elementary school texts did not feature theological messages, but they encouraged practices conservatives rejected. The teacher's edition of Heath's primary-level English book *Communicating*, for instance, encouraged educators to use "open-ended questions" and to "bring [students'] intuitive knowledge to the fore,"[75] even in lessons on basic grammar—a subject conservatives thought best taught authoritatively. Generalizations about over 300 volumes prove difficult, but on the whole, the books did push educators towards innovation, and they did not include stories that affirmed the worldview of the protesters. After reviewing sixty representative social studies textbooks, New York University professor Paul C. Vitz declared, "Religion, traditional family values, and conservative political and economic positions have been reliably excluded from children's textbooks."[76] In spite of publishers' claims to the contrary, the textbooks privileged an outlook at odds with that of the protesters.

And while experienced educators considered the books "harmless at worst," they failed to grasp that the West Virginia protesters, like the Gablers, credited the books with the ability to transform their children.[77] In fact, Moore herself underestimated the passion with which ordinary folks opposed the books. When she cajoled the board into removing the new language arts curriculum for a thirty-day review period, she expressed elation, as even a temporary suspension of the books represented a greater triumph than she had hoped for. Some of her supporters, on the other hand, expressed disgust. "Why should we settle for one thing less than we've been hollerin' for?" said one. "It's the difference between Heaven and Hell for our children."[78] In the minds of protesters, textbooks that exposed students to a liberal worldview could doom their children to adopting a value system at odds with their parents. An interviewer asked anti-textbook minister Charles Quigley if he thought "all these negative things like increase in crime and so on are due to the schools." Quigley responded, "Yes, definitely so. I believe that . . . they taught them crime right in them books."[79] Quigley's comment signaled anti-textbook activists' fear that their cultural, political, and religious values might not survive the onslaught of liberalism in the classroom.

The boycott highlighted the importance of conservatives' sense that textbooks undermined parents' rights. When opponents accused the protesters of censorship, conservatives said such accusations deflected attention from the central issue. The controversy, said one writer, has "nothing to do with 'book burning' or freedom of inquiry for students. The students, after all, are already locked in to a compulsory setting, with reading matter selected for them by adults. The question at issue is which adults will do the selecting, and what particular set of values will be brought to bear in making the decision."[80] Conservative parents felt liberal experts had rebuffed their participation in decisions concerning public schools, and even some of their opponents agreed. An article by the liberal Protestant magazine *Christian Century* conceded, "Rarely are either parents or students allowed to share in policy-making. . . . In an attempt to upgrade the quality of our schools, emphasis has shifted more and more toward professional expertise."[81] Experts barred the door to conservative parents, who felt that such a stance conflicted with democratic principles.

This populist sentiment—that parents had both the skill and the right to choose public school curricula—represented the chief legacy of the West Virginia controversy for the family values movement. One protester told an interviewer that the goal of the boycott was to "get this government down to where they'll listen to us little old hillbillies."[82] The government's unwillingness to do so allowed conservatives to frame a textbook protest as a referendum on who ought to control children's education.[83] As competing forces threatened to fragment the protest in late September, conservative political leaders provided anti-textbook forces with the compelling narrative of "parents' rights." Poll after poll showed a majority of Kanawha parents opposed to the books, and when parents finally won the opportunity to say whether their children could use the books, they overwhelmingly disapproved of them. While critics bewailed the triumph of censorship, conservatives celebrated the ways parents had retaken control over the education of their children.

Textbook Battles and the Family Values Movement

Parents' rights became an essential cog in the family values agenda conservatives would use in their drive for control of national politics. As textbook protests sprouted up across the country—a 1975 *New York Times* article listed details on textbook controversies in 17 states—conservatives increasingly felt the public schools taught that "children must be weaned away from the narrow mind-set of their families."[84] "Educators no longer worry about whether a child can write. They worry about what the child writes, what the attitude is toward a particular subject," said activist Onalee McGraw. "It's no longer 'See Susie and her mother.' It's 'Susie lives in a slum. How does Susie relate to her mother? How do you relate to your mother?'"[85] Conservatives instinctively connected the "realism" in the controversial textbooks to an assault on their parental prerogative. And that, said conservatives, represented an attack on the framework of authority laid out in scripture. "Parents' rights come from God by way of the natural law," said one author. "The existence of the family unit presupposes parental rights; continuation of civilized society presupposes the existence of the family unit."[86] When public schools, through their use of liberal textbooks, threatened God's law, conservative Christians had no choice but to respond.

It remains difficult to judge to what degree the Kanawha protest—or, for the matter, the Gablers' campaign—represented a Christian movement. Certainly most of the anti-textbook forces claimed membership in conservative churches: Moore's husband was a Churches of Christ minister, and protest leaders Marvin Horan, Ezra Graley, Charles Quigley, and Avis Hill all served Protestant churches.[87] Protesters couched their struggle in religious terms, carrying handmade placards that read "Out with the Devil" and complaining of books that treated the biblical story of Daniel in the Lion's Den as a myth.[88] Yet anti-textbook leaders often refrained from casting their campaign as simply a battle pitting Christians against secularists. In June 1974, over 12,000 people signed a petition that asked schools to remove textbooks that "deal with religion in any manner—its beliefs, rituals, or literature." The petition argued, "Inasmuch as it has been held unconstitutional for a tax-supported school to promote religious belief, we hold that it is equally unconstitutional to promote religious disbelief."[89] That is, if books could not promote Christian faith, neither could they attack it.

Protesters' ability to situate their demands in secular language, even as they fought for religious ideals, represented another important legacy of the controversy. West Virginia protesters, using language Christian right leaders would employ in the late 1970s and early 1980s, said the books "indoctrinate your children in ideas totally alien to the American way of life" and "appear to attack the social values that make up civilization." Moreover, the controversial texts went against "the moral and religious convictions of the vast majority of Americans."[90] Educators not only attacked the bedrock foundations of American society, they violated the principle of majority rule. But anti-textbook leaders rarely spelled out the content of their "moral and religious convictions," choosing a strategic ambiguity that allowed the protest to attract a broader following. On 12 November 1974, secular supporters of the protest formed a group called "Non-Christian American Parents" in order to counter the claim that all anti-textbook forces were fundamentalists. The group testified to conservatives' success in uniting Christian and secular forces against progressives. Not all Christians celebrated that development; one letter writer to *Christianity Today* who advocated Christian education complained that "when it comes to the everyday realities of life like work, education, play, economics and politics, we Christians tend to find our identity not in Christ but as Americans."[91] The writer wanted Christians to embrace a more explicitly religious discourse, to frame their battle as unambiguously Christian. Yet Kanawhans, along with the Gablers, chose a different path, one that portrayed their struggle as that of an embattled majority of ordinary Americans.

The alliance between conservative Christians and conservative politicians forged in the furnace of the book controversy presaged the emergence of the Christian right. Reflecting on the controversy twenty years later, Moore said, "I think that was sort of a beginning" to grassroots conservative movements that paved the way for the rise of the Christian right. Her fiercest opponent, Jim Lewis, grudgingly agreed. "It was being perceived . . . as some kind of crazy hillbilly battle, but it was much deeper than that. Right-wing politics and right-wing religion were coming together."[92] The one-year-old Heritage Foundation, a significant supporter of conservative politics, enthusiastically adopted the Kanawha County protesters' cause. *Human Events*, a conservative periodical closely aligned with the Heritage Foundation, said the textbook struggle made clear the growing alliance between secularism and liberalism. "Not only would many of these books offend religious fundamentalists because of obscene language and a seeming mocking of religion," it read, "but they should also offend many conservatives because of the astonishing left-wing bias."[93] Conservative politicians, seeing the way conservative Christians reacted to textbooks in West Virginia, pressed for politicization of evangelicals.

As in the Christian schools movement, battles over textbooks in various states created a national network of conservatives united against a common enemy. The Gablers' authorized biographer recalled a telling conversation that took place at the height of the West Virginia controversy. Alice Moore phoned the Gablers for support, and in the course of their conversation, she realized that Kanawha County had purchased editions of textbooks different from those used in Texas. "You mean your books don't even have 'damn'?" she asked Mel. "That's right," he responded, pointing out that publishers produced special Texas editions that did not include profanity. "Tell the publishers you want Texas editions," Norma suggested. "Arizona does that."[94] Norma's comment illuminated how their campaign against textbooks had taken on national dimensions. Conservatives were building alliances in their battles against publishers and public schools—battles that previously had remained local affairs. When the Gablers came to Kanawha County in October 1974, "a spontaneous local revolt became part of a national network long in operation but just fully savoring its power."[95] A conservative network stretching from California to West Virginia took up the cause of the Kanawha County protesters, who returned the favor by elucidating a vision of parental rights that became a prominent part of the family values agenda.

Evangelicals involved in the textbook protests showed political acumen that belied assumptions of evangelicals' longtime political dormancy. They created new organizations (like the Gablers' Educational Research Analysts) or latched onto existing ones (like the Heritage Foundation). Notably, few established church structures offered the protesters institutional support. Denominational periodicals avoided reporting on the West Virginia controversy.[96] Instead, the news media covered the controversy—extensively—with a mixture of fascination and horror, and politically conservative periodicals like *Human Events* adopted the textbook protest as their own.

The success of the Gablers and the Kanawhans showed that evangelicals could transform local politics, unite across regional boundaries, and create institutions to press their agenda. The populism at the root of the West Virginia controversy provided the anti-textbook movement with deep resonance among "ordinary" Americans. They shared a sense that the world they once knew was slipping away, and textbook protests gave them a chance to hold on to the past. (It is not surprising that most protesters, when pressed to give an example of a "good" textbook, pointed to the nineteenth-century McGuffey reader.) Battles in Texas and West Virginia cannot capture the wide range of motivations that stirred Christians to political action, but they certainly illuminated key features of a growing Christian right. As their opponents pressed liberal agendas, conservatives rallied around rhetoric of embattlement and parents' rights.

CHAPTER 3

Home Schools

Although conservative evangelicals who launched Christian schools and fought against textbooks won considerable success, they fought an uphill battle. After Supreme Court decisions in 1962 and 1963 declared prayer and devotional Bible reading in public schools unconstitutional, evangelicals' attempts to inscribe a Christian worldview in textbooks faced constant opposition. Christian schools offered religious education, but for conservative evangelicals they were often too expensive, too far away, or too similar to public schools. Moreover, Christian schools described their role as complementary to the family, since evangelicals believed education began at home. Some began to wonder why they should send their children to any school, Christian or otherwise. As one evangelical educator put it, if "education is the business of the family, why delegate it to the Christian schools?" Though Christian schools were "infinitely preferable" to public schools, conservative evangelicals sensed that home schooling provided an even better alternative.[1] By the 1980s, a growing number of white evangelicals were deciding to educate their children at home. Conservative Protestants had always comprised a majority of homeschoolers, and by 1990, they represented 85–90 percent of Americans who decided to educate their children at home.[2]

The home school represented a family values ideal: mothers providing for the nurture and education of children directly while fathers went off to work. The family values movement had sunk countless hours into fighting secularism in public schools and developing Christian schools, but its focus shifted in the 1980s. As homeschooling attracted more supporters and won mainstream acceptance, some conservative evangelicals began touting the home school as the best model for family values education. By keeping their children at home, evangelicals could embody the model family structure. Home schooling also enabled parents to resist sending their kids to "liberal" public schools, which evangelicals believed taught secular humanism and situational ethics. The family values movement drew on the increasing numbers of homeschoolers to promote "parents rights" in the 1980s. Beverly LaHaye, founder and president of Concerned Women for America (CWA), contended, "We cannot have strong families in this country if parents do not have the right to make decisions about the discipline, nurture, education, and religious instruction of their children." In 1985 CWA announced plans to introduce a Parents' Rights constitutional amendment to Congress. The amendment focused on parents' ability to "direct and control the rearing of minor children" and spelled out limits on the interpretation of child abuse, as conservative evangelicals worried that even the mildest form of corporal punishment might be construed as abusive.[3]

Motivation for such an amendment came in part from conservative evangelicals' sense that local governments intended to reprogram their children in "government schools." Alleged persecution of homeschoolers fueled these concerns. Periodicals such as *The Teaching Home, The CLA Defender* (Christian Law Association), and *The Christian Liberty Report* regularly trumpeted news of prosecutions against evangelical homeschoolers. Few states offered legal protection for homeschoolers in the early 1980s, though prosecutions were rare. Nonetheless, in 1983 conservative evangelical leader Michael Farris launched the Home School Legal Defense Association (HSLDA), which promised unlimited legal services to home school parents facing prosecution in exchange for a $100 annual membership fee. The creation of HSLDA and introduction of a parents' rights amendment signaled the importance conservative evangelicals attached to home schools. They saw homeschooling as the last resort from an educational system gone haywire.

Promoting homeschooling marked a final way the family values movement promoted its educational agenda in the late twentieth century. By the mid-1980s conservative evangelicals had developed a robust publishing industry that provided materials for parents who wanted to educate their children at home. Looking at curricula and periodicals reveals that evangelicals believed homeschooling embodied the family values agenda. It compelled families to structure their homes around traditional gender norms, as a stay-at-home mother nurtured and taught her children. Moreover, the perception of persecution encouraged homeschoolers to join political organizations that advocated for parents' rights. And, as their numbers grew, evangelical homeschoolers began to think of their children as future culture warriors. By the dawn of the twenty-first century, HSLDA trumpeted home schools as the breeding grounds for "Generation Joshua," which, following the example of the Old Testament leader, would "conquer the land" for God.[4] Looking at the emergence and growth of Christian homeschoolers reveals why conservative evangelicals took to homeschooling and how they appropriated the homeschooling movement to advance a family values agenda.

Criticizing Public Schools

The irony of evangelicals' predominance among homeschoolers in the twenty-first century is that the most famous early leader of the modern homeschooling movement came from the anti-establishment left of the 1960s. John Holt, a former teacher, articulated a countercultural critique of the conventional wisdom that children needed to attend school. High school attendance had approximately doubled every decade between 1890 and 1930. The Great Depression accelerated this trend, as jobs became harder and harder to attain. By 1950, over 75 percent of children aged fourteen to sixteen attended school. This dramatic uptick in school enrollment brought administrative challenges. Public school leaders responded by attempting to homogenize the school experience through consolidating school districts, administering standardized tests, and providing uniform curricula.[5]

All these developments seemed profoundly unhelpful to Holt, who wrote two books criticizing public schools in the late 1960s: *How Children Fail* (1964) and *How Children Learn* (1967). Together these volumes sold over 1.5 million copies. In them Holt made a compelling case against American schools—public and private—arguing that compulsory testing and a climate of fear made education nearly impossible. While Holt's observations rang true for many parents, education officials found him threatening. He railed against teachers' "deep lack of trust in children," arguing that it "poisoned the air of almost every kindergarten, nursery school, or day care center I have seen."[6] Middle and high schools were hardly better. Holt's frustration with schools grew so great that he began calling for an "underground railroad" to help children escape from them. Parents frustrated with their children's education began pulling them out of school and started teaching them at home. In response to these parents' requests for curriculum and community, Holt began publishing a four-page newsletter called *Growing Without Schooling* in 1977. It trumpeted home schools as the only way to honor children's rights.[7]

Even though conservative evangelical homeschoolers were more concerned about parents' rights, they were happy to discover Holt's newsletter. *Growing Without Schooling* was the only nationwide periodical devoted to home education in the late 1970s. The text-heavy, typewritten newsletter featured a wealth of information about how to teach children at home and, more important, helped create a nationwide network of homeschooling families. Holt corresponded with homeschooling families across the country and spent considerable amounts of his own money to sustain *Growing Without Schooling*. In the 1970s, as more and more evangelicals began teaching their children at home, they subscribed in growing numbers to Holt's magazine, in spite of reservations about his philosophy. "The best resource material is available from *Growing Without Schooling*," proclaimed the *Biblical Educator*. "Their perspective is that of a radical, ecologistic humanism, but many of the ideas found in their material are valuable for Christians to adopt."[8] Backhanded compliments such as these appeared in Christian school magazines during the late 1970s and early 1980s, as conservative evangelicals warmed to the idea of homeschooling. They depended on Holt's publication of curricular resources and teaching strategies. His ire toward public schools resonated with evangelicals as well.

Yet Holt's educational philosophy made a permanent alliance between evangelical and secular homeschoolers unlikely. By the mid-1970s, Holt had abandoned hope of reforming schools and had developed a philosophy called "unschooling." Upset at education's tendency to stifle creativity and squelch the joy of learning, Holt thought the best strategy was to leave children mostly to their own devices. He advocated an educational philosophy that depended on teachers' willingness to indulge their pupils' curiosity and abandon hard and fast conclusions in hopes of learning something new about the universe. He contended that children's innate curiosity would lead them to educate themselves. Indeed, he even labeled access to "self-directed learning" as "the most fundamental of all human rights," aside from the right to life itself. Holt's robust sense of children's potential led him to discourage all but the gentlest guidance in education.[9]

Conservative evangelicals, on the other hand, thought children needed strong discipline to reach their full potential. Mel and Norma Gabler, the textbook activists from Texas, criticized public schools' emphasis on "total reading freedom," or "the idea that children should have the right to read anything" they wish. San Diego pastor Tim LaHaye, a major figure in the Christian right who later became famous for co-authoring the popular *Left Behind* novels, explained why something like "total reading freedom" was such a problem in his 1983 book *The Battle for the Public Schools*. Just as his wife Bev thought schools challenged parental authority, Tim LaHaye argued that public education officials held "a basic humanistic misconception about man." He explained that "Humanists viewed man as good, as potentially perfectible" and saw "education as the key to that perfectibility."[10] Indeed, LaHaye and other conservative evangelicals believed that the "religion of secular humanism" had taken over American public educations. Humanism's belief in perfectibility encouraged schools to abandon traditional subjects and modes of discipline in hopes of fostering children's best instincts.

Such an approach conflicted sharply with conservative Christians' understanding of human nature. While evangelicals saw children as innocent and in need of protection, they also believed in the inherent corruption of human nature occasioned by the fall. Popular evangelical child psychologist James Dobson articulated this view of children in his 1978 bestseller, *The Strong-Willed Child*. After recounting a story in which a toddler tested her father's authority, Dobson wrote, "The entire human race is afflicted with the same tendency toward willful defiance that this three-year-old exhibited. Her behavior . . . is not so different from the folly of Adam and Eve," who "challenged the authority of the Almighty."[11] Christian belief in original sin meant that children, innocent as they appeared, possessed fundamentally corrupted souls in need of God's saving grace. Schools ought to protect children from materials that would further corrupt them (hence evangelicals' strident opposition to sex education) and should introduce them to the ways of God. Doing so required discipline. Conservative Christians portrayed public schools as sites of permissiveness, where "students are told there are no absolutes and that they are to develop their own value systems."[12] In the minds of conservative evangelicals, public schools encouraged "moral relativism," or the belief that no one value system should prevail.

Moreover, evangelical leaders pointed out how parenting experts and educational psychologists had discouraged corporal discipline, creating a culture of permissiveness that catered to kids' inherent selfishness. Whereas some researchers believed that religiously legitimated physical punishment caused children to develop a "perverted" understanding of God and authority, evangelicals thought otherwise.[13] Corporal punishment, wrote Dobson, "is not born of harshness. It is conceived in love."[14] Dobson and other evangelical leaders spelled out strict limitations on the application of physical discipline, arguing that parents should not spank children for forgetfulness or emotional reactions. Dobson did not advocate corporal punishment to the extent some of his critics supposed. But he did claim corporal punishment was a time-tested and necessary response to "willful disobedience." Dobson's claims resonated in the mid-1970s, a time when many conservatives felt the lax nature of punishment had fostered a culture of spoiled and disobedient children. The schools of the 1970s and 1980s seemed to foster permissiveness and lack of respect, as teachers and administrators could not physically discipline wild students.

Evangelicals, then, stood almost diametrically opposed to John Holt in their critique of public schools and their understanding of human nature. Where Holt faulted educators for not following curious children's insightful minds, conservative evangelicals thought teachers gave far too much ground. They called for teachers who would discipline their students, teach time-honored subjects and methods, and develop children's character. Evangelicals writing about education in the late 1970s and early 1980s believed that checking children's sinful impulses was a crucial component of education. They feared that public schools' humanism had created an indulgent curriculum that did not serve students' needs.

James Dobson on Raising Children Right

Most evangelicals in the late 1970s, however, viewed homeschooling with suspicion. They developed Christian schools and fought against liberal curricula in public schools, but few made the leap to homeschooling. For instance, Tim LaHaye admitted that his first reaction to the idea of teaching children at home was negative. He could not imagine keeping children away from school. But he later became one of evangelicalism's most visible advocates for homeschooling, and he came to narrate his initial skepticism as the result of an "educational propaganda machine," which has "conditioned us to believe that only [public schools] are 'qualified' to teach our children."[15] By the early 1980s, LaHaye had developed a comprehensive critique of public schools, viewing them as a hopeless cause. He advocated homeschooling alongside Christian schools as they only available avenues for conservative evangelicals who intended to rear their children in the way of the Lord.

Longtime homeschooling proponents Raymond and Dorothy Moore were instrumental in LaHaye's "conversion" to homeschooling. During the 1960s, Raymond Moore served as graduate research and program officer for the U.S. Department of Education. At a moment when most government officials were advocating lowering the compulsory schooling age and putting more money into programs like Head Start, Moore found himself growing increasingly disillusioned with public education. He left his post at the Department of Education in 1967 and launched a research group to study the effects of schooling on early childhood development. Five years later, the Moores published their results in *Harper's*; their paper was reprinted in *Reader's Digest* and the *Congressional Record*. They found that "many of the problems early schooling is supposed to solve"—such as "crime, poverty, addiction, malnutrition, and violence"—"actually exist because children right now are being forced into schooling too early."[16] In *Harper's* the Moores advocated delaying schooling until seven or eight. At a moment when virtually no one challenged the worth of public education, the Moores' position stood out. The *Harper's* article "elicited one of the largest responses in that magazine's history."[17]

The Moores' critique echoed conservative evangelical beliefs about the ways schools had violated parents' rights. If Holt wanted to protect children from schools' stifling discipline, the Moores feared schools had wrested away parents' educational prerogative. In particular, they believed mothers ought to serve as the chief instructors of their children.[18] "Mothers must be encouraged to be mothers," they wrote in a 1980 *Christian Life* article. "Instead of increasing subsidies to nurseries, day-care centers, and other substitute playpens, we should consider tax credits or outright grants that will keep the mother at home. . . . It is time to repopularize motherhood."[19] The Moores contended that home schools provided the ideal environment for education and the proper ordering of families. Since they saw education of children as a primary responsibility of mothers, they viewed homeschooling as the ideal mode of instruction. Homeschooling relieved families of the financial burden presented by Christian schools, and it put the mother in her rightful role as the family's chief pedagogue.

This view of mothers emanated in part from the Moores' faith in Seventh-day Adventism. Ellen G. White, founder of Seventh-day Adventism, wrote in 1900, "If you are a mother, train your children for Christ. This is as verily a work for God as is that of the minister in the pulpit."[20] These sentiments appealed to Dorothy Moore, whose experience teaching remedial reading to California public school students convinced her that early exposure to formal education did more harm than good. She had converted to Adventism in college and found herself agreeing with most of White's teaching about motherhood and the education of children. Like countless homeschoolers who would follow them, the Moores' religious faith provided important motivation for them to take control of their children's education.

Evangelicals, however, occasionally identified Seventh-day Adventism as a cult.[21] Indeed, in the first half of the twentieth century, the Moores' doctrinal commitments would likely have ostracized them from other conservative Protestants. But almost no evangelicals in the early 1980s criticized the Moores' Adventism when describing their homeschooling research. This lack of comment—alongside evangelicals' (temporary) willingness to collaborate with John Holt—reflected a strategy of "co-belligerence" that prevailed in the late 1970s and 1980s. Evangelical theologian Francis Schaeffer disseminated the notion of co-belligerence, which encouraged evangelicals to cooperate with any allies in a "culture war" against secularism. The dire straits conservative evangelicals found themselves in, argued Schaeffer, demanded collaboration with any and all allies willing to fight alongside evangelicals. In this instance, evangelicals could not afford to wait for doctrinally pure allies in the battle against public schools, which they identified as a "public enemy."[22] The theological differences among evangelicals and Seventh-day Adventists remained important; indeed, theological motivations underpinned evangelical critiques of public schools. But unlike earlier generations of conservative Protestants, late twentieth-century evangelicals cooperated with doctrinal foes.

It helped that the Moores came with the blessing of James Dobson. His 1970 bestseller *Dare to Discipline* almost totally refuted John Holt's philosophy. "Heredity," wrote Dobson, "does not equip children with proper attitudes; children will learn what they are taught." Holt's encouragement of children's natural curiosity appeared as neglectful permissiveness in Dobson's view.[23] But Dobson liked the Moores. In 1977, he invited them to appear on his widely syndicated radio show, *Focus on the Family*. The Moores reported on their research showing that schools stifled early childhood development, and they argued that educating children at home yielded far better learning outcomes for young children. Many listeners agreed. Dobson reported, "We received more mail in response to those programs than any we had ever aired, with better than 95 percent of the letters being highly favorable."[24] Perhaps as a result of that response, Dobson recorded more than twenty subsequent shows with the Moores. In a 1983 article, he wrote, "I have reviewed the research basis for Dr. Moore's perspective on today's children and find it valid." Homeschoolers "tend to catch and pass their age mates when enrolled for the first time at eight or ten years of age. . . . I believe the home school is the wave of the future."[25] Dobson's endorsement gave the Moores a wide audience among evangelicals.

Moreover, Dobson framed homeschooling as a way of furthering family values. In books like *Dare to Discipline* and *Parenting Isn't for Cowards*, he advocated an authoritarian family structure as a necessary response to the libertine counterculture of the 1960s. "Permissiveness," he wrote, "has not just been a failure; it's been a disaster."[26] He cited his experience as a professor of pediatrics at the University of Southern California School of Medicine in the 1960s as instrumental in shaping his views on the family. "Divorce, abuse, and other forms of familial strife were tearing lives apart," he wrote. Dobson's diagnosis of family breakdown in American society resonated with evangelicals, who bought many of the two million copies *Dare to Discipline* sold.[27] Dobson, then, was hardly interested in homeschooling as a way of preserving children's rights. Indeed, he explicitly criticized Holt in his 1978 *The Strong-Willed Child*, saying Holt's views on child-rearing made (liberal) pediatrician and author Benjamin Spock seem "downright oppressive" in comparison.[28] Conversely, the Moores echoed the family values agenda championed by Dobson. We must "encourage development of policies that renew the family and restore authority and responsibility to the home," they wrote. "If we do not take strong action to reverse the breakdown of families, America will not survive the twentieth century as a democratic society."[29] Like Tim LaHaye, Dobson seemed wary of homeschooling for most of the 1970s, and sent his oldest child to early kindergarten. But the Moores' research, alongside their views on the family, swayed him. By the early 1980s, Dobson regularly depicted homeschooling as an element in the larger family values agenda.

Dobson's support of homeschooling resembled his approach to other issues, and this made him the single most important figure in promoting family values. His approach, especially in the first half of his public career, depended on an apolitical appearance. He cultivated a large and devoted following by dispensing child-rearing advice on his weekly radio show, and he often demurred from political statements in the 1970s and 1980s. Unlike Falwell, who had a ready comment on every hot-button issue during those years, Dobson positioned himself above the fray. Although Focus launched a political advocacy group, the Family Research Council, in 1981, the bulk of the organization's efforts went toward Dobson's radio show, counseling hotline, and mail correspondence. By 1988, Focus received 1.8 million pieces of mail annually, the vast majority from distressed mothers and wives. A small army of trained "correspondents" responded to the mail with Dobson-approved resources. Focus on the Family correspondents dispensed advice for free, and financial appeals were minimal. For instance, Focus correspondents mailed books to listeners in exchange for "suggested donations" rather than fixed prices. The organization attracted enormous financial support in this manner; Focus on the Family's annual budget eclipsed $100 million in 1995.[30]

Dobson's appeal among evangelicals deserves examination. Trained in psychology, he never embraced the popular parenting trends promoted by Benjamin Spock. Spock's 1946 book, *The Common Sense Book of Baby and Child Care*, had become something of a sacred scripture among both pediatricians and parents; only the Bible itself outsold Spock's text the decade after its publication. In it Spock encouraged parents to trust their instincts, and to let their children explore the world around them. Spock drew on the psychoanalytic theories of Sigmund Freud, though he used plainspoken language rather than Freudian terminology. Dobson respected Spock, but the evangelical psychologist disagreed with Spock's premises. (Dobson also respected Freud—at least enough to name the family dachshund after the founder of psychoanalysis—but he disagreed with Freud, too.[31]) Dobson understood children as gifts from God, but also as willful, disobedient, and narcissistic. Like other evangelicals, he believed humans' sinful natures manifested themselves even among children. Moreover, he argued for the importance of clear lines of authority. In Dobson's mind, Spock's permissive parenting styles—or at least, parents' misapplication of them—had contributed directly to the cultural tumult of the 1960s. Though admitting he had little evidence to support such a claim, Dobson wrote, "the defiant youngster is in a 'high risk' category for antisocial behavior later in life. . . . He is more inclined toward sexual promiscuity and drug abuse and academic difficulties."[32] Dobson advised parents to begin taming such children as toddlers, lest their offspring contribute to the weakening of social mores that was sweeping the nation.

Although he kept his denominational affiliation muted, Dobson's background in the Church of the Nazarene filtered into his parenting advice. Nazarenes belonged to the Wesleyan tradition, and they focused in particular on the potential of "entire sanctification," or the removal of the impulse to sin. Nazarenes believed that original sin had corrupted all humans; salvation had the potential to remove that corruption. After a Christian's salvation, sin became something that was personal and voluntary. More than most evangelicals, Nazarenes believed in the possibility of human perfection. They believed the Holy Spirit could release Christians from sinful impulses. First, however, Christians had to recognize that humans' natural instincts had been corrupted by sin. Dobson hailed from a tradition that could not abide Spock's permissive parenting advice, given Nazarenes' belief in the pervasiveness of sin. His parenting advice urged mothers and fathers to help their children understand the boundaries they could not cross. These boundaries would start children on the path to perfection by removing some of the sinfulness that all children inherited from Adam and Eve. In short, Dobson's Nazarene faith taught him that the first step in creating adults who renounced sin was to mold children who knew that they could not indulge every impulse.

Because all evangelicals did not share Nazarenes' belief in the possibility of human perfection, Dobson never elaborated on his particular theological heritage to his listeners. Rather, he dispensed his advice as that of a medical professional who had become convinced that wrongheaded parenting theories were endangering America. *Dare to Discipline* served as Dobson's response to the 1960s. He suggested that poor parenting was a major cause of the sexual revolution, growth of drug use, and proliferation of pornography. Evangelicals concerned about these developments found in Dobson an expert they could trust. He shared their belief that society had gone off track, and his solutions for America's problems resonated widely. All evangelicals agreed with Dobson's beliefs about the ways sin had corrupted humanity, and most felt the best way forward involved restoring traditional authority structures. Dobson's parenting advice played directly into these beliefs. Moreover, Dobson and Focus had become a lifeline for millions. He built a massive following by helping parents and families out of crisis situations—doing so with a mixture of professional psychology and evangelical beliefs. Dobson's radio show stood out among evangelical broadcasts, as he eschewed fire-and-brimstone in favor of avuncular if firm parenting advice. Dobson never shied away from providing his views, but he never came across as blustering. Here was an expert evangelicals could trust, someone who carried the imprimatur of an elite education yet retained his evangelical faith.

As Dobson's influence grew, he became less reticent about commenting on political issues. Launching the Family Research Council in 1981 signaled Dobson's desire to effect changes in policy-making. Yet throughout the 1980s he resisted campaigning for most right-wing causes, in spite of repeated invitations from Paul Weyrich, who had been instrumental in convincing Falwell to launch Moral Majority. In 1989, Dobson told the *Washington Times*, "We never talk about anything but the family. We never endorse a political candidate. And we do very little with legislation."[33] Dobson's statement understated his increasing activism, but Focus on the Family earned its following by responding to listeners' phone calls and letters about family crises, not through political agitation. Still, Dobson understood politicking as part of his strategy for strengthening the family. As he

Figure 5. James Dobson became the most prominent promoter of
family values. Reprinted under GFDL license, courtesy of Focus of the
Family.

became convinced of an issue—as with the importance of homeschooling—he
marshaled considerable resources to promote his point of view. Evangelicals who
tuned into Dobson's radio show *Focus on the Family* for tips on raising children
would hear him decry government intrusions on family life. In the late 1980s, he
served on the Attorney General's Commission on Pornography, weighed in on
The Last Temptation of Christ, and protested proposed civil rights legislation he
thought would inhibit religious freedom. Focus launched Family Policy Councils
to lobby state legislatures and began publishing *Citizen*, which provided pro-
family analysis of public policy. By the late 1980s, Dobson and Focus were increasingly involved with national and state-level politics.[34]

This politicking came together under the banner of family values. Dobson earned credibility among evangelicals because Focus actively and carefully responded to listeners' crises, and his organization grew because he was a smart and hard-driving leader. But he also had the foresight—or good fortune—to speak the language of family values with the credibility of a doctor and the heart of an evangelical. His books and videos on parenting and marriage offered a timely message for conservative evangelicals. As evangelicals became convinced that restoring traditional family life was key to saving the nation, Dobson provided strategies for how to raise their children right. His embrace of homeschooling fit well with his larger program of promoting clear lines of parenting authority and restoring power to traditional families.

Dobson's embrace of homeschooling signaled changes in the home education movement. Whereas John Holt and the Moores focused mainly on the ways public schools negatively affected early childhood education, Dobson saw homeschooling as a way for parents to preserve authority in a culture run amok. Other evangelicals narrated their homeschooling similarly. For instance, in 1983 North Carolinians Peter and Carol Duro decided to teach their children at home because public schools fostered "humanism" and "immorality," and the local Christian school "was radically different [from them] in doctrine." The Duros, who had recently moved south from Maine, "believe that the Lord led them to North Carolina . . . for this very purpose"—that is, to fight for parents' rights to teach children at home.[35] Stories like the Duros' appeared with increasing regularity in evangelical educational magazines during the 1980s. While these stories always mentioned the high quality of home education, they focused on homeschooling as a religious calling. Conservative evangelicals like Dobson and the Duros subtly but noticeably shifted rhetoric about homeschooling, focusing on the ways homeschooling promoted the family and defended religious values rather than on educational outcomes.

Evangelical homeschoolers' motivations for removing their children from schools varied, but depicting home education as a religious calling attracted thousands of homeschooling converts and transformed the movement. Researchers estimated that the movement grew tenfold over the course of the 1980s. Precise numbers were (and are) hard to come by, but the children of conservative evangelicals made up a significant majority of the nation's 500,000 homeschoolers in 1990.[36] Holt's unschooling philosophy persisted among a minority of homeschoolers, but his star had faded for conservative evangelicals.[37] A homeschooling movement born in response to the poor educational outcomes of public schools had witnessed the influx of conservative evangelicals who championed the family values movement. By the late 1980s, these white evangelical homeschoolers controlled American homeschooling.

Making Homeschooling Legal

Evangelicals interested in homeschooling had many questions about its legality. Compulsory schooling laws existed in almost every state, and Christian school magazines often featured stories about the persecution of homeschoolers. The most notable instance of persecution came in 1979, when Utah authorities fatally shot John Singer, an excommunicated Mormon who had taken multiple wives. Singer had removed his children from Utah public schools in 1973 after seeing a picture in his daughter's textbook that portrayed Martin Luther King, Jr., as a "great American patriot" like George Washington and Betsy Ross. Singer, whom the Church of Jesus Christ of Latter-day Saints excommunicated in 1972, believed the picture of King, Ross, and Washington violated church teaching against racial mixing. He withdrew his children and built a one-room schoolhouse on his heavily fortified farm. Courts had awarded custody of some of the children on the farm to the previous husband of one of Singer's wives. Singer refused to relinquish these children and, as a result, found himself confronted by ten police officers while on a trip to the mailbox in January 1977. Singer pulled out a gun; officers shot him six times.[38]

Singer's case, which featured polygamy, Mormonism, and custody battles, should have repelled evangelicals. His lifestyle and theological beliefs put him far beyond the pale. But homeschoolers could not help but feel some connection to Singer, whose legal troubles stemmed partly from his refusal to send his children to school and to apply for a waiver—something he and other homeschoolers saw as government intrusion on their parental prerogative. Singer refused to appear in court to defend himself against truancy charges, resulting in a contempt of court citation that compelled officers to arrest him. What happened when officers served that arrest warrant further complicated Singer's case. Why did the police need such a show of force to issue a simple arrest warrant? Why did the autopsy turn up entry wounds in Singer's back, if the officers had shot in self-defense? Questions like these filled conspiracy-laden reports about the government's "attack" on Singer's

religious freedom and parental rights. News reports focused on Singer's combination of exoticism (multiple wives) and quaintness (a one-room schoolhouse on his property).[39]

Press like this made Singer into a hero for anti-government activists—
and for homeschoolers. Evangelicals convinced of the government's determination to control their children found Singer's story irresistible. *The Alarming
Cry*, a small fundamentalist magazine, described Singer's death as "the cul-
mination of a six-year battle to educate his own children."[40] Stories lionizing
Singer—a polygamist ex-Mormon—showed up in conservative evangelical
periodicals across the country, signaling both the co-belligerence of the family values movement and the shared sense that the government intended to
take children away from their parents. By omitting some details about Singer's beliefs and framing his story through the lens of parental rights, conservative evangelical homeschool advocates made him into an early martyr for
the homeschooling movement.

Although Singer was an extreme example, a number of homeschoolers
did face legal prosecution in the early 1980s. One early case involved Ruth
and Peter Nobel, a couple from Dorr, Michigan, who had decided to teach
five of their seven children at home. A 1980 *Washington Post* feature story on
the Nobels noted that their children were working above grade level and followed a precise daily schedule. Like Peter and Carol Duro, the Nobels viewed
public schools as "out of the question" and said they withdrew their children
from a local Christian school because of "doctrinal differences." When county
education officials asked Ruth to take a required teacher certification exam,
she refused on religious grounds. Authorities subsequently issued a warrant
for the Nobels' arrest. They turned themselves in and went to court. Washington, D.C., lawyer and evangelical activist John Whitehead represented
them and won a surprising decision when the Michigan judge ruled that the
key issue in the case was the Nobels' right of religious freedom. "For [Ruth]
to accept certification would not make her a better teacher," wrote the judge.
Certification would "interfere with her freedom to exercise her religious beliefs."[41] This decision validated the Nobels' decision to fight compulsory
schooling on First Amendment grounds.

The Nobels had little legal precedent on which to build their case. Previously, courts had ruled against homeschoolers who refused to comply with
both compulsory schooling laws and requirements to obtain a license. According to the federal courts, Americans had to send their children to school
or become certified to teach their kids at home. The Amish were the only

Christians who merited an exception to this rule. In 1972, the U.S. Supreme Court ruled in *Wisconsin v. Yoder* that Old Order Amish, who believed secondary education fostered pride, held a First Amendment right to remove their children from schools after those children completed the eighth grade. The Court carefully circumscribed the *Yoder* decision, pointing out the Old Order Amish possessed "a history of three centuries as an identifiable religious sect" and provided "informal vocational education" for high-school age children. Writing for the majority, Justice Warren Burger declared, "probably few other religious groups or sects could make" the case for avoiding compulsory schooling because it violated their right to freely exercise their religion.[42] As Burger predicted, evangelical homeschoolers lost court battles tried on First Amendment grounds—all of which referenced *Wisconsin v. Yoder*—in Illinois, West Virginia, Alabama, North Carolina, and North Dakota. These decisions followed a similar pattern: the court would concede the sincerity of homeschoolers' religious convictions and then note how their invocation of *Wisconsin v. Yoder* failed to account for the way the Supreme Court had circumscribed that ruling. As a result, courts in a half dozen states refused to find that compulsory schooling laws violated the First Amendment rights of homeschoolers. [43]

Homeschoolers had only somewhat better luck arguing that compulsory schooling laws violated the Fourteenth Amendment, which protects citizens' rights to equal protection and due process. Home school advocates frequently cited a pair of Supreme Court rulings from the 1920s: *Meyer v. Nebraska* (1923) and *Pierce v. Society of Sisters* (1925). These rulings referenced the due process clause of the Fourteenth Amendment to protect parents' rights to determine how to educate their children. Homeschoolers were particularly fond of quoting *Pierce*, which held, "The child is not the mere creature of the state."[44] They less often pointed out a more recent case that dramatically expanded rights protected by the due process clause: *Roe v. Wade* (1973), which protected women's right to terminate a pregnancy. At least one evangelical homeschooler did note the irony, pointing out "the strongest precedent for a right to teach a child at home is *Roe v. Wade*."[45] *Roe* declared that parents possessed "fundamental" privacy rights that protected decisions about procreation, parenthood, and child rearing. The court decision in *Roe* depended on the exact interpretation of the Fourteenth Amendment that homeschoolers were attempting to make. They drew on a similar rationale to argue that parents held fundamental rights to make decisions about their children's education. But since *Roe* paved the way for legalized abortion, most homeschoolers refused to invoke that precedent in attempting to establish their parental rights. Instead, they turned to the older decisions in *Pierce* and *Meyer* to make their case. The Supreme Court has not ruled on whether the Fourteenth Amendment protects homeschooling, and lower courts have typically disagreed with homeschoolers' Fourteenth Amendment arguments.[46]

Homeschoolers' constitutional arguments won their most famous hearing in *Mozert v. Hawkins County Board of Education*, a four-year legal saga that was not, on its surface, related to homeschooling at all. In *Mozert*, seven evangelical families sued the public school system of Hawkins County, Tennessee. The schools had adopted a Holt, Rinehart, and Winston reading series for grades 1–8 in early 1983. Vicki Frost, the mother of four children, discovered stories in her daughter's sixth-grade Holt reader that promoted "evolution, 'secular humanism,' . . . 'futuristic supernaturalism,' pacifism, magic, and false views of death." Frost and other plaintiffs (including Bob Mozert, whose name appeared as lead plaintiff) argued that that compelling their children to read such material violated the parents' free exercise rights. Lower courts agreed with the plaintiffs, but the Sixth Circuit Court of Appeals ultimately decided that "mere exposure" to religious pluralism did not violate the plaintiffs' First Amendment rights.[47]

At stake in *Mozert* was a question that occupied Christian school promoters, evangelical critics of public school textbooks, and homeschoolers: do public schools preach a religion of secular humanism? The plaintiffs' attorney Michael Farris thought the answer to this question self-apparent. "Our job," he wrote, "is to lead the courts and society to this inevitable conclusion: education inherently involves the inculcation of values."[48] Farris believed the Holt reading series promoted the values of secular humanism; indeed, his argument rested on the conviction that these textbooks were fundamentally religious. By featuring "passages that expose their children to other forms of religion . . . that contradict the plaintiffs' religious views without a statement that the other views are incorrect," the books, according to Farris, promoted the religion of secular humanism. In other words, the books did not merely teach toleration; they preached a value system that contradicted evangelicals' exclusive truth claims. While plaintiffs conceded that they could not violate non-Christians' right to practice other religious faiths, they believed books like those in the Holt series established a religion of secular humanism, which taught above all the relativity of truth claims. For evangelicals, the Holt series represented a government attempt to establish a religion in public schools, something expressly forbidden by the First Amendment. The Sixth Circuit of Appeals disagreed. Justices held that the books taught "*civil* toleration of other religions" rather than "*religious* toleration of other religions" (a distinction lost on the plaintiffs).[49] *Mozert*, then, was the most notable judicial denial of conservative evangelicals' contention that the state was teaching a new religion in public schools. Convinced that these schools intended to re-program their children, many evangelicals responded by taking them out of schools altogether.[50]

While *Mozert* denied evangelicals' claims about the religious nature of secular humanism, the case featured two important legacies for homeschooling and the family values movement. First, as in the West Virginia and Texas textbook protests, a mother of school-aged children spearheaded the public campaign. In this case, Vicki Frost led the charge against the Holt reading series. Like Alice Moore and Norma Gabler, Frost depicted herself as a mother scandalized by what her children had to read in public schools. This posture was crucial. Among conservative evangelicals, motherhood had become an idealized role for women, a role under attack by feminists and liberals. Sticking up for motherhood stood at the center of the family values agenda. And mothers sticking up for their children carried special resonance. Indeed, the embattled mother stood as both a symbolic counterweight to feminists and a fearsome political foe. In campaign after campaign, women who embraced their identity as mothers won significant gains for the Christian right. Though Vicki Frost lost the battle in *Mozert*, she won valorization as a mother fed up with a government encroaching on her domain. Other mothers took cues from Frost, Moore, and Gabler, standing up for their children against the educational establishment.

Second, the lead attorney in the case, Farris, established his nascent Home School Legal Defense Association (HSLDA) in the aftermath of *Mozert*. A graduate of Gonzaga Law School, Farris had launched his legal career prosecuting abortion clinics and pornographers. He tried cases against the ACLU on behalf of Concerned Women for America and Moral Majority, two prominent organizations in the Christian right. His fiery rhetoric in the courtroom annoyed judges but appealed to conservative evangelicals. *Mozert* convinced Farris that establishing parental prerogative in educational decisions demanded a concerted and relentless national effort. After *Mozert* he devoted considerable energy to getting the fledgling organization off the ground.[51] Having made a splash with his trial work, Farris would soon become the most prominent and most polarizing figure in the homeschooling movement.

Evangelical Homeschooling
Organizations and Family Values

The premise behind HSLDA was simple and successful. For an annual fee of $100, homeschooling families could become members of the organization, which offered a subscription to HSLDA's *Home School Court Report* and guaranteed legal representation in the event state authorities challenged the family's right to teach at home. Many members also subscribed to *Teaching Home*, where Farris regularly contributed a "Legal Update" section. Farris used *Teaching Home* and *Home School Court Report* to spotlight cases involving prosecution of homeschoolers and stress the urgency of constant vigilance against government intrusions on parental rights. A 1984 issue of *Teaching Home*, for instance, reported that the HSLDA had "successfully negotiated settlements for a number of families from California, Oklahoma, Texas, Washington, Indiana and other states. We have provided attorneys in Texas, Ohio, Arkansas, Oklahoma, and California."[52] One year later, an article compared homeschoolers facing legal battles in Ohio, Michigan, and Texas to the biblical prophet Nehemiah, who exhorted Israelites to "take their load with one hand doing the work and the other holding a weapon." The "weapon" in this battle was the legal representation provided member families by HSLDA, which, according to *Teaching Home*, spent "tens of thousands of dollars to defend the rights of home-schooling families." The article ended with an exhortation for readers to join or renew their membership to HSLDA: "Teach your children with one hand, and show them how to hold a weapon in the other. Then send the proceeds to the Home School Legal Defense Association."[53]

The militarism was not accidental or even euphemistic: HSLDA consciously promoted the idea of a "culture war" raging between liberal educational elites and homeschoolers. Evangelical theologian Francis Schaeffer had helped popularize the notion, and Farris and the HSLDA adopted it with gusto. Moreover, the organization could point to a number of ongoing legal battles as evidence for the widespread persecution of homeschoolers. HSLDA defined itself as the sole nationwide organization protecting the rights of homeschoolers. And even as more and more states passed statutes recognizing the legitimacy of homeschooling (according to HSLDA, 30 had done so by 1988), the organization depicted homeschooling as a long way from full legal acceptance. As Farris put it in a 1988 article, "This is a long, long fight we have ahead of us. Complacency, at this point, in any state, is just plain foolish."[54] By portraying the movement as embattled, Farris and HSLDA encouraged members to continue their financial support and to engage in legal campaigns around the country.

As a result, HSLDA became the most well funded and widely known homeschooling organization—as well as the most controversial. The notion that homeschooling was risky business in the late 1980s did not sit well with all homeschoolers. Many homeschooling veterans—especially those who had followed John Holt—felt Farris both exaggerated the amount of persecution faced by homeschoolers and usurped the credit due pioneers like Holt and the Moores for building the movement. Whereas *Teaching Home* painted a picture of near-constant persecution, the movement's rapid growth suggested homeschooling was becoming easier each year. Moreover, movement veterans resented the HSLDA's overtly political stance and assumption of authority. Critics intimated that Farris was late to a fight that was mostly over. Most states had made at least rudimentary accommodations for home education by 1985, and movement veterans worried that HSLDA's polemical style was both unnecessary and insulting. *Growing Without Schooling*, for instance, declared that John Holt (who died in 1985) had always wanted homeschooling "decentralized, open to all, and local." Holt Associates refused to endorse the National Center for Home Education (an offshoot of HSLDA) on account of its "politically right-wing" agenda.[55] In an issue of *Teaching Home*, Farris struck back. "Home schooling has many diverse adherents," he admitted, "but there are clear majority views on a great number of issues. . . . The majority of home schoolers are born-again Christians. . . . Numbers speak. The majority rules. That's the American way."[56] HSLDA had begun on a shoestring in 1983, but by 1990 its membership fee structure and articulation of evangelical mores catapulted it ahead of longer-tenured organizations.

Ironically, some of the most notable critics of Farris and HSLDA were Raymond and Dorothy Moore, without whose support HSLDA would have foundered in infancy. In 1982 Farris met the Moores on Dobson's radio show, and the Moores frequently referred their supporters to HSLDA in the early 1980s. These early referrals allowed HSLDA to get on its feet. But the organization's polemical and overtly religious tone did not sit well with the Moores, who had spent years researching early childhood education and portrayed homeschooling as the best option for young children. They viewed the emphasis on court battles and political campaigns as a distortion of what homeschooling was all about. In their 1988 book *Home School Burnout*, the Moores attacked "movement insiders" who promoted anti-government ideology and used scare tactics to recruit members. HSLDA was the obvious target.[57] Six years later, the Moores published *The Successful Homeschool Family Handbook*, in which they attacked "curriculum rushers," "zealots without wisdom," and "bandwagoners." They omitted any mention of HSLDA in the chapter "How Home Education as a Movement Was Born." They referred to John Holt as a "warm personal friend" and talked at length about his vision. They also argued that homeschooling leaders from various states "are not interested in supporting a national organization."[58] The Moores distanced themselves from Farris and HSLDA, viewing the new organization as a political front that had perverted the original ideals of homeschooling.

Philosophical differences over the nature of homeschooling precipitated the split between Farris and the Moores. While some evangelical homeschoolers worried about the Moores' Adventist faith, the more important distinction lay in differing approaches to teaching at home. The Moores decried the increasing regimentation of homeschooling, and they disliked the proliferation of homeschooling curricula. They wrote, "We wish now that we could eliminate the word *school*" from homeschooling, and they lamented the increasingly profit-driven homeschooling curriculum industry.[59] Whereas Holt and the Moores saw homeschooling as a way of breaking children free from conventional education, increasing numbers of evangelical parents copied educational structures in their living rooms, to the point of buying surplus school desks and saying the pledge of allegiance each morning. Parent-teachers cycled through a litany of subjects each day, replicating the format of the traditional school day. A homeschooling mother from Iowa wrote to praise an evangelical homeschooling video series for creating a "classroom atmosphere" in her home.[60] The new look of homeschooling was—in method, at least—increasingly similar to the schoolrooms parents had abandoned.

In this more "conventional" form of homeschooling, curriculum played an essential role both in structuring the "school day" and in uniting evangelical homeschoolers. The most notable early curricula came from the Christian Liberty Academy Satellite Schools (CLASS), which by the mid-1980s enrolled the largest number of K-12 "correspondence students" in the country. Homeschoolers prior to the mid-1980s had been largely decentralized and often used makeshift curricula, so the number of students using CLASS materials was still relatively small (around 20,000 nationwide).[61] But CLASS's rhetoric and rigor signaled a shift among homeschoolers. John Holt would never have described children as correspondence students, just as the Moores would never have countenanced the rigorous curricula supplied by CLASS. Yet conservative evangelicals considering homeschooling found the CLASS materials appealing. They brought a "Christian worldview" to conventional educational materials. In short, CLASS allowed conservative evangelicals to break free of the unconventional ideas of Holt and the Moores. Its focus on authority and structure more closely resembled the family values agenda.

Founded by Illinois pastor Paul Lindstrom, CLASS emanated from a particular strain of conservative Protestantism known as Christian Reconstructionism, a small faction of the larger Reformed tradition. Reconstructionists believed Jesus would come again only after Christians had rebuilt his kingdom on earth. (This view, known as postmillennialism, contrasted sharply with the majority evangelical view, premillennialism, which held that Christ would come again to establish his kingdom on earth.) As a result, Reconstructionists tended to advocate a theocratic view of government and believed education must train children in a holistic Christian philosophy. As the most prominent Reconstructionist, Rousas John Rushdoony, put it, "religions that fail to dominate and control education and law quickly become fading relics of the past."[62] More than most conservative evangelicals, Reconstructionists saw a deep and abiding conflict between secularism and Christianity. The CLASS curriculum, then, reflected a view of history, philosophy, and economics that emphasized this conflict and trained students to adopt a "Christian worldview" when approaching any subject. The CLASS website stated, "As the foundational book, Scripture is the only infallible rule for faith and practice, for grammar and literature, for mathematics and science, for health and physical education, for geography and history, and for social studies and the arts." It promised that CLASS curricula would "train Christian warriors and leaders who will go forth in the power of the Holy Spirit to win decisive victories."[63] This sense of scripture as the only fount of truth and of Christians at war with nonbelievers meant CLASS curricula lacked the inclusivity and openness of earlier homeschooling materials. It promoted an exclusive and hardline mentality that increasingly characterized evangelical homeschoolers after the mid-1980s.

Yet CLASS did not remain tightly confined within the small world of Reconstructionists; it became a clearinghouse for evangelical curricula produced by non-Reconstructionist outfits like Bob Jones University Press and A Beka Books. Both publishers had produced extensive curricula for Christian schools, and CLASS's reach into the evangelical homeschooling market appealed to them. CLASS, for its part, found that BJU Press and A Beka

Books produced materials homeschooling families found appealing and use-
ful. In fact, as families adopted series from BJU Press and A Beka Books, they
increasingly abandoned CLASS and ordered books directly from the publishers. The curricular materials that found their way into evangelical homeschoolers' hands, then, offered a mixture of competing theological viewpoints.
Reconstructionists at CLASS focused significant attention on "biblical" economics and the need for Christians to establish theocratic control over government. BJU Press offered a comparable focus on maintaining a "Christian
worldview," but its origins lay in writing creationist science textbooks. And
the very title of A Beka's world history volume—"Towards the End"—
signaled its premillennialist theology, a far cry from the postmillennialism of
the Reconstructionists.[64] The texts these organizations produced had many
similarities, but the subtle theological differences signaled the variety of
evangelical homeschoolers. A 1991 study of homeschoolers put it, "The people behind the proliferation of [homeschooling curricula] come from a wide
variety of philosophical backgrounds. . . . Such materials are often sorted into
rather simplistic categories as either 'Christian' or 'non-Christian.' "[65] The
"Christian" category tended to encompass a large majority of evangelicals,
but they hailed from an array of theological homes.[66]

Evangelical homeschoolers, then, could never claim theological consensus. But they did evince a strong coherence built at least in part on family
values. The very structure of homeschooling dictated this. In nearly all homeschooling families, the mother bore the lion's share of instructional responsibilities while the father left the house for work. Homeschooling made
it virtually impossible for both parents to work and inscribed a "traditional"
division of labor in the family. Mothers who fought for control over their
children's education in schools, like Norma Gabler and Alice Moore, won
support because evangelicals assumed mothers should control their children's education. But homeschooling went farther in instilling the family values ideal by forcing mothers to control their children's education directly.
Women like Ruth Nobel in Michigan and Carol Duro in North Carolina won
support because they faced government opposition for trying to carry out
mothers' most basic task: the care, nurture, and education of their children.

Moreover, curricula and publications bore out evangelical homeschoolers' assumptions about the family. Michael Farris's book *The Homeschooling
Father* featured chapters like "Helping your Helpmeet," "Fulfilling Your Role
as Protector," and "Spiritual Leadership Is Not Optional." These terms reflected a complementarian outlook on marriage, the belief that husbands and

Figure 6. Evangelical publishers like A Beka Books ran advertisements in John Holt's Growing Without Schooling newsletter that trumpeted the "Christian" vision of homeschooling curricula without referencing the specific theological emphases of the publishers. Reprinted with permission of HoltGWS LLC © 2014.

wives filled distinct yet complementary roles. The husband provided protection and support, whereas the wife focused on childrearing and domestic responsibilities as a "helpmeet" for her husband. Raymond and Dorothy Moore, though far more progressive on most issues, also advocated complementarian arrangements in their volume *The Successful Homeschool Family Handbook*. Homeschooling simply assumed mothers would care for the children during the "school day." Mothers served as the lead instructors in virtually all homeschooling arrangements. Conservative evangelical homeschoolers developed a clear articulation of family authority (parents over children, husbands over wives) to complement their focus on a more structured homeschooling experience.

By the late 1980s, then, a discernible group of evangelical homeschoolers had coalesced, and their philosophy cohered in part because of a commitment to family values. Mary Pride, whose regularly updated *Big Book of Home Learning* served as a clearinghouse for evangelical homeschooling curricula, aptly captured the ethos of evangelical homeschooling. Pride's 1985 book, *The Way Home: Beyond Feminism, Back to Reality*, argued that motherhood was essential to women's identity and outlined Pride's experience with homeschooling. She criticized feminist organizations like Planned Parenthood and the National Organization for Women. "Homeworking is the biblical lifestyle for Christian wives," wrote Pride. "Homeworking, like feminism, is a total lifestyle. The difference is that homeworking produces stable homes, growing churches, and children who are Christian leaders." As one of a growing number of evangelical anti-feminist tracts (many written by women), *The Way Home* placed mothers on a pedestal and viewed homeschooling as an integral part of Christian womanhood. The homeschool could not survive without faithful and intelligent mothers tending their brood. *The Way Home* served as an empowering text for scores of homeschooling mothers.[67]

While homeschooling advocates like Pride focused most of their praise and advice on mothers, homeschooling fathers also received attention. Gregg Harris, whose Christian Life workshops became a phenomenon among conservative evangelical homeschoolers in the late 1980s (and who, like Farris, had an ugly break-up with the Moores), wrote an article for *Teaching Home* on how fathers played an integral role in homeschooling. Harris assumed fathers ought to lead their families, but he also implored fathers to invest in the emotional and spiritual lives of their children. "There is something that happens in the hearts of men when we consciously make time for children."[68] This model of emotionally engaged fatherhood resembled the message of

Promise Keepers, an evangelical men's movement that grew rapidly in the 1990s. It marked a partial break from the masculinity of previous generations: men were still supposed to lead, but they were to do so with a tender embrace rather than with an iron fist.[69] The nature of homeschooling encouraged this view of fatherhood. Educating children at home—done well—was a mighty task. Mothers bore the brunt of the load, but homeschooling publications constantly insisted on the importance of engaged fathers. The male leadership advocated by conservative evangelical homeschoolers was neither distant nor ham-fisted.

Homeschooling, then, inscribed the family values agenda even more thoroughly than did Christian schools or battles over public school textbooks. In homeschooling, conservative evangelicals made their clearest statement that children were not wards of the state, and that parents ought to have full control over education. Homeschoolers launched court battles in which they articulated the notion of a secular state at war with conservative Christianity—and specifically with conservative Christian *families*. These families fought back by bringing education into the home and assigning distinct, complementary roles to all members of the family. Christian right leaders like Jerry Falwell decried a "vicious assault" on American families and contended, "families educating their children in moral principles have carried on the traditions of this free republic."[70] Many homeschoolers could affirm Falwell's observations about families. Homeschooling was the fullest extension of the family values agenda within the realm of education, and its continual growth among evangelicals since the mid-1980s suggested the deep resonance of that agenda within conservative Protestantism.

The Joshua Generation

As the ranks of conservative evangelical homeschoolers grew, they became a more and more attractive political base. Whereas the homeschoolers of the 1980s were too disorganized and independent to provide for large-scale politicization, the movement of the 1990s featured more robust national organizations and coherence. HSLDA continued to attract new members at 25 percent a year (even as it regularly lost 18–20 percent of its membership annually—after all, the legal defense it promised was not as important after 1990, when every state had laws permitting homeschooling in some form). Homeschooling conventions and curricula sprouted across the country.

Numbers were notoriously hard to pin down, but even conservative estimates suggested 1 million children were being homeschooled by the early 2000s.[71] A majority of homeschoolers continued to identify as evangelicals throughout the 1990s. By the turn of the century, conservative homeschoolers represented a substantial portion of the evangelical population.

HSLDA, as one of the largest and wealthiest homeschool organizations, attempted to mobilize its base to campaign for conservative candidates and causes. Farris launched Patrick Henry College in 2000 near Washington, D.C., with the express hope of training homeschoolers for political service. Farris used $400,000 from HSLDA accounts to start Patrick Henry; another $9 million came from private donors (with Tim LaHaye providing one of the largest donations). Farris said he started the college in response to two constituencies: homeschool parents who wanted to send their children to a college that reflected their values and conservative congressmen wanting to hire homeschoolers as interns. Patrick Henry students began appearing in government offices almost immediately, and the school attracted national attention when it placed nine students in the George W. Bush White House (five as interns, four as volunteers). The ethos of Patrick Henry reflected none of the laissez-faire atmosphere of early homeschoolers; students described the place as intense. One student petition called for the library to open before 6:00 A.M. so students could begin studying earlier. Farris dreamed of mobilizing homeschoolers to influence government, and Patrick Henry gave them a clear avenue into Republican Washington.[72]

Farris titled his manifesto for Patrick Henry "Generation Joshua," a designation he applied to twenty-first-century evangelical homeschoolers across the country. Recalling the Old Testament leader Joshua, who was called by God to reclaim the land of Israel, Generation Joshua would reclaim America for God. As in Christian schools and in campaigns against public school textbooks, conservative evangelical homeschooling materials described the United States as a place where Christian values had once reigned supreme. The sordid state of popular culture and the legalization of "anti-Christian" practices like abortion and gay rights derived from the increasing godlessness of America. Generation Joshua would arrest the secularization of American society and put God back in rightful control.

HSLDA sent out student volunteers from Generation Joshua in the 2004 elections. *Home School Court Report* detailed the work of homeschoolers in Indiana, where a group of twenty "Generation Joshua members worked long hours to help push [Republican challenger Mike] Sodrel in the battle for

Indiana's 9th Congressional District." Likewise, a "student action team" helped South Dakota Republicans oust longtime Democratic Senator Tom Daschle. And HSLDA claimed partial credit for helping George W. Bush win Ohio, thanks to Generation Joshua teams in Tuscarawas and Cuyahoga Counties. A seventeen-year-old on the South Dakota team reported, "I believe I was able to make a difference in the course of our nation."[73] HSLDA, to be sure, had reason to overstate its influence. The homeschooling volunteers made up a tiny fraction of the get-out-the-vote effort on election day. Yet the connection between homeschooling and politics had never been quite so explicit. By 2004, HSLDA had reoriented itself as a political action committee. If the children were the hope of the future, homeschoolers who had imbibed the ethos of conservative evangelicalism had to transform the nation. And politics provided the clearest path for them to do so.

These developments within HSLDA occurred even as homeschooling was diversifying. In the late 1980s and 1990s, conservative evangelicals acquired both numerical majorities and curricular dominance among American homeschoolers. While conservative evangelicals continued to produce much of the homeschooling curricula in the 2000s, a new crop of non-evangelicals was flocking to the movement. Homeschoolers in 2005 looked more like the ideologically diverse array of homeschoolers in 1985 than the more homogeneous evangelical homeschooling movement of 1995. And racial diversity was slowly increasing as well: a 2003 study pegged African American membership in the movement at 5 percent—still low but up from 1 percent in the late 1990s.[74] Moreover, the rise of the internet made do-it-yourself curricula more attainable for many homeschoolers and offered the possibility of new initiatives like "cyber-charters," online schools that attracted thousands of homeschoolers. HSLDA balked at cyber-charters and worried about the diversification of the movement. By 2010, the trend among homeschoolers seemed to be toward fragmentation.[75]

Yet the early conservative evangelical homeschoolers—alongside their counterparts who established Christian schools or fought against liberal public schools—provided an important model for the family values movement. It was in battles over education where conservative evangelicals developed rhetoric and ideologies to compete with late twentieth-century liberals and learned to mobilize for political battle. The family values agenda resonated in the realm of education because parents' control over their children was so crucial. Fights over children inevitably aroused emotion, and in arguing about who controlled education—whether in public schools, private schools, or home schools—conservative evangelicals hit on a way of describing the world that put them at odds with "enemies of the family." By asserting the primacy of the family and the rights of parents to control their children's education, the family values movement's educational battles provided early and sustained places of political engagement and signaled evangelicals' belief that families were the bedrock of society.

PART II

MOTHERS

CHAPTER 4

Abortion

Mothers commanded respect in the family values movement. They promoted Christian schools, championed the fights against liberal textbooks in Texas and West Virginia, and defended their rights to educate children in home schools. Women like Alice Moore, Norma Gabler, and Vicki Frost leveraged their roles as mothers to fight for their kids. This was not a new strategy. For over a century, Americans had assumed women held unique gifts in the realm of child-rearing. Early Americans valorized the "republican mothers" who fostered the values of the American Revolution in their offspring; nineteenth-century theologians talked about the centrality of "Christian nurture" and the importance of a feminine touch in the home. Temperance activists fought alcohol on behalf of battered mothers and children, while anti-lynching advocates promised to "teach our children at home, at school and at church a new interpretation of law and religion."[1] In these movements and others, Americans of widely different political persuasions reflected a common assumption: mothers held unique ability and power in the rearing of children. The mothers at the center of the family values movement, then, premised their activism on a long tradition of women whose political power derived from motherhood.

But in the mid-1970s motherhood itself seemed under attack. The 1973 Supreme Court decision *Roe v. Wade* gave women the right to terminate a pregnancy. At the same time, "second-wave" feminists championed an Equal Rights Amendment (ERA) to the U.S. Constitution. According to its detractors, the ERA was an assault on motherhood, as it suggested that women should focus on pursuing equality outside the home rather than on preserving their prerogatives within it. Likewise, a large faction of conservative Christians saw legalized abortion as an unnatural attack on women's biological destiny. Evangelicals believed God had created men and women to fulfill particular roles. Biology confirmed for them that motherhood was women's role. Abortion and feminism—along with the birth control pill, about which evangelicals were more circumspect—made motherhood more optional than ever before. Family values proponents could not abide that.

By the middle of the 1970s, mothers had become a major part of politically conservative campaigns. "Housewife populists" in southern California had spearheaded campaigns against communist influences and liberal education activists in the 1950s. As the conservative movement coalesced in the 1960s, these housewives had become a crucial demographic for political conservatism. Conservative political action group meetings featured well-coiffed women in pumps and pantyhose, serving as a visible rejoinder to the braless and bell-bottomed women of the counterculture. In the words of one historian, these housewife populists cultivated a "cult of wholesomeness that introduced nuclear family-style suburban domesticity into political performance."[2] Appealing to mothers became a major strategy for GOP candidates like Barry Goldwater and Richard Nixon. But the appeal did not turn on women's issues such as reproductive rights or violence against women. Rather, politicians appealed to conservative women's maternal instincts, as a way of garnering the support of a critical constituency.[3]

As conservative evangelicals came to believe that motherhood itself was under attack, the family values movement went to battle on behalf of these mothers. Grassroots political campaigns against *Roe* and the ERA represented the most visible sites of this fight for mothers. These campaigns took place alongside the campaigns for Christian education. Evangelicals' battles for children and their defense of mothers depended on one another. Home school advocates defended parents' rights just as pro-life organizations decried abortion as an easy way out of motherhood. By 1980, the family values movement took it as a given that defense of the family demanded support for parents' rights and opposition to abortion.

Yet that connection is not intuitive. After all, shouldn't "parental rights" include the right to postpone or avoid parenthood? Shouldn't people on a crusade for family values support feminists, who argued for daycare and higher pay for working mothers? Liberals fought to broaden the definition of "family values" throughout the 1970s. Most famously, Democratic President Jimmy Carter convened a White House Conference on Families near the end of his term in office, in 1980. Carter declared that the conference would "examine the strengths of American families, the difficulties they face, and the ways in which family life is affected by public policies."[4] He recruited a panel of organizers and asked them to focus on how government policy might better support family life. The diverse group of conference organizers Carter assembled insisted that a conference on families must examine the pressures facing homosexual and single-parent families, and they refused to define family as a heterosexual, two-parent household. These decisions led conservative Christian political leaders to repudiate the meeting. Jerry Falwell's political action group Moral Majority dubbed it "the Anti-Family Conference," and Alabama governor Fob James announced his state would not send any delegates "because the conference appears to oppose Judeo-Christian values." Conference speakers, declared the *Moral Majority Report*, were "activists who hold the traditional family and its morals in contempt." As a result, according to religious conservatives, the White House Council on Families would "heap scorn and ridicule on the American family."[5]

As Carter found out in his ill-fated White House Conference, by 1980 the "family" was no longer a neutral term. To most evangelicals, "family values" meant opposition to abortion, opposition to feminism, and refusal to see anything but the heterosexual, two-parent family as a legitimate family. By painting their opponents as enemies of the family, movement leaders gave their sectarian agenda the potential for wide appeal. Longstanding divides— between Catholics and evangelicals, or between political activists and conservative Christians—broke down as the Christian right rallied supporters of the "traditional family." Believers who had once defined their vision in biblical terms recognized the political power of recasting their agenda as a matter of family values.

Locating opposition to abortion and feminism as a defense of motherhood was a key step in the definition of "family"—and in the construction of the family values movement itself. Evangelicals forged a connection with conservative Catholics on these two issues, and that connection facilitated the growth of the family values movement. Whereas the campaigns for Christian schools and home schools happened largely in the world of conservative Protestantism, arguments against abortion and the ERA spanned the Protestant-Catholic divide. Conservative evangelicals and Catholics came together in defense of motherhood, creating a definition of "family values" that came to dominate political debate.

Learning to Oppose Abortion

Abortion has stood at the center of the family values movement for three decades. No other issue has commanded as much political attention in conservative evangelicals' fight for family values. Christian right fundraising letters from the 1980s and 1990s called post-*Roe* abortions a holocaust and enjoined Christians to get involved with politics in order to stop the slaughter. Groups like the National Right to Life Committee graded congressmen on the strength of their opposition to *Roe v. Wade*. And conservative Protestant leaders named abortion as *the* critical issue that awakened them from long political slumber. "The abortion issue," recalled Southern Baptist leader Al Mohler, "is the stick of dynamite that exploded the issue."[6] Likewise, Jerry Falwell said that on "the morning of January 23, 1973"—the day after the *Roe v. Wade* decision—"I felt a growing conviction that I would have to take my stand."[7] Though it took several years for Falwell to follow through on his conviction, abortion clearly occupied the central role among the constellation of issues Christian right leaders spotlighted in their political mobilization of evangelicals.

Yet evangelicals' initial response to *Roe v. Wade* hardly matched their recollections of immediate indignation. Falwell issued no statements on the decision until 1975, a silence he attributed to preoccupation with a government investigation of his organization's finances in 1973.[8] Polls of Southern Baptists in the half-decade before *Roe* showed an overwhelming majority in favor of "therapeutic abortion," albeit not "abortion on demand." Though some conservatives in the Southern Baptist Convention agitated for a stronger stand against abortion after *Roe*, moderates blocked discussion of an anti-abortion resolution at the 1974 convention.[9] *Christianity Today*, the flagship evangelical journal launched by Billy Graham in the 1950s, took a strong stand against abortion under the direction of editor (and Southern Baptist minister) Harold Lindsell. But most evangelical Protestant leaders did not grasp the political implications of *Roe* prior to 1975. While grassroots pro-life activists expressed indignation about the *Roe* decision, most evangelical Protestant leaders and institutions responded tepidly at first.[10]

Two factors contributed to this initial response to *Roe*. First, the language the Court used to legitimate abortion drew on a conservative rationale, as it guarded individual rights against an invasive government. The Fourteenth Amendment, said the Court, "protects against state action the right to privacy." In other words, the Supreme Court employed an individual rights rationale that favored women's prerogative in reproductive choices against the state's interference. Early abortion foes knew that by defining abortion as an issue "belonging to the *private* sphere, more like a religious preference than a deeply held social belief," the Court's decision appealed to those who rejected government interference in private decisions.[11] Evangelicals, who had developed sensitivity to government intrusion on their beliefs, increasingly guarded against any attempts to infringe their religious liberty. By framing abortion as an individual right, the Court predisposed religious and political conservatives to support *Roe*. For instance, the Southern Baptist Convention premised its initial support for *Roe* on the convention's historic support for the separation of church and state.[12]

Second, and more important, Catholics spearheaded the earliest campaigns against abortion.[13] In the early 1970s, approximately 70 percent of the members of the National Right to Life Commission claimed membership in the Catholic Church.[14] Catholic leadership of the pro-life movement made it less likely that conservative Protestants would join it. A 1984 study of the pro-life movement found that few activists had expressed any public opposition to abortion before 1967 (when California legalized abortion), and almost all the earliest activists were Catholic. Catholics' majority in the pro-life coalition persisted at least through 1978.[15] Given the historic enmity between Catholics and conservative Protestants, it is hardly surprising that evangelicals felt some discomfort about joining the pro-life movement in the early 1970s. As evangelical theologian Harold O. J. Brown put it, "At that point, a lot of Protestants reacted almost automatically—'If the Catholics are for it, we should be against it.'"[16] Pro-life groups did receive a surge in Protestant membership after the *Roe* decision—especially from younger women with small children—but on the whole, evangelicals seemed hesitant to enter the pro-life coalition until the mid-1970s.[17]

That stance changed—dramatically—in the late 1970s, paving the way for abortion to become the crucial issue of the family values movement. While most conservative evangelicals came late to the fight against legalized abortion, their conversion to the pro-life cause transformed the debate over abortion in America. The success of pro-life activists in mobilizing evangelicals depended in part on appeals to family values. Making a decision to terminate a pregnancy did, in the mind of conservative evangelicals, end a life, but it also intruded on family matters. Teenagers could defy their parents; wives could decide the matter apart from their husbands. And abortion made motherhood a matter of choice rather than destiny. All these elements marked abortion as an enemy of the family.

Indeed, pro-life activists succeeded so well at changing the rhetoric of the abortion debate that their opponents in the pro-choice camp had begun to use pro-life slogans by the 1980s. For instance, pro-choice campaigns in Arkansas and Alabama argued that bans on public funding for abortions represented a government intrusion on a family decision.[18] Pro-choice advocates discovered that framing their campaigns as "protecting a woman's right to choose" was a losing strategy in areas where evangelicals dominated. Instead, they adopted the language of family values to defend *Roe*. But to their chagrin, conservative evangelicals had transformed the abortion debate by the early 1980s. While *Roe v. Wade* has survived for over four decades, its opponents have leveraged legalized abortion to reenergize conservative evangelicals in national politics. Pro-life activism is "the most visible and dominant type of Christian right activism."[19] Leaders of the family values movement have successfully mobilized conservative evangelicals against *Roe* in part because they see it as a threat against the family.

Evangelicals who claimed that abortion was *the* motivating factor for their political transformation were rewriting history. Few evangelicals paid much attention to *Roe v. Wade* when the decision came down in January 1973. But the evangelicals who did criticize abortion prior to the mid-1970s provided an important framework for later pro-life activism. Among these early evangelical critics was L. Nelson Bell, a former medical missionary to China whose daughter Ruth married Billy Graham in 1943. A conservative southern Presbyterian, Bell played a role in the emergence and development of twentieth-century evangelicalism. After launching the *Presbyterian Journal* in 1942, Bell helped Graham start a nondenominational periodical for evangelicals in 1956 called *Christianity Today*, which quickly outpaced most denominational journals in circulation, notably the liberal *Christian Century*. Bell's regular column, "A Layman and His Faith," spelled out conservative positions on a host of issues. He opposed drug and sex education in public schools, and he supported efforts to retain (or return) prayer to the classroom. When Bell weighed in on international affairs, he typically voiced conservative support for the government. "A Layman and His Faith" did not touch on political topics every week, but Bell's occasional essays on politics revealed a decidedly conservative voice.

Doctors like Bell had long controlled administration of legal abortions in the United States. In the late nineteenth century, American Medical

Association members successfully campaigned to have abortion defined as a medical procedure, permissible only at the discretion of physicians. By 1900, every state had passed a law forbidding abortions, though all but six states allowed exceptions for "therapeutic abortions" necessary to preserve a pregnant woman's health. This meant that any woman seeking a legal abortion was at the mercy of a doctor's decision about the threat posed to her by pregnancy or childbirth. As recently as 1967, women across the country had almost no control over whether they could obtain a legal abortion. Every state provided for imprisonment of doctors who performed abortions the state deemed unnecessary—though the definition of "unnecessary" varied, from requiring the mother's life to be in danger to more lenient standards in states that permitted therapeutic abortions. Either way, physicians largely controlled who could obtain an abortion, and by the middle of the twentieth century the abortion rate in the United States was historically low.[20]

That situation changed dramatically in 1967, when California passed the Therapeutic Abortion Law (also known as the Beilenson Bill). This law allowed doctors to apply a "broad construction" of an 1872 statute permitting therapeutic abortions. In theory, doctors and lawmakers expected a mild increase in the number of abortions, as physicians still ostensibly made the final decision about whether to perform an abortion. In practice, the number skyrocketed, as women became the agents deciding when abortions would happen. Between 1967 and 1971, the rate of legal abortions in California increased 2,000 percent. By 1971, 99 percent of women requesting an abortion were granted one, and one in three pregnancies ended in a legal abortion. This unanticipated jump in the abortion rate played an instrumental role in converting California governor Ronald Reagan—who had signed the Beilenson Bill—into a pro-lifer. As one sociologist put it, "for the first time in over a century, medical control of abortion was becoming nothing more than a legal fiction. By 1971, women in California had abortions because they wanted them, not because physicians agreed they could have them."[21]

L. Nelson Bell was horrified by this transformation, both as a doctor and as a Christian. When the *Presbyterian Survey*, the official publication of the Presbyterian Church (U.S.), ran a 1972 article in favor of legalizing abortions, Bell responded with disgust. "The choice of an interview with an abortions agent as the lead article," wrote Bell, "is almost unbelievable. Equally distressing is this Presbyterian minister's cavalier statement that a fetus is not a person." As scriptural support for his contention that a fetus is a person, Bell referenced Luke 1:41, in which Elizabeth felt her child "leap" within her womb when her sister Mary, the mother of Christ, entered the room. Pro-life Christians have cited this passage as a biblical justification for opposing abortion. It suggests to them the presence of life before birth and impels them to view abortion as the taking of life. Bell drew on this view of fetal life to inform his medical practice. He admitted he had performed abortions in the past but claimed he did so only with no viable alternatives.[22] As such, he unequivocally rejected arguments for loosening the strict abortion laws in place. Bell thought doctors ought to retain control over abortions, knowing that losing control would transform abortions from an unfortunate but occasional medical necessity into a frequent end for unwanted pregnancies. Bell's view reflected evangelicals' assumptions about authority. Whereas pro-choice advocates saw Bell's argument as a patriarchal and paternalistic approach that left (mostly male) physicians in control of female bodies, pro-life evangelicals like Bell thought it spoke to the importance of clear lines of authority. Without doctors controlling decisions regarding when to terminate pregnancies, Bell knew the number of abortions would skyrocket.

The huge uptick in abortions created a dire moral crisis for those, like Bell, inclined to see abortion as murder. It also helped establish the bifurcation of the abortion debate that persists in the twenty-first century. Whereas pro-choice advocates saw abortion opponents as oppressors, pro-lifers saw abortion rights advocates as baby killers. The dissonance between the two sides of this dispute made it nearly impossible for combatants to find common ground. Someone like Bell was either oppressor or hero, depending on where one fell in the abortion debate. The title of a 1992 study of abortion attitudes among the American population—*Between Two Absolutes*—signaled the polarity of this debate.[23]

This polarization came about in part because pro-choice activists began talking about abortion as a right. Whereas the Beilenson Bill theoretically kept ultimate decisions about abortions in the hands of doctors, in practice women in California controlled nearly all abortion decisions after 1967. As this reality was becoming clear, pro-choice activists began mobilizing to repeal all laws restricting abortion, arguing that the ability to terminate a pregnancy was a fundamental right of women. "When we talk about women's rights, we can get all the rights in the world . . . and none of them mean a doggone thing if we don't own the flesh we stand in," said a member of the Society for Humane Abortions. "I consider the right to elective abortion, whether you dream of doing it or not, is the cornerstone of the women's movement."[24] Because an unplanned pregnancy could short-circuit a woman's career, earning ability, and power, women's right's groups increasingly saw abortion rights as the centerpiece of their struggle for equality. Without the ability to control reproduction, they argued, women remained subject to the patriarchal structures that had governed society for centuries.

The Supreme Court decision in *Roe v. Wade* used the language of individual rights to defend women's right to have an abortion. The case began in 1969 when Sarah Weddington and Linda Coffee, feminist attorneys in Texas, decided to challenge that state's abortion ban. They filed a class-action lawsuit against Dallas district attorney Henry Wade on behalf of an anonymous pregnant woman, Jane Roe (later identified as Norma McCorvey). The case wended its way through lower courts before the U.S. Supreme Court heard oral arguments in 1971. The case hinged on whether terminating a pregnancy was a woman's right. The Court thought it was. In January 1973, the Court issued its decision. "This right of privacy . . . founded in the Fourteenth Amendment's concept of personal liberty and restrictions upon state action . . . is broad enough to encompass a woman's decision whether or not to terminate her pregnancy," wrote Justice Harry Blackmun for the majority.[25] The decision exceeded the hopes of even some of the strongest pro-choice advocates. It reversed a century of statutes that had placed abortion decisions in the hands of doctors and gave women near-total control over whether to terminate a pregnancy. *Roe v. Wade* invalidated abortion laws in 46 states. In its far-reaching decision, the Supreme Court declared that abortion on demand, in the first trimester, was an individual right of women. The Court's decision, in short, transformed the landscape of abortion in America.

The pro-life movement was slow to respond at first, in part because pro-life groups simply did not exist in large numbers in 1973. Prior to *Roe*, the burden of changing the law was on pro-choice groups, which mobilized to a greater extent than did pro-life groups. As a result, the decision caught abortion opponents flat-footed. On the morning after the decision, the *New York Times* story about opposition to *Roe* cited the opposition of Catholic cardinals and an officer of the pro-life group Right to Life. Their comments were sad rather than defiant. Cardinal Cooke of New York called the decision an "unspeakable tragedy," while Barbara Meara, president of a Bronx right-to-life group, noted the "ironic" nature of the court's decision to "sanction the destruction of life" at a moment when "this country is trying to improve the lot of so many people."[26] Missing in the immediate aftermath of *Roe* were bold calls for pro-life action—for the simple reason that pro-life groups were not yet mobilized. Anti-abortion activists later made excuses for their lack of action in the first years after the decision. For instance, a Baptist minister who later became involved in pro-life activism said that in 1973, "I was busy, in a busy, growing pastorate and finishing a doctor's degree and all kinds of things."[27] Similar statements have appeared from many strong abortion opponents, signaling their awareness of and discomfort with the tepid initial response to *Roe*. Given the centrality of abortion to the family values coalition, this quiescence is surprising. But given the legal standing of abortion before *Roe*, the lack of immediate pro-life mobilization begins to make more sense. Social movements struggle to sustain themselves to preserve the status quo. Before 1973, pro-life groups could only point to California as an example of what *might* happen to abortion laws. But prior to *Roe*, no one—even pro-choice activists—could imagine the scope of the Supreme Court decision.

Furthermore, Americans in the 1970s considered opposition to abortion a "Catholic issue." Newspapers repeatedly turned to Catholic religious leaders for pro-life comments, and Catholics comprised the majority of members in pro-life organizations.[28] Catholic leadership of the pro-life coalition stemmed from at least three factors. First, Catholic opposition to all forms of birth control made opposition to abortion a logical and necessary position. Church doctrine taught that all sexual acts had to admit at least the possibility of conception. As a result, when birth control became widely available in the twentieth century, Catholic leaders opposed all forms of contraception. By the mid-1960s, liberal Catholics hoped the Church's teaching would change. And they had reason to hope: in 1965 the Second Vatican Council affirmed a host of progressive reforms, which included saying mass in the vernacular and admitting that non-Catholics possessed "many elements of sanctification and truth." But the Church did not budge on birth control. In his 1968 encyclical *Humanae Vitae* ("Of Human Life"), Pope Paul VI declared, "Each and every marital [sexual] act must of necessity retain its intrinsic relationship to the procreation of human life."[29] Protestants, on the other hand, had long supported birth control and family planning.[30] As a result, plenty of Protestants viewed abortion as part of a larger system of birth control; hence, even if they had moral qualms about the procedure, they did not feel compelled to oppose it.

Second, most mainline Protestant church leaders expressed solidarity with the women's movement and approval of the *Roe* decision. In 1970 the Presbyterian Church (U.S.) Board of National Ministries accepted a $50,000 gift in order to establish a Committee on Therapeutic Abortions. The

Presbyterian General Assembly approved a position paper advocating for "medical intervention" in "problem pregnancies" for all who "desire and qualify for it." The leadership of the Presbyterian Church advocated making therapeutic abortions accessible to everyone, not just to wealthy individuals.[31] Southern Baptists, a more conservative lot that was somewhat less sanguine about abortion, passed a resolution affirming a "high view of the sanctity of human life." Still, the SBC called for "legislation that will allow the possibility of abortion under such conditions as rape, incest, clear evidence of severe fetal deformity, and carefully ascertained evidence of the likelihood of damage to the emotional, mental, and physical health of the mother." After *Roe*, the SBC refused to hold a vote on a resolution condemning abortion at its 1974 and 1975 national convention meetings. While leadership of Protestant bodies skewed more liberal than the laity, the women's movement had won broad support among mainline denominations. The quest for abortion rights seemed bound up with women's desire for full equality—a cause most Protestants supported in the first half of the 1970s.

Third, Protestants had a long history of opposing Catholics, no matter the issue. In 1966 the National Council of Catholic Bishops formed the Family Life Division, which remained the only national pro-life group until *Roe*. Five months after the decision, activists met in Detroit and formed the National Right to Life Committee, which inherited much of the infrastructure and personnel of the Catholic Family Life Division. Delegates elected a Methodist (Marjory Mecklenburg) in order to highlight the NRLC's distance from the Catholic hierarchy, but most Protestants remained skeptical. As late as 1980, NRLC membership was 70 percent Catholic.[32] Protestants' reluctance to join partly derived from their anti-Catholicism. Evangelicals (including Nelson Bell) had publicly opposed the election of John F. Kennedy in 1960 on account of his Catholicism. Bell, in fact, had likened Catholicism to "an octopus [that] covers the entire world and threatens those basic freedoms and those constitutional rights for which our forefathers died."[33] Just over a decade later, Bell was trying to convince fellow Protestants that the anti-freedom octopus had, in this one case, gotten it right. Bob Holbrook, president of Baptists for Life, wrote a 1975 pamphlet called, "Is Abortion a One-Religion Concern? NO!" He promised readers an investigation of the " 'Catholic' issue of abortion" that would convince them to join with their long-time foes. But the need for Holbrook to write such a pamphlet testified to the reluctance most Protestants expressed regarding opposition to abortion.[34] The lack of theological, institutional, and historical rationale for Protestants to join

Catholics in the fight against abortion hampered the pro-life movement for
at least a half-decade after *Roe*.

Francis Schaeffer and the "Catholic Issue"

Evangelical theologian Francis Schaeffer sought to change that. Born and
reared among conservative Presbyterians in Pennsylvania, Schaeffer established a Christian community called L'Abri ("the shelter") in Switzerland
during the 1950s. From L'Abri, Schaeffer published his views on a variety of
subjects. He rejected fundamentalism's notion of "purity," the desire to remain separated from doctrinal rivals, as misguided and even heretical. Christians, he contended, needed to engage with doctrinal foes and secular culture
as part of a holistic presentation of the gospel. "The Lordship of Christ," he
argued, "covers *all* of life and *all* of life equally." He presented conservative
Christian views on a host of subjects, from the environment to the arts.
Schaeffer contended that "secular humanists" had embedded an anti-
Christian philosophy in American laws and government. Now, he argued,
Christians had to fight back.[35]

By the end of the 1970s, Schaeffer had emerged as the foremost evangelical opponent of abortion, which he portrayed as the primary issue demanding Christian response. In *Whatever Happened to the Human Race*, which
Schaeffer co-wrote with future surgeon general C. Everett Koop, he argued,
"Of all the subjects relating to the erosion of the sanctity of human life, abortion is the keystone." Schaeffer contended that the permissibility of abortion
meant America had abandoned respect for human life. The book connected
abortion to a host of dehumanizing practices, including euthanasia, torture,
and suicide. The final pages of *Whatever Happened to the Human Race* featured various figures pictured in cages: African American slaves, Jewish immigrants, a handicapped girl, and a premature infant. Schaeffer concluded,
"we must stand against the loss of humanness in all its forms." He saw abortion as murder of innocents, and his book popularized that interpretation
among conservative Protestants.[36]

Perhaps more important, Schaeffer disseminated a view of political involvement that encouraged—even demanded—that evangelicals cooperate
with non-evangelicals to achieve political success. He advanced the notion of
a culture war, and he suggested that political quiescence was untenable in the
face of practices like abortion. He argued that evangelicals needed to adopt

"co-belligerence," or cooperation with non-evangelicals, as a political tactic. In *A Christian Manifesto*, he wrote, "It is time for Christians and others who do not accept the narrow and bigoted humanist views rightfully to use the appropriate forms of protest."[37] Schaeffer believed that the dire straits in which Christians found themselves in the late 1970s demanded cooperation with all who would join the fight against abortion. Evangelicals responded. A comment by Jimmy Draper, president of the Southern Baptist Convention in 1982–84, typified Christian right leaders' view of Schaeffer's influence: "Francis Schaeffer was the first one to say, hey, listen, there's a war going on with our culture, and our worldview's in danger, and we need to stand for the things that God has revealed to us."[38] Evangelicals' embrace of Schaeffer's culture war ideal represented the critical step in mobilizing conservative Protestants against abortion.

Jerry Falwell emerged as the foremost proponent of Schaeffer's doctrine of "co-belligerency." Falwell's leadership of the movement was surprising. In the 1960s he had advocated political quiescence and fundamentalist "separation" from doctrinal rivals. But he changed in the late 1970s. In *Moral Majority Report*, he wrote, "In itself, the political process is not 'dirty.' It has been corrupted by wicked, sinful men and by the neglect of God's people to be the moral conscience of our leaders." Christians, he said, must fight "the spiritual war where Satan is active—in the political arena."[39] And in order for conservative Protestants to fight successfully in the political arena, they would have to cooperate with those whose theology differed from theirs. Falwell contended, "those of us in the leadership of Moral Majority are aware of the vast theological issues that separate Catholics, Protestants, Jews, Mormons, etc. We are not fighting to unite any of these factions. We are fighting to maintain religious freedom of this nation so that we can maintain our religious practices regardless of how different they may be."[40] These words reflected Schaeffer's influence. Schaeffer called Falwell in 1978 to encourage him in his efforts against moral decay in America.[41] Falwell subsequently popularized many of Schaeffer's views through his books, periodicals, and public appearances.

In May 1979, Falwell inaugurated the political action group Moral Majority. That month, a handful of conservative Republicans, including a Catholic (Paul Weyrich) and a Jew (Howard Phillips), met with Falwell at the Holiday Inn in Lynchburg to discuss forming a political action committee. Weyrich reportedly coined the new group's name, and Falwell emerged as the leader.[42] In an early promotional brochure, Moral Majority described its philosophy as "pro-life, pro-family, pro-moral, and pro-America." The brochure also suggested that a coalition of at least 170 million "moral" Americans existed: 50–60 million "idealistic moralists," more than 60 million "religious moralists," and 60 million born-again Christians.[43] The organization clearly intended to reach all these groups, crossing once unbridgeable divides.

Most notably, Moral Majority targeted Catholics for cooperation. Falwell claimed that 30 percent of Moral Majority's budget came from Catholic contributions, and *Moral Majority Report* regularly published letters and articles from Catholic supporters.[44] "I do hope others will join me in giving you our prayerful support (which I have already given you)," wrote one Catholic nun. "I think Dr. Jerry Falwell is brave, devoted to Christian living and unafraid to speak out."[45] Falwell's advertisement of Catholics' support displayed his commitment to political alliances with non-fundamentalists. Moreover, Catholics' strong and consistent stance against abortion endeared them to evangelicals who had grown increasingly strident in their pro-life position by the end of the 1970s. In his 1987 autobiography, Falwell celebrated Catholics' early opposition to *Roe* and lamented, "the voices of my Protestant Christian brothers and sisters, especially the voices of evangelical and fundamentalist leaders, remained silent" in the first few years after the decision.[46] Aligning himself with abortion's earliest opponents reflected his wholesale adoption of Schaeffer's doctrine of co-belligerency.[47]

Cooperating with Catholics was not a trivial step for Falwell to take. This new alliance triggered the breakup of some older ones. Fundamentalist stalwart Bob Jones, Jr., issued a denunciation of Falwell and Moral Majority. In a letter to alumni of Bob Jones University dated 10 June 1980, Jones censured Falwell's alliance with anti-feminist activist Phyllis Schlafly ("a devout Roman Catholic") and called him "the most dangerous man in America as far as Biblical Christianity is concerned." Jones viewed cooperation with Catholics as an unpardonable breach of fundamentalist "separation." As a leader of southern fundamentalists, Jones's condemnation of Moral Majority effectively excommunicated Falwell from the rightmost flank of conservative Protestantism. Stung by the criticism, Falwell replied, "I am indeed considered to be 'dangerous' to liberals, feminists, abortionists, and homosexuals, but certainly not to Bible-believing Christians. . . . God has called me to do what I am doing today."[48] He rejected the proposition that his political activities compromised his faith, yet he understood that building alliances with Catholics had occasioned turmoil among his spiritual compatriots. The legalization of abortion, in Falwell's estimation, made that turmoil unavoidable. *Roe*, he said, showed him "that this time preaching would not be enough." He decided, "it was my duty as a Christian to apply the truths of Scripture to every act of government."[49] Political action was no longer taboo—it was essential.

Motherhood and Abortion

In order to recruit evangelicals to the pro-life coalition, activists connected opposition to abortion with defense of the family. Mildred Jefferson, an African American physician who had become the first black female graduate of Harvard Medical School in 1951, saw abortion as the first step on a slippery slope to a genderless society. She wrote, "Today, it's the unborn child and tomorrow it could be the notion that men and women are interchangeable."[50] Jefferson did not explain why acceptance of abortion would lead to androgyny, though she might have anticipated conversations about genetic engineering. More explicit discussion about abortion's threat to gender roles came in the Family Manifesto, a lengthy policy statement released by several Christian right organizations in the mid-1980s. These groups declared, "We proclaim that parental responsibility for reproductive decisions is joint. Hence we deny that reproduction is solely a 'woman's choice.' "[51] The document's authors used the language of pro-choice advocates to show how *Roe* threatened the family structure authorized by the Bible. By relegating the family's primary function—reproduction and rearing of children—to private decisions women could undertake apart from their husbands, *Roe* posed a threat. Conservative Christians perceived the language of *Roe*, which described abortion as a "woman's choice," as a direct assault on the gendered family order instituted by the Bible.

Portraying abortion as an assault on motherhood was crucial. In 1984, a landmark sociological study of pro-life and pro-choice groups discovered a high degree of correlation between the primary occupations of women and their position in the abortion debate. Women who worked outside the home were more likely to support abortion rights. Homemakers, in contrast, felt that abortion devalued motherhood, which had once represented women's social and biological destiny. After *Roe*, motherhood became simply one of several choices available to women.[52] This choice, in the eyes of abortion foes, demeaned the mothering roles most of them cherished. They believed abortion fostered "a world view that deemphasizes (and therefore *downgrades*) the traditional roles of men and women." Female abortion foes' experience as mothers and homemakers predisposed them to reject *Roe*'s disregard for their family values.[53]

By portraying abortion rights as an assault on motherhood, populist evangelical leaders like Jerry Falwell were able to create a joint evangelical-Catholic coalition that eluded earlier Protestant foes of abortion like Nelson Bell. This was surprising, given that Bell came from a wing of evangelicalism that historically was more open to ecumenical cooperation. Falwell emerged from a fundamentalist Baptist tradition that took a hard line against any kind of theological compromise. But he represented a new face of fundamentalism. He embraced Catholic allies who had stood against abortion for decades. Moreover, by 1980, abortion rights foes had found a winning strategy in describing abortion as an assault on motherhood. Falwell's *Moral Majority Report* described a woman seeking an abortion as "reluctant mother to be" and identified feminists as "the most outrageous creation of the me-decade."[54]

This characterization of women as selfish and irresponsible fit perfectly into the solidifying notion of "family values." God had given each person a role to play, and one's gender largely determined one's adult responsibilities. Women, according to this interpretation, needed to accept their biological destiny as mothers. *Moral Majority Report* shocked readers with uncorroborated evidence that 97 percent of all abortions took place for reasons of "convenience and economy," representing the triumph of "selfishness and greed."[55] For readers of *Moral Majority Report*, statistics like these confirmed their suspicion that women getting abortions were taking the easy way out. Women needed to accept responsibility for their sexual activity, but more basically, women needed to be mothers. A Moral Majority petition to the U.S. Congress said that abortion in the first trimester was legal if "the mother wants the baby killed."[56] Such an incendiary description of abortion rights highlighted the dominant stereotype of the women who would shirk their God-given responsibility: they would kill rather than become mothers. In 1981, Dr. Jefferson, who served as president of the National Right to Life Committee in 1975–1978, told a congressional hearing, "the obstetrician and the mother" were becoming "the worst enemy of the child."[57] In the first ten years after *Roe*, few pro-life evangelicals took into consideration the exigencies that drove women to seek abortion in such large numbers. This would change over time, as evangelicals launched hundreds of "crisis pregnancy centers" and began to grapple with the circumstances that made abortion such an attractive option for so many. But in the early years of evangelical pro-life politics, writers described women seeking abortions as reluctant and irresponsible at best.

This understanding of women signaled the importance evangelicals attached to women becoming mothers. Yet high abortion rates suggested that many American women did not want to become mothers. If women sought abortions at such a high rate—somewhere between one-quarter and one-third of pregnancies ended in abortion in the early 1980s—how could conservative evangelicals hold on to the notion that motherhood was every woman's God-given destiny? The answer depended on evangelical theology and the family values ideal. Evangelicals believed women seeking abortion were seeking a way out of the consequences of sexual sin. While a large percentage of abortions happened among women who were already caring for a child (and a somewhat smaller percentage among married women), the family values movement portrayed abortion largely as the choice of unmarried women seeking to delay or reject parenthood. These women had flouted evangelical beliefs about the immorality of premarital sex, and they now wanted out of the consequences. Such behavior did not exactly surprise evangelicals, who had long emphasized the pervasive nature of sin. But the U.S. government's sanction of abortion rights in *Roe* suggested a sea change in American values. To evangelicals, the Supreme Court had offered women an easy way out.

This posture reflected the family values movement's sense that feminists and pro-choice advocates had upset the legal structures that had held human sinfulness in check for centuries. In 1981, conservative evangelical politicians supported a Family Protection Act that would require parental notification any time a minor sought "abortion-related services." It also demanded that the armed forces require soldiers separated from their families to "send home a predetermined allowance for spouses each month."[58] In both instances, the family values movement insisted on government mandates that guarded against humans' sinful proclivities. Legalized abortion, in this line of thinking, was an invitation to immorality. Family values called for clear lines of authority that made wives subject to their husbands' authority and, more broadly, placed men above women. The abortion laws that had governed the Unites States from the late nineteenth century until the mid-1970s had implicitly upheld these authority structures, as a (mostly male) medical profession controlled women's access to abortion. *Roe* obliterated that legal structure and set women free to elect abortions for whatever reasons they saw fit. Defenders of family values saw *Roe* as a sign of a society in decline because, to them, the decision sanctioned sinfulness. Legalized abortion meant men and women could indulge in sexual activity outside marriage without consequences.

Of course, the rhetoric Christian right leaders deployed in opposition to abortion did not portray *Roe* solely as an assault on motherhood. Moral Majority flyers talked about a "holocaust" and compared abortion advocates to defenders of slavery. "In 1857 the U.S. Supreme Court voted 7 to 2 that a slave was not a person but the property of his owners," read one such flyer, invoking the *Dred Scott* decision. Likewise, said Moral Majority, "in 1973 the U.S. Supreme Court voted 7 to 2 that an unborn human being was not a person but the private property of his mother. . . . Again, the self evident truth of the right to life, liberty, and the pursuit of happiness was denied."[59] Spurred by Schaeffer's vision, evangelical leaders in the early 1980s had characterized abortion as an unmitigated evil. Their ability to do so depended on a host of factors, including the far-reaching nature of the *Roe* decision and the subsequent spike in abortions performed in the United States.[60]

The description of abortion as an infringement on fetuses' right to life went hand in hand with the notion of abortion as an attack on mothers. As more and more evangelicals came to describe fetuses as "unborn babies," they came to understand abortion as an attack on the most vulnerable members of the family by their reluctant mothers. Furthermore, science seemed to confirm evangelicals' conviction that life began in the womb, not outside it. Medical advances in the 1970s and 1980s allowed infants born prematurely to survive in more cases, and in 1978 British doctors facilitated the first successful birth of a "test tube baby," Louise Brown. Pro-life evangelicals cited these developments as proof that fetuses were unborn babies.[61] They pushed for a Human Life Bill in 1981 that would define human life as beginning at conception. The bill failed, as did many similar successors introduced in Congress by pro-life legislators. But by the early 1980s, evangelicals understood fetuses as babies and pregnant women as mothers. The language of the pro-life movement brought campaigns against legalized abortion into the rhetorical framework of family values.

Because evangelicals viewed the abortion issue through the prism of family values, they showed more ambivalence about in vitro fertilization (IVF). IVF allowed women to have embryos surgically implanted after fertilization. During the last quarter of the twentieth century, this process became a standard—if expensive—option for couples struggling to become pregnant. IVF allowed women to become mothers. Given evangelicals' emphasis on motherhood, it would make sense for them to endorse the procedure. IVF, however, almost always resulted in the destruction of embryos. This put pro-life evangelicals in a difficult position, as it pitted their rationales for opposing abortion against one another. On the one hand, consistent pro-life thinking demanded that conservative evangelicals consider all embryos as persons. The destruction of embryos during IVF procedures could not be sanctioned, and many pro-lifers repudiated the procedure. On the other hand, women who sought IVF fit well into the family values model, as they went to great lengths to embrace motherhood. While some evangelicals voiced reservations about embryo-destroying processes, many more stayed silent. As one evangelical bioethicist put it, "IVF kind of snuck up on evangelicals. We weren't paying as close attention as we should have."[62] By the mid-1980s, abortion was clearly beyond the pale for evangelicals. IVF occupied a much murkier position in the framework of family values.

Evangelicals' increasing unanimity in opposition to abortion coincided with the Republican Party taking the lead in opposing *Roe*. This was not a foregone conclusion. A large majority of Catholics identified as Democrats, and a substantial faction of Democratic legislators opposed *Roe* in the 1970s. In the 1980 election, voters identifying as pro-life actually favored the Democratic candidate, Jimmy Carter, over the Republican nominee, Ronald Reagan. Pro-life voters remained equally divided between the two parties until 1979.[63] But the trend was toward the GOP. In the mid-1970s, Republicans led the fight against *Roe*. Political conservatives initially made outlawing federal funding of abortions a priority. In 1976 Henry Hyde, a Republican representative from Illinois, introduced legislation that would forbid Medicaid coverage of abortions except when the mother's life was threatened. Congress adopted the Hyde amendment one year later, with the added provision that women who were the victims of rape or incest could receive government aid for abortions. Politically conservative outlets like *Human Events* danced around the abortion controversy at first, suggesting a certain level of discomfort with the increasing prominence of right-to-life groups. *Human Events* even fretted that President Jimmy Carter's "remarkable firmness" in support of the Hyde Amendment might "bring the right-to-life supporters into the Democratic fold."[64]

But the Republicans' support of a constitutional amendment that would ban abortion secured the support of the majority of pro-life activists. In 1975, Republican senator Jesse Helms introduced a Human Life Amendment (HLA) to Congress. While it never passed, in 1980 the HLA won a spot on the Republican platform. Conservative Christian leaders painted opponents of the HLA as supporters of abortion, regardless of their stated personal views. Most notably, evangelical activists slammed Jimmy Carter for his rejection of the HLA. Falwell, typically, pressed the issue most forcefully: "If [Carter] does not stand where I say he does," said Falwell, "then a simple declaratory statement that he favors the Helms amendment . . . would quickly clear him with everyone."[65] Carter's claims to be pro-life did not convince abortion opponents when he failed to support the amendment.

By the early 1980s, ambivalence about abortion had mostly disappeared among conservative Protestants. In a 1982 resolution, the Southern Baptist Convention declared, "Both medical science and biblical references indicate that human life begins at conception. . . . [We] affirm that all human life, both born and pre-born, is sacred, bearing the image of God."[66] That statement summed up the feelings of most evangelicals. Abortion had become analogous to murder, and conservative rhetoric turned toxic. Moral Majority commentator Cal Thomas wrote, "the pro-abortionists will stop at nothing to continue the slaughter."[67] Evangelical and Catholic pro-life groups portrayed pro-abortion candidates as accomplices to crime. The rhetoric about abortion highlighted the ways political developments had reified the divide between "pro-life" and "pro-choice" in the late 1970s.

Yet the escalation in the Christian right's anti-abortion rhetoric in the early 1980s obscured both an early hesitancy to engage the issue and the connection of pro-life positions to a program of family values that coincided with conservative Christians' worldview. "Pro-life activists believe that men and women are intrinsically different," wrote sociologist Kristin Luker. "They subscribe quite strongly to the traditional belief that women should be wives and mothers *first*."[68] The correlation of "traditional" understandings of gender roles and opposition to abortion reflected the efforts of Schaeffer, Falwell, and other Christian right leaders to connect *Roe* with a widespread assault on "family values." It also helps explain why the Christian right demonized the women's movement in the years after *Roe*, just as feminism appeared poised to win wide acceptance among evangelicals.

CHAPTER 5

Feminism

Many abortion rights advocates hailed from the ranks of the women's movement, which won notable gains during the 1970s. The United Nations designated 1975 as International Women's Year, sanctioning the movement's goal of making women full and equal participants in civil societies. During that year, the UN convened a summer conference in Mexico, which produced a report emphasizing women's contributions to peacemaking and tying their full participation in governments to the promotion of disarmament.[1] Some U.S. feminists derided the IWY as a token gesture, but mainstream media endorsed the achievements and mission of feminism. For instance, *Time* said, "feminism has transcended the feminist movement. In 1975 the women's drive penetrated every layer of society, matured beyond ideology to a new status of general—and sometimes unconscious—acceptance."[2] The women's movement had won a new measure of popular support. Feminists seemed poised to accelerate their drive for full equality.

Evangelicals initially appeared excited about the advances of feminism. A 1974 editorial in *Christianity Today* endorsed the Equal Rights Amendment, and a survey in the same issue reported that Christians favored it by a 3–1 margin.[3] Evangelicals in 1974 also witnessed the publication of Letha Scanzoni and Nancy Hardesty's *All We're Meant to Be: A Biblical Approach to Women's Liberation*, which became the most important text in the nascent evangelical feminist movement. Scanzoni and Hardesty's book deployed some familiar feminist arguments, such as the contention that cultural conditioning, not biology, played the largest role in creating notions of "masculine" and "feminine." But unlike most second-wave feminists, Scanzoni and Hardesty enlisted the support of the Bible. They wrote that "from the beginning" of the church, "women participated fully and equally with men." The church must therefore "face up to the concrete implications of a gospel which liberates women as well as men."[4] Although many of Scanzoni and Hardesty's conclusions parroted the claims feminists had been making for years, their use of biblical arguments in support of "women's lib" awakened Christians to the possibility that the Bible might support feminism. Feminist Alice Matthews described *All We're Meant to Be* as "a shot heard round the evangelical world." She recalled, "once books and journal articles appeared by reputable evangelical feminist scholars writing and speaking within the limits of accepted evangelical interpretive guidelines, shock waves coursed through the evangelical scholarly community."[5] Scanzoni and Hardesty enabled conservative Christians to claim biblical support for feminist positions.

While not all evangelicals agreed with Scanzoni and Hardesty, some of the most prominent ones conceded the fundamental worthiness of the women's movement. *Christianity Today* editor Harold Lindsell—a staunch conservative—admitted, "women, evangelical or not, have legitimate grievances." He believed that women "should have the same rights as men; equal pay for the same jobs; [and] the right and freedom to pursue any career."[6] Likewise, former *Christianity Today* editor Carl F. H. Henry declared, "this is a moment in history . . . when able evangelical women are needed in all the professions and vocations now opening to both sexes—medicine, law, the mass media, politics, and much else."[7] Neither of these conservative stalwarts agreed with Scanzoni and Hardesty's contention that the Bible sanctioned the ordination of women. Indeed, the debate over women's ordination divided— and continues to separate—evangelical churches. Yet Lindsell and Henry's measured outlook on the broader women's movement reflected evangelicals' initial openness to the advances of feminism.

But not all conservative Protestants were on board with the women's movement. During the 1970s, anti-feminist evangelicals argued that feminists rejected biblical gender norms and violated family values. The key leader of this movement, Catholic activist Phyllis Schlafly, voiced the central belief of the anti-feminists. "What the liberals and the feminists are really afraid of," she wrote, "is not the right wing but the eternal truth that the traditional family is still the best way to live, and that babies still need mothers in the home."[8] According to Schlafly, feminists could not abide the biological truth that women wanted mostly to be mothers.

Many of Schlafly's followers were evangelicals, who witnessed and participated in a theological debate about gender that erupted in the 1970s. Evangelicals hashed out the meaning of scriptural passages concerning gender in a series of articles and books. Conservative Christians involved in these debates identified as either complementarians or egalitarians. Complementarians, who rejected feminism, argued that the Bible laid out complementary roles for men and women. According to complementarians, feminist campaigns to move women out of the home and into the workplace demeaned the honor ascribed to motherhood by the Bible. Egalitarians, on the other hand, contended the few biblical passages arguing against women's full and equal participation in society were concessions to the patriarchal order of the first century. The real message of the Bible, they argued, was one of equality. Egalitarians argued that Jesus preached a radical message of gender inclusivity—that the Bible supported feminism.

As this theological debate raged, the battle over the Equal Rights Amendment emerged as a major issue in American politics. Passed by Congress in 1972, the ERA provided for constitutional protection against discrimination on account of sex. The amendment appeared well on its way to ratification by three-quarters of the states. Yet a vocal and well-organized STOP ERA campaign emerged in the mid-1970s, arguing that it would embed anti-family provisions in the Constitution. The STOP ERA movement succeeded in defeating ratification in several state legislatures, largely because legions of anti-feminist women opposed the ERA. One key leader of anti-feminists, Concerned Women for America founder Beverly LaHaye, wrote, "ERA will invalidate all state laws which require a husband to support his family" and make it "unconstitutional to pass any law that differentiates between men and women."[9] The political opposition to feminism, like the theological opposition, depended on a sense that the women's movement's success would invalidate gender difference and result in the failure of families. The surprising and widespread opposition to feminism among both theological and political conservatives meant that by the end of the 1970s feminists had become archenemies of family values crusaders.

Egalitarians and Complementarians

Conservative evangelicals' fight against feminism began almost as soon as first-wave feminism emerged in the nineteenth century, and continued throughout the twentieth century. In 1941, fundamentalist stalwart John R. Rice published the memorably titled book, *Bobbed Hair, Bossy Wives, and Women Preachers*. The subtitle indicated that the book would settle the answers to "significant questions" by turning to the "word of God." Not surprisingly, Rice discovered in the Bible that "God simply did not intend for a woman to have a place of authority or leadership over men or to teach men."[10] Rice argued that women should not possess authority over men inside or outside the church, and he drew on "straightforward" readings of scripture to support his interpretation. Though few fundamentalists were as prominent or as colorful as Rice—his *Sword of the Lord* newsletter reached 100,000 in circulation in the 1950s and regularly lampooned religious liberals—most fundamentalists and conservative evangelicals rejected feminism as un-Christian. The theological debates of the early twentieth century had "embedded the principle of masculine leadership and feminine subordination in salvation history itself and . . . uplifted order as the highest principle of Christian life and thought."[11] While a few female preachers achieved celebrity among conservative Protestants, the bulk of early twentieth-century evangelicals assumed that scripture endorsed men's authority, especially in the pulpit.

The rise of second-wave feminism in the 1960s and 1970s, however, attracted evangelical support. This support scandalized conservative evangelicals, who assumed that fidelity to scripture demanded that Christians reject feminism. These anti-feminist evangelicals frequently identified as inerrantists, who believed that the Bible had no errors. In 1976, Harold Lindsell, an inerrantist and editor of *Christianity Today*, published *The Battle for the Bible*, which accused some evangelicals of believing "the Bible has errors in it." While Lindsell and his supporters resisted charges that they were "wooden-headed literalists," inerrantists almost always preferred the most literal (and least figurative) reading of scripture.[12] This meant that Lindsell criticized Christians who understood the Bible in figurative, allegorical, or metaphorical ways—especially when it came to certain passages about gender. Lindsell lambasted Christians who believed that scriptural texts were not always as reliable as contemporary academic research in matters of history, geography, and science. Lindsell argued that this position put non-inerrantists in an untenable position. "The best that can be said," he wrote, "is that some who hold to errancy do not go beyond errors of science and history." Yet they had started down a slippery slope. Lindsell believed that the gap between evangelicals who maintained a belief in inerrancy and those who did not "will become enormous in due season, and the differences will increase as other doctrines, now believed, are tossed overboard, discarded with the doctrine of infallibility."[13] In *Battle for the Bible*, Lindsell argued that abandoning inerrancy would lead to loss of faith.

Lindsell's book occasioned an outpouring of comment. *Christianity*

Today, not surprisingly, carried advertisements for *The Battle for the Bible* that urged evangelicals to "read it and act!" Critics worried that Lindsell's book would launch internecine war. Indeed, the very title of his book suggested inerrantists welcomed a fight. Donald Dayton, another evangelical professor, penned a critique of *The Battle for the Bible* in *Christian Century*. "Evangelicals," said Dayton, "are jittery, feeling that the book might herald a new era of faculty purges and denominational splits." Dayton's words proved prophetic, as the Southern Baptist Convention divided over inerrancy in the decade following publication of *The Battle for the Bible*.[14] Lindsell did not apologize. In a subsequent book he wrote, "If to stand for the truth of Scripture is divisive, than I am divisive. So be it."[15] Lindsell divided evangelicalism into two camps: those who believed in inerrancy and those who did not.

This bifurcation forced evangelicals to make a decision: one either affirmed biblical inerrancy or rejected it. According to inerrantists, conditional endorsements of biblical inerrancy simply masked heresy. Moderates like Dayton complained that Lindsell "ignores contrary evidence" and "shows little awareness of the blurring of lines."[16] Yet Dayton's position proved more difficult to defend rhetorically. Moderates did not want to appear to doubt the Bible's trustworthiness, yet they also wanted to deal forthrightly with some of scripture's apparent inconsistencies. Their claims to believe in the Bible's authority necessarily entailed more nuance than Lindsell's simple statement, "All scripture must be true."[17] Inerrantists characterized their position in rhetorically favorable ways that made opponents seem hostile to scripture.

Among evangelicals, affirming biblical inerrancy became the signal of orthodoxy on other positions, notably opposition to women's ordination. The decade between 1975 and 1985 had witnessed a dramatic upsurge in the number of ordained women. Women like Rev. Nancy Sehested, who served as pastor for Southern Baptist churches in Georgia and Tennessee, argued that ordination of women signaled an overturning of sinful patriarchy and improper scriptural interpretation. Conservatives disagreed. "I believe there are many opportunities for women to be engaged in ministry and serving the Lord," said Southern Baptist leader Morris Chapman. "It's simply that I believe the Bible teaches that . . . the role of pastor in the church [is] to be a male."[18] Opposing women's ordination emerged as the foremost marker of one's commitment to biblical inerrancy, as conservative evangelicals argued that scripture affirmed men as the only legitimate leaders of their churches.

The centrality of women's ordination to the inerrancy debate revealed the ways conservative evangelicals favored a populist approach to scriptural texts, whereas moderates argued for contextualized interpretation, which treated the Bible as a historical document situated in first-century Palestine. This populist hermeneutic privileged the simplest, most direct interpretations of scripture. Conservatives allowed little room for gray areas, preferring an unflinching confrontation with God's revealed word. For instance, moderate evangelicals viewed Paul's blunt directive, "I suffer not a woman to teach, nor to usurp authority over the man, but to be in silence," as a culturally specific command that did not apply to twentieth-century believers.[19] On the other hand, conservatives saw Paul's words as a timeless statement of divine hierarchy that placed men above women. They charged liberals with unwillingness to face up to the hard realities of scripture. "What do you think?" wrote one conservative about the passage. "Is verse 13 hard to understand? Or are [liberals] unwilling to accept what it says?"[20] Defenders of inerrancy read the Bible in particularly populist ways, often fixating on verses that ascribed authority to men and interpreting those passages in the most direct manner possible.

While conservative evangelical arguments against women's ordination relied mainly on scriptural passages proscribing women's role in the church, conservatives also thought that the biblical promotion of men's authority simply affirmed the reality of creation. They believed that God commanded men to lead churches because men were better suited to the task. Sehested argued that conservatives had so biased evangelicals against the idea of female pastors that a woman hearing God's call to the pulpit would not know what to think. "WHO, ME?" asked Sehested's hypothetical woman. "You gotta be kidding! I'm a woman! I've got a high voice and no hair on my chest. I'm emotional, I cry, and I can't think straight."[21] Sehested's parody caricatured conservative gender norms, but it nonetheless revealed a fundamental reality: conservative evangelicals believed men were uniquely gifted to lead their churches. "Pastors must make their personal identity appealing," wrote one conservative, "by emphasizing their own masculinity."[22] Statements like these suggested the assumptions underlying conservative evangelicals' opposition to women's ordination. They believed that God had endowed men and women with particular gifts. To ignore that reality in pursuit of a superficial equality was, in the minds of conservative evangelicals, to deny the reality of creation.

Conservative evangelicals' opposition to women's ordination reified the definition of "inerrancy." Al Mohler, president of Southern Baptist

Theological Seminary, described how this happened. Mohler believed that throughout American history, evangelicals "believed in biblical inerrancy [and] wouldn't understand why anyone wouldn't believe in biblical inerrancy."[23] But prior to the 1970s, few issues emerged to test that view. When feminists began making inroads in evangelical churches, inerrantists responded. Mohler himself admitted that his commitment to inerrancy sharpened as a result of a conversation with evangelical stalwart Carl F. H. Henry about women's ordination. On a walk around Southern Seminary in 1980, "Dr. Henry looked at me with a look of intellectual shock and asked me how, if I held to the inerrancy of Scripture, I could possibly hold to the egalitarian position. I tried to defend it and discovered that I didn't have much ammunition."[24] Mohler highlighted a basic issue in the "battle for the Bible": inerrancy became an issue only when cultural developments—specifically feminism—brought it into focus. As he pointed out, believing the Bible to be without error became synonymous with opposition to women's ordination. To be sure, evangelical leaders like Mohler gave extensive and nuanced presentations that defended inerrancy with linguistic and historical evidence. Yet their arguments gained traction among rank-and-file evangelicals only when it became clear that moderates' reading of scripture coincided with feminism. Mohler recalled that when he was a seminary student, moderate professors mocked letters from laypeople that asked them to make definitive statements about key political issues. Mohler thought, "You don't get it. [Grassroots evangelicals] don't care what else you believe if you're wrong on these issues."[25] Scriptural inspiration was not an academic problem. One's stance on biblical inerrancy mattered because of the worldview it signaled. Belief in inerrancy came to coincide with belief in "biblical" notions of gender that ascribed authority to men and rejected attempts to normalize female leadership.

Conservative evangelicals felt a particular burden to codify biblical gender norms because the movement known as evangelical feminism had grown in stature throughout the 1970s. Taking some cues from the secular women's movement, evangelical feminists advocated for the full and equal participation of women in all aspects of contemporary life. They argued that women could occupy all the offices men currently controlled, and they wanted equality of representation and compensation in American government and business. Yet unlike most of their secular counterparts, evangelical feminists anchored their advocacy in a particular reading of scripture, and they did not consider Christianity a hopelessly patriarchal religious tradition. Evangelical

feminists favored egalitarian readings of scripture and campaigned for wom-
en's ordination, and they charged conservative evangelicals who were opposed to feminism with misrepresenting biblical teaching.[26]

Just as Lindsell's *Battle for the Bible* served as a foundational text for inerrantists, Letha Scanzoni and Nancy Hardesty's 1974 book *All We're Meant to
Be* supplied evangelical feminists with their own first principles. In 1969,
Scanzoni, a freelance writer who had contributed articles on women's role in
the church to Christian magazines, recruited Hardesty, a professor at Trinity
College (Deerfield, Illinois), to collaborate on a book about women in Christianity. They began their text with a chapter addressing the creation narrative,
in which God created humans as male and female. This narrative historically
had resulted in Christians understanding gender as integral to human identity. Scanzoni and Hardesty suggested that this understanding created a polarity between male and female and inevitably resulted in comparison of one
sex to the other. Their reading of scripture, on the other hand, indicated that
Jesus had liberated humanity from a polarizing division between the sexes.
They argued that Christianity could provide a "solution to the problem of
suspiciousness and separation between the sexes" because "men and women
stand on equal footing as fellow members of the kingdom of God."[27] They
based this conviction on the belief that the kingdom of God transcended
gender in the sacred realm, a belief best expressed in Galatians 3:28: "There is
neither Jew nor Greek, there is neither slave nor free, there is neither male
nor female; for you are all one in Christ Jesus."

Scanzoni and Hardesty acknowledged other biblical passages that seemed
to put men in a position of authority over women, and they spent the majority of the book addressing and rebutting claims that Christianity sanctioned
patriarchy. Several chapters detailed the liberating effects of Christianity for
first-century women, suggesting that the messages of Jesus and writings of
Paul empowered women to claim roles denied them by Roman society. Scanzoni and Hardesty pointed out the integral role of women in Jesus' life and
ministry—not just as caretakers but as preachers of the good news as well.
And they took on the Pauline passages that seemed to restrict female authority in marriage and the church. "Those who think in terms of duties, roles,
and hierarchies," wrote Scanzoni and Hardesty, "misuse" Ephesians 5, which
enjoins wives to submit to their husbands. They pointed out that Ephesians 5
laid out "an altogether new ideal of marriage" in which the husband sacrifices
himself for his wife as Christ sacrificed himself for the church. This passage,
according to Scanzoni and Hardesty, revealed the "interdependence of the

sexes" within the bounds of marriage. They argued that Christians had incorrectly fixated on words like "head" and "subject" and, as a result, had misunderstood the meaning of the passage.[28]

This interpretation of scripture reflected Scanzoni and Hardesty's dissatisfaction with evangelicals' reading of the Bible. The second chapter of *All We're Meant to Be* featured a discussion of hermeneutics, the principles for interpreting scripture. Like Lindsell, Scanzoni and Hardesty were concerned that Christians read the Bible faithfully. Unlike Lindsell, they prioritized passages that emphasized egalitarian elements of the gospel message. They stressed the biblical texts' origins in a patriarchal first-century culture and cautioned against reading them without contextualization. Concerned that Christians used scriptural "proof texts" to discriminate against women, Scanzoni and Hardesty claimed, "any teaching in regard to women must square with the basic theological thrust of the Bible."[29] This hermeneutical approach stood at odds with the "straightforward" reading of scripture long prized by conservative evangelicals. Scanzoni and Hardesty borrowed in part from personalism, a tradition in which philosophers and theologians viewed personhood as carrying an inviolable dignity that demanded respect. For Scanzoni and Hardesty, this meant Christian theology must treat women as full and equal persons—a message they found throughout the Bible. Personalism, however, conflicted with other theological traditions that ascribed more authority to God, tradition, and scripture. As a result, Scanzoni and Hardesty's reading of scripture stood somewhat at odds with the hermeneutical traditions at the heart of evangelicalism.

In spite of this, *All We're Meant to Be* launched a movement that grew and diversified over the next decade, attracting support from evangelicals of all stripes. By the mid-1980s, a growing number of conservative Christians considered themselves "egalitarians," who believed that the Bible ordained equal roles for men and women (even if they shied away from calling themselves feminists). Many egalitarians congregated in a group known as Christians for Biblical Equality, which attracted support from evangelical intellectuals and helped Christians in various denominations advocate for women's ordination. For instance, Southern Baptists witnessed a twenty-fold increase in the number of ordained female pastors between 1974 and 1983.[30] Timothy Weber, a church historian, believed that in the early 1970s, "nearly all conservative Christians had concluded that a high view of the Bible and 'women's lib' were essentially incompatible." But by 1989, Weber thought, "it will not be long before the majority of evangelicals are egalitarian." Weber rooted his confidence in the belief that a proper reading of scripture showed that "its ultimate aim is to promote egalitarianism in Jesus Christ." He expected that evangelicals, who listed a high view of scripture among their most important beliefs, would increasingly see that the Bible supported the fundamental aims of feminism.[31]

Weber's expectation assumed that the reading of scripture used by evangelical feminists would convince a majority of evangelicals to follow their lead, but it did not. This resulted largely from a division between egalitarians and conservatives over the nature of the Bible. Two major disagreements about scriptural interpretation separated the groups. First, egalitarians believed that a holistic reading of scripture demonstrated that early Christians rejected the prevailing patriarchal gender norms of first-century Judaism, whereas conservatives believed a straightforward reading of Pauline texts showed that scripture endorsed male leadership. One feminist author argued, "no well-informed ecclesiastic or church body has today the right to proclaim that 'Scripture irrevocably condemns' birth control, abortion, homosexuality, or women's equality to men."[32] Evangelical feminists believed that responsible interpretation of scripture must account for the ways both Jesus and Paul relied on women in ministry and challenged the patriarchal culture in which they lived. But more conservative evangelicals focused on seemingly straightforward Pauline passages that called for females' submission to male authority.[33]

Second, and more important, conservative evangelicals believed scripture endorsed hierarchy, whereas egalitarians read the Bible as, well, egalitarian. In *All We're Meant to Be*, Scanzoni and Hardesty connected conservative defenses of gendered order to past hierarchical arrangements. "Those who declare that the gospel offers women spiritual equality in Christ but not in this world," they wrote, "find themselves arguing along with [those] who wrote in defense of slavery."[34] Weber agreed, though he avoided a direct reference to slavery. "The debate over women's roles in the church is the latest episode in a centuries-long conflict between advocates of egalitarian and hierarchical worldviews," he wrote.[35] Egalitarians repeatedly referenced slavery as an example of an unjust hierarchy that previous generations of Christians had defended by citing a straightforward reading of the Bible.

But that did not stop twentieth-century conservatives from sanctioning hierarchy. Although nineteenth-century Christians had mistakenly used the Bible to support slavery, they said, that did not render scripture's endorsement of gendered hierarchy irrelevant. According to conservatives, biblical defenses of slavery ignored that God had never established the "peculiar in-stitution." They regarded slavery as a sinful system that Christians had helped to abolish.[36] Conversely, God had established both the family and the church. And God had given instructions for how to govern those institutions: men should lead them. Conservatives argued that this in no way compromised the equality of men and women. After all, wrote Stephen Kovach, "scripture teaches the eternal subordination of Jesus to God the Father . . . [but] this does not make him inferior to the Father in essence and dignity. The same may be true for women or any other person in a different or 'subordinate' role in the church today."[37] Kovach summed up most conservative evangelicals' view of scripture. They believed that the Bible endorsed hierarchies.[38]

Evangelicals who defended a gendered order argued for complementar-ianism, the belief that scripture outlined clear and distinct roles for men and women. Complementarians differentiated themselves from egalitarians, though they took pains to avoid calling women inferior or otherwise imply-ing belief in the unequal worth of men and women. "Yes, there is equality of personhood. Yes, we are both created in the image of God. Yes, we both come to God in the same way," said complementarian Dorothy Patterson. "But we have also a responsibility of how we relate to one another and that's submis-sion and headship."[39] Complementarians defended the essential equality of men and women, even as they argued that women ought to submit to male leaders (whether husbands or pastors).

In 1987, complementarians codified their beliefs in a document called the Danvers Statement.[40] It held that "the emergence of roles for men and women in church leadership that do not conform to Biblical teaching . . . backfire[s] in the crippling of Biblically faithful witness." Moreover, signers charged that egalitarians presented a "threat to Biblical authority as the clar-ity of Scripture is jeopardized and the accessibility of its meaning to ordinary people is withdrawn into the restricted realm of technical ingenuity." In the face of the egalitarian threat, the Danvers Statement affirmed "distinctions in masculine and feminine roles," including "the husband's loving, humble headship" and the restriction of "some governing and teaching roles" within the church to men. The Bible did not simply acknowledge differences be-tween men and women; it stipulated that men assume leadership roles in families and churches.[41]

Complementarians further clarified their stance in the 1991 volume *Re-covering Biblical Manhood and Womanhood*. Editors John Piper and Wayne Grudem billed their five-hundred-page tome as "a response to evangelical feminism." They solicited essays from seminary professors throughout the country, each dealing with a particular facet of biblical teaching concerning gender. The main contention of evangelical feminists—that men should not exercise authority over women in either home or family solely on account of their gender—met with harsh critique in *Recovering Biblical Manhood and Womanhood*. In his analysis of Genesis 1–3, Raymond Ortlund contended that the creation story established both the principle of male-female equality and the rule of male headship. "In the partnership of two spiritually equal human beings, man and woman," wrote Ortlund, "the man bears the primary responsibility to lead the partnership in a God-glorifying direction."[42] In a subsequent essay, George W. Knight spelled out the ramifications of this arrangement. "God has called men to serve as leaders in marriage and the church, and women to submit themselves willingly to their leadership."[43] By enlisting a lineup of leading evangelical intellectuals to write sustained defenses of male headship, *Recovering Biblical Manhood and Womanhood* reinforced the conclusions of the Danvers Statement, which the book reprinted in an appendix. Authors for the volume unanimously concluded that God established distinctions between men and women during creation, and that faithful biblical witness must reflect those distinctions by assigning men alone to leadership roles in churches and families.

Indeed, conservative Southern Baptists thought biblical teachings about gender so important that their 1998 revision of the Baptist Faith and Message—the first revision since 1963—included only one new section: one on the family. Passed in 1998, the section on the family asked the wife "to submit herself graciously to the servant leadership of her husband," whereas the husband was "to provide for, to protect, and to lead his family."[44] This "submission statement" attracted considerable attention from national media. The *New York Times* published a front-page story noting that the amendment passed "overwhelmingly." The *Times* also pointed out that four years earlier, Roman Catholic bishops had drafted a statement on the family that called for "mutual submission" of wives and husbands.[45] Southern Baptists would have deflected criticism had they simply adopted that language. But Southern Baptist conservatives rejected the language of mutual submission (and rarely followed Catholics' lead, in any case). They believed an official endorsement of men's leadership in families honored scriptural teaching. More important, conservatives felt that holding the line on gender roles was the foremost difference between them and their moderate opponents. CBMW president Tim Bayly said, "Christians are being tested in this matter in a way that we're being challenged on few other issues today."[46] Southern Baptist conservatives believed their firm stance on gender marked them as faithful to the Bible.

Conservative evangelicals' complementarian viewpoint made explicit a hierarchical gendered order. Whereas previous generations had relegated women to subservience through unspoken cues and social customs, conservative evangelicals opposed to feminism explicitly barred women from leadership roles through a particular reading of scripture. Complementarians did authorize some leadership roles for women. Dorothy Patterson, a self-described "homemaker and adjunct faculty member" who has served on faculty at both Southeastern and Southwestern Baptist seminaries, became a leading spokesperson for the complementarian position. Patterson prefaced talks to mixed-gender audiences by saying, "I see there's some men here, but I've been asked to come and to share with you women."[47] This disclaimer indicated her allegiance to the complementarian position that women should not instruct men in the church, even though some men might hear her talk. Patterson, to be sure, did not often address mixed-gender gatherings; she spent most of her time teaching female-only audiences. But her affirmation of conservative gender teachings, alongside her marriage to conservative Southern Baptist leader Paige Patterson, enabled her to carve out a prominent, if unofficial, leadership role within conservative evangelicalism.

Dorothy Patterson's leadership of evangelical women opposed to egalitarianism signaled the importance of female opposition to feminism in both intra-evangelical debates and in the broader culture. Indeed, the complementarian movement depended on women advocates. In 1979, Susan Foh wrote *Women and the Word of God* as a response to egalitarians. She began with a simple question: "Can We Believe the Bible?" This opening gambit signaled complementarian orthodoxy. Foh determined to show that feminism simply did not accord with scriptural teaching. "Biblical feminists," argued Foh, "do not believe that God has given us his word true and trustworthy."[48] By ignoring the hard passages about gender, biblical feminists, according to Foh, made "human reason" the "final authority." Foh's book became a touchstone for anti-feminist evangelicals, who repeatedly cited her as an authority on the proper reading of scripture.

Other evangelical women provided cultural rejections of feminism. One of the most radical anti-feminists, Mary Pride, offered a scathing rebuttal of evangelical feminists in her 1985 book, *The Way Home: Beyond Feminism, Back to Reality*. More than most evangelicals, Pride argued that "homeworking" was integral to women's identity, and that women working outside the home were perverting their gender identity. Drawing on passages from Deuteronomy, Pride contended that parents' "responsibility to teach our children their moral and spiritual values cannot be delegated."[49] Mothers played an essential (and non-negotiable role) in fulfilling this responsibility. Pride labeled feminism a big "con game" and preached that wives held a particular burden to sacrifice themselves daily for the well being of their husbands and children. She painted "liberated" women as selfish and lazy. Being a woman, said Pride, meant abandoning foolish hopes for parity in the workplace and rededicating oneself to the rigors of homeworking, which is what God created women to do.

Pride dismissed objections to her argument. She had little patience with people who claimed that families with only one working parent faced financial hardship. Although she thought Americans' "present repressive Socialist laws do force us into costlier lifestyles," Pride suggested that couples worried about the costs of child rearing held misplaced priorities. She noted how her college professor father's "embarrassingly small salary" nonetheless supported seven children, including camping trips and figure skating lessons. As for worries about overpopulation—common in the 1970s and early 1980s—Pride stated bluntly, "Overpopulation does not exist. *Unbelief does.*"[50] According to Pride, women who rejected their divinely ordained roles as wives and mothers, including evangelical feminists, did not really believe what the Bible said. Scripture promised a world of abundance for men and women who followed God's commands. Pride and others like her contended that the problems plaguing Christianity involved an unwillingness to confront the hard truths of the Bible. According to complementarians, nowhere did Christians reject the Bible's teaching more than in their misguided endorsement of feminism.

The ERA Debate

The internecine battles among evangelicals over gender roles and women's ordination took place alongside and in response to second-wave feminism. The "first wave" of feminist activism came in the late nineteenth century, when activists like Susan B. Anthony and Elizabeth Cady Stanton campaigned for women's right to vote and to hold property rights and for equality in marriage. Many first-wave feminists drew on Christian teaching for support, though their critics often derided them as anti-religious. For instance, Stanton's

Woman's Bible, published in 1895, offered feminist interpretations of certain passages of scripture and argued for a liberated reading of the Christian Bible. "We have made a fetich [sic] of the Bible long enough," she wrote. "The time has come to read it as we do all other books, accepting the good and rejecting the evil it teaches."[51] Such a selective approach to scripture displeased Stanton's conservative critics, who contended that the *Woman's Bible* preached heresy. In spite of criticism from both evangelicals and biblical scholars, the book became a bestseller. First-wave feminism, then, depended in part on showing how Christianity supported women's rights.

Second-wave feminism, which won its greatest acclaim in the 1970s, was more wary of religious faith. Although women like Scanzoni and Hardesty argued that the Bible supported feminist teaching, the most prominent second-wave feminists disdained what they saw as the patriarchal culture of Christianity. Mary Daly, a feminist theologian at Boston College, condemned "Christian idolatry" that put Jesus at the center of faith. She thought that women's liberation demanded that believers reject the centrality of Christ and embrace an androgynous spirituality. Daly proposed a "castration" of Christianity that would remove "the myths of sin and salvation" that placed believers at the mercy of a male savior. In short, Daly demanded that spirituality accommodate women's liberation. She saw no future for a Christianity with Jesus at the center.[52] Such a radical reinterpretation of traditional Christianity alienated evangelicals and, for many, marked second-wave feminism as a rejection of scripture.

Yet the efforts of evangelical feminists to maintain a more orthodox reading of the Bible alongside a commitment to women's liberation did pay dividends. In the early 1970s, a majority of Christians seemed supportive of the overarching goal of second-wave feminism: enabling women to achieve equality in all walks of life. Conservative Christians' openness to feminist advances in the early 1970s depended in part on the seemingly benign wording of the Equal Rights Amendment, feminism's most notable policy goal. The ERA, which passed Congress in 1972, read like a simple guarantee of women's full and equal participation in modern society:

Section 1. Equality of rights under the law shall not be denied or abridged by the United States or by any state on account of sex.

Section 2. The Congress shall have the power to enforce, by appropriate legislation, the provisions of this article.

Section 3. This amendment shall take effect two years after the date of
ratification.

Most evangelicals felt that the ERA represented the fulfillment of women's
push for equal rights. Thirty states ratified the amendment within a year of its
passing by Congress. At least thirty-eight states needed to ratify ERA in order
for it to be added to the U.S. Constitution. In early 1974, ratification seemed
overwhelmingly likely.

Yet conservative Christian activists led by Phyllis Schlafly blunted and
eventually halted the ERA's momentum. Schlafly, a Catholic from Alton, Illinois, won the hearts of conservative Republicans in the 1950s and 1960s by
opposing communism and nuclear disarmament. *A Choice Not an Echo*, her
1964 book endorsing conservative senator Barry Goldwater for the GOP
presidential nomination, sold more than three million copies and solidified
her place as the "sweetheart of the silent majority."[53] She emerged as the exemplar of "ordinary" women's opposition to ERA. Given the increasing importance conservative Christians attached to abortion, Schlafly's Catholicism
actually became an asset in winning some Protestants' allegiance. She deftly
combined evangelical language with a vision of political cooperation. Schlafly told supporters, "We have the power of God's help. . . . We have the power
of truth. . . . We have the power of voluntary teamwork."[54] Evangelicals had
long concerned themselves with the movement of the Spirit and with defense
of truth, and Schlafly emphasized how following God's leadership involved
"voluntary teamwork." As in the abortion debate, conservative Catholics and
evangelicals came together to oppose second-wave feminism.

Schlafly and other leaders of the Christian right framed their campaigns
as means of giving voice to an embattled majority—a populist message that
resonated among conservatives. Eagle Forum, an organization Schlafly
launched in 1975 to combat feminists, claimed 42,000 members ("greater
than the 40,000 members claimed by the nation's largest women's lib organization") within one year of its inauguration.[55] Yet in spite of its popular appeal, Eagle Forum worried that the federal government would figure out a
way to ratify the amendment against what it believed the majority of women
desired: rejection of the ERA. President Ford, for instance, "skewed" his
39-member National Commission on the Observance of International Wom-
en's Year "in favor of those who dote on *Ms.* Magazine and think the essence
of womanly grace is Bella Abzug." Likewise, by funding the National Commission, the U.S. Congress appropriated $5 million to a "militant, feminist

lobby."[56] This rhetoric proliferated among conservative evangelicals who saw feminists as a threat.

These conservative Catholics and evangelicals found in the ERA a political target that crystallized the anti-family goals of feminists. They agreed with Schlafly that the amendment was "anti-family, anti-children, and pro-abortion."[57] Schlafly contended that ERA's benign appearance masked its sinister potential. She claimed to support "any necessary legislation" needed to redress inequalities between women and men in employment opportunities or income, but Schlafly thought all the necessary legislation had already passed Congress.[58] "There is no way," she wrote in the politically conservative magazine *Human Events*, that the ERA "can extend the effect of the Equal Employment Opportunity Act of 1972 . . . the Education Amendment of 1972 . . . [or] the Equal Credit Opportunity Act of 1974." Rather, "the Equal Rights Amendment is a big takeaway of the rights that women now have. It will take away the right of a young woman to be exempt from the draft . . . invalidate the state laws that make it the obligation of the husband to support his wife financially . . . [and] wipe out the right [for a wife] to receive Social Security benefits based on her husband's earnings."[59] Writing for the *Moral Majority Report* a few years later, Schlafly described ERA to evangelicals in more dire terms. ERA, she wrote, would eliminate "the traditional family concept of husband as breadwinner and wife as homemaker," restrict motherhood to "the very few months in which a woman is pregnant and nursing her baby," and embed "the first anti-family amendment in the Constitution." She also argued that the amendment would protect bigamists, legalize prostitution, and defang rape laws. In short, "the social and political goals of the ERAers are radical, irrational, and unacceptable to Americans."[60]

Most of Schlafly's charges depended on tenuous and unlikely legal developments. She arrived at her conclusions based on a reading of the law that emphasized the most extreme possible eventualities of ERA ratification. In the article for *Moral Majority Report*, Schlafly used the book *Sex Bias in the U.S. Code*, authored by future Supreme Court justice Ruth Bader Ginsburg and Brenda Feigen-Fasteau, as "a good index to what the ERA would do." While Schlafly rightly highlighted that the federal government funded *Sex Bias*, concluding that the book would provide the blueprint for post-ERA legislation required a leap of logic. Schlafly based her assertion on Ginsburg's status as one of the nation's "most widely-quoted pro-ERA lawyers" and Feigen-Fasteau's role as "director of the Women's Rights Project for the ACLU." The federal government funded their study, but *Sex Bias* was an advocacy document. The preface of *Sex Bias* admitted that an ongoing Department of Justice study of gender discrimination in U.S. laws would ultimately decide which of the book's recommendations to follow. Schlafly's usage of the study allowed her to exaggerate the potential effects of ERA.[61]

This sleight of hand reflected Schlafly's political skill, and it worked well because a large subset of evangelicals felt that feminists misrepresented their hopes and desires. Women, argued Schlafly, wanted to tend their homes and care for their families. The acronym of her anti-feminist coalition, STOP ERA (Stop Taking Our Privileges), revealed the organization's philosophy. Convinced that the ERA would make it impossible for women to assume the roles of wife and homemaker—the privileges most STOP ERA members desired to protect—activists mounted a massive campaign aimed at state legislators. A typical anti-ERA letter sent to Ohio legislators read, "Those women lawyers, women legislators, and women executives promoting ERA have plenty of education and talent to get whatever they want in the business, political, and academic world. We, the wives and working women, need you, dear Senators and Representatives to protect us." And then, tellingly: "We think this is the man's responsibility."[62] STOP ERA materials reflected a gender essentialism that placed men in the role of providers and protectors, while women appeared as domestically inclined nurturers. Some STOP ERA campaigns featured well-coiffed conservative women bringing freshly baked sweets to legislators' offices. The contrast between conservative women's femininity and feminists' aggressiveness was not lost on lawmakers. According to historians Donald Mathews and Jane Sherron DeHart, "the perceived lack of civility of 'women's libbers' seemed to offend" U.S. Senator Sam Ervin, "possibly because it indicated disrespect for themselves as well as other women." Ervin, the Senate's chief opponent of ERA, felt that "'physiological and functional differences' between the sexes [were] so natural and sacred as to have had a moral economy based upon them."[63] STOP ERA members agreed with Ervin's assessment and, taking their cue from Schlafly, took pains in both word and deed to highlight their femininity.

Yet these domestic desires did not prevent them from entering public life—especially when feminists were threatening the sanctity of home and family. It is instructive that the most famous picture from Schafly's 1952 campaign for Congress featured her in an apron cooking breakfast. She ran this picture in a bid for legislative office—not exactly a domestic responsibility. Schlafly constructed a public persona that emphasized the primacy she gave her family, even as she undertook larger and larger political initiatives.

Figure 7. Catholic activist Phyllis Schlafly led the STOP ERA
movement in a 1977 demonstration at the White House. Photo by
Warren Leffler, courtesy of Library of Congress, Prints & Photographs
Division, U.S. News & World Report Magazine Collection,
LC-DIG-ds-00757.

Indeed, her contention that women wanted most to tend their homes and
care for their families demanded that she give primacy to her role as wife and
mother. It was jarring for feminists to encounter a woman who held degrees
from Washington University and Harvard (as Schlafly did) posit that men are
inclined to pursue "higher intellectual activities," whereas women "tend more
toward conformity than men—which is why they often excel in such disciplines as spelling and punctuation."[64] Declarations such as this caused an ex-
asperated Betty Friedan to tell Schlafly, "I'd like to burn you at the stake!"[65]
But the conservative Christian women who flocked to Schlafly's banner understood her point. Women could engage in public affairs and intellectual
activities, but their primary desire was to care for home and family. They
perceived feminism as a denigration of women's noblest calling. Schlafly's political activities seemed legitimate to anti-feminist women because she framed
them as a defense of her right to be a wife and mother.

Indeed, Friedan's frustration with Schlafly signaled the late 1970s polarization among American women she helped create. Friedan's 1963 blockbuster *The Feminine Mystique* did more than any single book to spark second-wave feminism. In the book, Friedan talked about the shackles of suburban "housewifery," which imprisoned women in a domestic "concentration camp." Many second-wave feminists cited *The Feminine Mystique* as the book that awakened their desires for full equality in the public sphere. They felt oppressed by the domestic demands expected of women and demanded the choice to pursue a career. Conversely, conservative evangelicals committed to motherhood as a divine duty felt that Friedan denigrated women's highest calling. In article after article, evangelicals opposed to feminism noted that God had created women to serve as "helpmeets" for their husbands. They argued that the Creation story established clear and distinct roles for men and women, with women designed to bear, rear, and nurture children. With the emergence of Schlafly on the national stage, these women found their champion—and a target for their frustration with feminism: the Equal Rights Amendment. Conservative evangelicals claimed they supported "superior rights" for women and suggested the ERA would remove "rights" currently enjoyed: the right to avoid military combat, the right to stay home with children, and the right to expect support from their husbands. The appropriation of feminist language and the assertion of "rights" that feminists saw as limitations created a rift among women. Feminism became a lightning rod that divided evangelicals.

The conservative evangelicals who opposed feminism did not acknowledge the ways white, middle-class mores shaped their opposition. They built their opposition to the women's movement on a model of family life infused by nineteenth-century Victorian sentimentality. Historian Grant Wacker has even suggested, "Victorian culture is ineradicably encoded in the genes of evangelical religion."[66] Confronted by new configurations of work and home life in the urban environments spawned by the Industrial Revolution, Victorians forwarded a notion of "separate spheres" for men and women, where men dominated the workplace and women tended the home. Anti-feminist evangelicals reinforced this ideology by suggesting that the creation story commanded this Victorian division of labor. They longed for an era before the sexual revolution and second-wave feminism, where men and women understood their various roles, and where popular culture supported the order of creation.

Scholars have demonstrated that this image of a "golden past" is a fiction. In her book *The Way We Never Were*, Stephanie Coontz called the "traditional family"—with a breadwinning father, stay-at-home-mother, and well-scrubbed children—"an ahistorical amalgam of structures, values, and behaviors that never coexisted in the same time and place."[67] In particular, Coontz argued that the "nostalgia trap" that led many Americans to valorize the stability of family life in the 1950s ignored the deep prejudices confronting minority families, the anxieties produced by the Cold War, the financial pressures on the majority of families, and the limited choices afforded to most women. While the postwar prosperity of the 1950s did mean good times for many American families, the decade was not as peachy as conservative evangelicals remembered. Their nostalgia, combined with a scriptural warrant for anti-feminism, created a golden age of families that never existed.

Nonetheless, this imagined past held great sway in the minds of many Americans. The opposition to ERA emanated from a deep sense of alienation among conservative evangelicals. This sense emerged from their belief that feminists wanted to do away with women's domestic desires and to obliterate the family. As in the abortion debate, women who opposed ERA had a worldview fundamentally different from the feminists who supported the amendment. Specifically, conservative Christians rejected feminists' claim that physiological traits represented the only meaningful differences between the sexes, because they believed the Bible delineated clear distinctions between men and women. "We proclaim that male and female were established in their diversity by the Creator," said the authors of Moral Majority's "Family Manifesto." This created diversity, the authors contended, "extends to psychological traits which set natural constraints on gender roles. . . . The role of the male is most effectively that of provider, and the role of the female one of nurturer."[68] In conservatives' minds, feminists' rejection of gender essentialism challenged the created order. God had ordained certain roles for men and women, and the ERA threatened them. Conservatives worried that the ERA would mandate government-funded daycare and paternity leave, measures they believed would denigrate women's primary responsibility for rearing children. (One Moral Majority radio commentator referred to the possibility as "Big Mother" government.[69]) Convinced that "women's lib . . . flies in the face of the Scriptures," conservative Christians increasingly viewed the ERA as a frontal assault on faith and family.[70]

Not all evangelicals endorsed the Christian right's anti-feminism, but the STOP ERA forces mustered enough support to defeat the amendment. Only one state (Indiana) ratified ERA after 1975, and four (Nebraska, Tennessee,

Idaho, and Kentucky) voted to rescind their initial ratification of the amendment. Fifteen states never ratified ERA. A 1978 effort by feminists to extend the deadline for ratification won them extra time but alienated some state legislators who felt the deadline extension unfair. Subsequent, widely publicized campaigns in Illinois, North Carolina, and Florida resulted in defeat for ERA supporters, and the deadline for ratification finally arrived on 30, June 1982. Without the necessary number of states ratifying the amendment, the ERA was dead. Schlafly marked the occasion with a celebratory "Rainbow Dinner" in Washington, D.C., where she symbolically buried the Equal Rights Amendment in a grave dug by the pro-family movement.[71]

Anti-Feminism and the GOP

Schlafly's success in the STOP ERA movement betokened new political alignments. Just as the anti-abortion movement pushed evangelicals to mute their longstanding hostility to Catholics, opposition to feminism and the ERA demanded cooperation across previously unbridgeable divides. These divides included not only those between Catholics and Protestants but also those between southerners, Midwesterners, and Californians. Whereas southern politics in the 1950s and 1960s fixated on the struggle to overcome segregation, the fault lines of the 1970s occurred more often in the realms of gender and sexuality. New cleavages in American politics created new alliances (and new enemies), though the political realignment of the 1970s depended on shifts that took place during the civil rights struggle. The battles over school desegregation, busing, and states rights had caused a pair of important transformations. First, white southerners broke with the national Democratic Party, which had supported the civil rights movement. Second, the racial demagoguery that characterized southern politics during the Jim Crow era ceased to be a viable strategy. Race, of course, still mattered greatly in the configuration of American politics. But the ostensible aims of white southern politicians had changed. As a result, conservative evangelicals in the South increasingly found political champions in surprising locales like California and in the Republican Party.

The battle over the ERA illustrated these new alignments. Women in the Old South became the backbone of the STOP ERA movement, forming an alliance with a northern Catholic that their mothers would have found abhorrent. The near total absence of comment from evangelicals on Schlafly's

Catholicism marked an important transition in American Christianity. Prot- estants who just fifteen years earlier had worried about the dangerous men- ace of Rome behind John F. Kennedy's bid for the presidency now stood squarely behind a Catholic champion of anti-feminism. The regional bound- aries dividing southerners from the rest of the nation faded into the back- ground as women joined forces to defeat the ERA. The states that rejected the amendment included Alabama, Arizona, Arkansas, Florida, Georgia, Illinois, Indiana, Louisiana, Mississippi, Missouri, Nevada, North Carolina, Okla- homa, South Carolina, Utah, and Virginia. The disproportionate representa- tion of the Old South demonstrated the importance of conservative evangelical southerners to the STOP ERA coalition, yet this list of states also indicated the linkages among conservative activists in the Midwest and Sun- belt that defined the Republican Party in the second half of the twentieth century. The alliance of women opposed to ERA signaled the shifting land- scape of religion and politics in America.[72]

The STOP ERA campaign also illustrated the symbolic and strategic im- portance of family values rhetoric to late-twentieth century conservatism. Activists from the National Organization for Women (NOW) admitted that in 1972, "We just didn't realize it was going to be that difficult" to secure pas- sage of the ERA.[73] For liberals, the ERA seemed a commonsense approach to ratifying female equality. But conservatives painted it as anti-family. In the context of increasing drug use, sexual revolution, rising crime, and a sense of cultural decline, conservative evangelicals identified the family as the crucial institution guarding against societal collapse. Schlafly's ability to convince a formidable coalition of women that feminists aimed to take away their rights as wives and mothers spelled doom for the ERA. The sense that feminism threatened family values resonated across the southern half of the nation, where conservative crusaders from Arizona to Virginia put the brakes on ratification.

It was telling, then, that the paradigmatic figure of the conservative counter-revolution, Ronald Reagan, emerged from the Sunbelt spouting op- position to the ERA. Reagan had supported the amendment earlier in the 1970s, but by 1980 he realized the political folly of endorsing a measure his conservative base saw as anti-family. Reagan assured women that he opposed gender discrimination, but on the campaign trail he mouthed the concerns of STOP ERA protesters who worried that the amendment would make women subject to the military draft and impose hardships on women who chose to remain at home with their children. Reagan's election in 1980 heralded the demise of the amendment's chances for ratification. According to NOW, Reagan's inauguration marked the first time a sitting president opposed the ERA since its introduction in the 1920s. More important, a number of conservative state legislators elected on Reagan's coattails strengthened opposition to the amendment in capitals across the nation. None of these new lawmakers dared support an "anti-family" amendment.

The bulk of the opposition to the ERA, however, came from conservative women. Two women in particular illustrated the alliance between evangelicals and Republicans that was forged in the fires of family values activism. Beverly LaHaye, whose husband Tim had championed the Christian school movement in southern California throughout the 1970s, founded Concerned Women for America in 1978. By 1984 CWA reported a membership of 365,000, which was, officials proudly noted, over 100,000 more women than belonged to NOW.[74] It had grown on the strength of opposition to the ERA. LaHaye's earliest CWA materials included a pamphlet called "To Manipulate a Housewife." The pamphlet featured quotes from feminists connecting the ERA to the preservation of abortion rights, approval of divorce, and atheism. In the accompanying letter, LaHaye called the ERA the "first major step" in a movement that "does not want the traditional family life of a father, mother, and children to continue." She addressed the letter specifically to housewives and signed it "Author, Lecturer, Mother, and Pastor's Wife." LaHaye, like Schlafly, emphasized her identity as wife and mother. She represented a conservative evangelicalism that had come to view the family as under attack by a vocal and pernicious faction of feminists.[75]

While LaHaye symbolized a more aggressively partisan evangelicalism, Reagan White House official Dee Jepsen signaled the ways the Republican Party was changing in response to conservative evangelicals. Reagan appointed Jepsen to the Public Liaison Department in 1982 as leader of his administration's outreach to women's organizations. These organizations were aghast. Jepsen had opposed the ERA and *Roe v. Wade*. Moreover, she had not worked outside the home before coming to Washington as an unpaid aide to her husband, Senator Robert Jepsen. Groups like NOW thought her appointment was a slap in the face to feminists. Jepsen was an important concession to conservative evangelicals, who were dismayed by the lack of action on social issues by the Reagan administration. She voiced the critique of feminism that family values crusaders had sounded over the previous decade. "More than 90 percent" of American women, she reported, "wanted to marry and have children. Though some would have us believe that marriage and motherhood are 'out of fashion,' it seems that in reality, most of America's women don't agree."[76] Jepsen told of conversations with countless women who said feminists "just don't speak for me."[77] These conservatives found their champions in leaders like Schlafly, LaHaye, and Jepsen—women who had achieved public notoriety but insisted that their essential identities were those of wife and mother. These wives and mothers insisted that feminism threatened to destroy the family, and they targeted ERA as emblematic of the anti-family aims of the women's movement.

By the end of the 1980s, anti-feminist women had become an integral part of the Republican coalition. The GOP's longtime support of the ERA had disappeared, shoved aside by a faction of conservatives who understood feminism as an assault on motherhood. The influence of anti-feminist women manifested itself most notably at the 1992 Republican convention in Houston. Although insurgent candidate Pat Buchanan failed to unseat incumbent President George H. W. Bush in the primaries, Buchanan's opening night "culture war" speech defined the Republican Party as the home of family values. According to Buchanan, Bill and Hillary Clinton "compared marriage and the family as institutions to slavery" and represented "radical feminism. The agenda that Clinton and Clinton would impose on America," he continued, "is not the kind of change we can abide in a nation that we still call God's country."[78] Buchanan's jeremiad resonated in the convention hall and across the conservative landscape, even as it likely scared away some moderates who might have helped Bush's faltering reelection campaign. Buchanan's speech also revealed how successfully conservatives had tarred feminists as enemies of the family.

PART III

FATHERS

CHAPTER 6

Gay Rights

According to conservative evangelicals, mothers were not the only parents under assault. Beginning in the 1970s, a vocal cadre of family values crusaders argued that America's greatest need was for strong fathers. "If America is going to make it," James Dobson told a Focus on the Family seminar in 1981, "it will be because husbands and fathers begin to put their families at the highest level of priorities and reserve some of their time and energy for leadership in their own homes. There is no subject that I feel more strongly about than this one."[1] Dobson's words typified rhetoric heard throughout the country in church auditoriums, conservative political rallies, and stadium events for men. Traditional family values required strong fathers. Fathers led families, and families suffered when fathers abdicated their God-given responsibilities. "The solution to family problems," said evangelical leader Edwin Cole, "must begin with the father."[2]

The stress on strong fathers depended on complementarian understandings of gender. Just as God had ordained women to act as wives, mothers, and homemakers, God had created men to serve as spiritual leaders, protectors, and providers. Spiritual leadership demanded that men lead their families in both corporate and private worship, setting the example for their wives and children to follow. Conservative evangelicals located the dictum for male leadership in the Bible, where they emphasized passages like Ephesians 5:23, "For the husband is the head of the wife, even as Christ is the head of the church" (KJV). Evangelicals read these passages as confirmation of men's prerogative in the family. When speakers like Dobson and Cole implored men to tend their wives and children sensitively, there was no doubt about who was in charge.

Conservative evangelicals' scriptural understanding of fathers' roles fit nicely with cultural stereotypes about manhood. Manhood required strength, wisdom, power, and virility. Though evangelicals cautioned against violence and licentiousness, they worried more about a lack of vitality among American men. Indeed, conservative evangelicals' diagnosis of America's decline often located the nation's failings in men's flabbiness. As Jerry Falwell put it, "We have weak men who have weak homes, and children from these homes will probably grow up to be weaker parents leading even weaker homes."[3] Falwell located the problems that beset American society—from drug abuse to pornography to prostitution—in the lack of strong masculine leadership. He demanded that men take their God-given responsibility to serve as strong leaders and fathers, and he vouched for politicians who exemplified manhood. Falwell and other conservative evangelicals were looking for men who seemed to honor biblical understandings of fatherhood and cultural notions of masculinity.

Too often, conservative evangelicals believed that a new type of man threatened the cultural dominance of strong fathers: gay men. According to the family values movement, family values excluded homosexual activity by definition: the only family sanctioned by God, the church, and scripture involved heterosexual parents and children. Gays and lesbians, in this reading, flouted "God-given" sexuality in pursuit of a hedonistic alternative lifestyle. Worse yet, evangelicals believed gays preyed on children. Throughout the 1970s, 1980s, and 1990s, Christian right periodicals repeatedly spotlighted an alleged link between homosexual behavior and pedophilia. Conservative evangelicals accused gay men of trying to "recruit" children to the "homosexual lifestyle." The most famous crusade against gay rights in the 1970s took the name, "Save Our Children." Because gays and lesbians could not have their own children, the thinking went, they had to draft the kids of others. "Most of us, while feeling sorry for the homos," said one Christian right leader, "believe they should not be given posts of importance, lest our children come to regard the gay life as 'normal.'"[4] Whereas adults could identify the ways homosexual behavior flouted traditional family arrangements, children might be convinced homosexuality was an acceptable "alternative lifestyle." Conservative evangelicals could not abide that.

Examining conservative evangelicals' response to the gay rights movement illuminates yet another facet of family values. The growth of the gay rights movement represented a perfect storm for evangelical activists, who were increasingly convinced that liberals were making a "vicious assault on the American family."[5] Gay rights upended both gender and sexual norms. Gay men's perceived effeminacy seemed to threaten cultural norms of masculinity, and homosexual relationships, by definition, violated conservative evangelicals' sexual standards. Evangelicals believed that sex outside marriage was sinful, and that marriage existed only between a man and a woman. Conservative evangelicals believed homosexual relationships presented an existential threat to the "traditional family." Though a few evangelicals pointed out that the statistically larger trends of divorce and heterosexual sex outside marriage presented greater threats, homosexual behavior loomed larger for most evangelicals. Fighting gay rights (and later, gay marriage) became one of the most prominent planks of the family values agenda.

The centrality of opposition to gay rights stemmed from several related factors. First, cultural proscriptions of homosexuality remained strong through the end of the twentieth century, allowing the Christian right to present opposition to the movement as a mainstream position. Second, gay men seemed to shirk both their duties as fathers and their masculinity, threatening conservative evangelicals' understanding of gender both as essential to human identity and as immutable. Men were supposed to be strong, disciplined, and heterosexual. Gay men, in conservative evangelicals' reckoning, were flamboyant, reckless, and homosexual. As such they fundamentally challenged evangelical assumptions about gender. Finally, gays and lesbians' alleged recruitment plan for children undermined parental authority and sexual norms. Gay rights, in short, threatened everything evangelicals held dear.

Conservative evangelicals leveraged Americans' discomfort with gay rights to push the family values agenda. Every time a Democratic politician made a concession to gay rights, conservative politicians and evangelical leaders blasted that politician as anti-family. Leaders of the movement rallied supporters behind campaigns against gay rights initiatives, and they sponsored ballot measures banning gay marriage to stimulate voter turnout. Meanwhile, mainline Protestant denominations began splintering in debates about the ordination of sexually active lesbians and gay men. In all these battles, the Christian right used the gay rights movement as a foil for family values. It represented everything the pro-family movement loathed.

From Homosexuality to Gay Rights

Throughout most of the twentieth century, the majority of Americans considered homosexuality an aberration.[6] States and localities passed a number of laws proscribing same-sex behavior and forbidding gays and lesbians from

attaining certain occupations.[7] As a result, gays and lesbians generally remained closeted. Widespread state sanction against same-sex behavior (and
even against same-sex desires) went hand in hand with cultural disapproval.
Major medical associations listed homosexuality as an abnormality, and
mainstream media rarely acknowledged gays. Conservative evangelicals believed that scripture proscribed homosexual behavior, and they—like the
vast majority of Americans—considered same-sex behavior a depraved phenomenon. In 1960, *Christianity Today* listed homosexuality as a "perversion"
similar to incest; an article four years later lamented "the alarming spread of
'overt homosexuality' in New York."[8] These brief mentions typified the magazine's treatment of same-sex activity prior to the late 1960s. Evangelicals worried about cultural acceptance of homosexual behavior (especially in places
like New York and San Francisco), but they wrote relatively little about the
issue, often because they endorsed the governmental and cultural attitude
that ostracized gays and lesbians.[9]

The gay rights movement challenged this legal and cultural persecution.
The movement grew in the period after World War II. During the war, gender
segregation, increased mobility, and distance from family loosened social
constraints normally imposed on gay men. After the war, as the constraints
tightened once again, a small number of lesbians and gay men attempted to
preserve the freedoms they had enjoyed during the war. They launched social
and cultural institutions—gay bars became some of the most important gathering places for the nascent gay rights movement—that helped establish networks and collective identity. As these institutions grew in the 1960s, the
country's politics grew increasingly tumultuous. Just as civil rights organizations campaigned to overturn discriminatory laws and behavior, gay rights
organizations began campaigning to overturn the federal government ban on
homosexual employees, to repeal sodomy laws, and to characterize homosexuality as a sexual orientation rather than a mental illness.[10]

These campaigns led to some modest gains for gay rights, but the movement exploded after the 1969 Stonewall Riots in New York. In the early
morning hours on 28 June, New York City police raided the Stonewall Inn in
Greenwich Village. Operated by the Mafia, the Stonewall Inn was one of the
few bars catering to gays in New York, and perhaps the only one that allowed
drag queens and dancing. Police raids on gay bars were common at the time,
and when police barged into the Stonewall Inn, they expected the raid to
follow normal procedures: they would arrest the drag queens and send the
rest of the patrons home. But several patrons resisted arrest, and over a

period of several hours, a crowd gathered outside the bar, forcing the police to barricade themselves inside. Riots continued sporadically for the next several days, accompanied by overt displays of effeminate behavior by protesters, including limp-wristed mock salutes and a transvestite kick line. Police cracked down on the protesters with violence, but the Stonewall riots marked a turning point. Gays were "out and proud," and they resolved to stay that way. The number of gay rights organizations skyrocketed from 50 in 1969 to over 800 by 1973.[11] These included the Gay Liberation Front and the Third World Gay Revolution—groups that explicitly connected gay rights to other civil rights organizations, which had grown more radical in the late 1960s. These new organizations took cues from both the radicalized civil rights organizations and the Stonewall protesters, making "coming out" a central element of gay identity. They intended to force the issue of gay rights, refusing to kowtow to societal proscriptions of homosexual behavior.

Evangelicals' relative quiescence about gays and lesbians in the years before Stonewall depended on the vast majority remaining in the closet, concealed from public view. "We make a distinction," wrote one conservative evangelical, "between the gay who is quiet and keeps his lifestyle to himself, and the exhibitionist."[12] The Stonewall protesters and members of new gay rights organizations typically fell in the latter category. Gay rights organizations' insistence on being "out and proud" alienated many conservative Americans, who were accustomed to homosexuals' relative obscurity. Their increasing visibility unsettled many Americans, as did gay rights activism, which had begun to pay dividends. In 1973 the American Psychiatric Association removed homosexuality from its list of mental illnesses, and sixteen states repealed sodomy statutes between 1971 and 1976. A 1975 *Time* magazine cover featured an Air Force officer declaring, "I am a homosexual."[13]

These developments frightened conservative evangelicals, who by the late 1970s talked about gays and lesbians as a sort of fifth column that had infiltrated the highest reaches of American government. This development echoed the "Lavender Scare" of the 1950s, in which conservative politicians painted gays and lesbians as threats to national security. A congressional investigation of "sex perverts" in the federal government coincided with and reinforced Senator Joseph McCarthy's hunt for communists in the State Department.[14] Three decades later, evangelicals were still sounding the alarm about gays in government. In 1980, Jerry Falwell recounted a conversation with President Carter. "I asked the president," Falwell said, "'why do you have known practicing homosexuals on your staff in the White House?' Carter replied, 'Well, I'm president of all the American people; I believe I should represent everyone.'" To that Falwell answered, "'Why don't you have some murderers and bank robbers and so forth?'" The Carter campaign subsequently released tapes that proved this exchange never occurred. When reporters challenged him, Falwell described his fabrication of the exchange as an "anecdote which we use not to specifically refer to what was actually said," a comment that created a firestorm about Falwell's credibility.[15] Yet his supporters questioned the media "attack" on their leader rather than his flimsy justification. The willingness of some evangelicals to grant Falwell latitude in this incident depended in part on their views of homosexuality. They saw gays and lesbians as a threat to America.

Throughout the 1970s and 1980s, conservative evangelicals did not pay as much attention to the gay rights movement as they did to abortion or feminism, but by the 1990s gay rights had become central to the Christian right agenda. The seeds of the Christian right's hostility toward gay rights were sown in the late 1970s. The relaxation of societal proscriptions of homosexuality, several high-profile gay rights campaigns, and a fear of "homosexual recruitment" of children conspired to make opposition to gay rights a key plank of the family values agenda. Moral Majority founder Jerry Falwell cited the prevalence and permissibility of homosexuality as a sign of America's downfall. "History proves that homosexuality reaches a pandemic level in societies in crisis or in a state of collapse," he wrote. "If homosexuality is deemed normal, how long will it be before rape, adultery, alcoholism, drug addiction, and incest are labeled as normal?"[16] One of his colleagues agreed. "There are absolutes in this world," said Moral Majority radio commentator Charlie Judd. "Just as jumping off a building will kill a person, so will the spread of homosexuality bring about the demise of American culture as we know it."[17] Explaining this hostility and fear demands understanding why evangelicals found so gay rights so threatening.

Save Our Children

One reason conservative evangelicals feared gay rights involved the widespread perception that gay men threatened children. Although few members of the Christian right accused gay men of pedophilia, they typically implied that men who engaged in homosexual activity preyed on young people's minds. In *Children at Risk*, Focus on the Family leader James Dobson suggested that the "family agenda of the left" intended to "teach students that gay and lesbian life-styles are no less moral than heterosexual relationships." He accused a Los Angeles City Schools program of providing "programs to recruit and support new converts" to homosexuality.[18] Coupled with conservative evangelicals' belief that public schools had adopted a secular humanist directive to liberate children from their parents' outmoded ways of thinking, the suggestion that schools promoted homosexuality threatened evangelical parents.

In particular, Christian right leaders insisted that for gay men and lesbians to survive, they had to recruit young children. In his 1980 polemic *Listen, America!*, Falwell unpacked the logic of this characterization. "Homosexuals cannot reproduce themselves, so they must recruit," he wrote. "Why must they prey upon our young?" Falwell drew on the words of Harold Voth, a leader of the National Association for Research & Therapy of Homosexuality, to answer his question. Homosexuals, explained Voth, were not fully mature. Being fully mature "include[s] the capacity to mate and live in harmony with a member of the opposite sex and to carry out the responsibilities of parenthood. Mature people are competent and masterful . . . they can replace themselves with healthy children who become healthy men and women." Falwell used this diagnosis to illustrate the threat gays posed to American families. Because homosexuals "prey on" the nation's children, the gay rights movement represented a brazen attempt to lure unsuspecting children away from their parents' sexual norms.[19]

Such "recruitment" obviously violated family values. Not only did men and women who engaged in homosexual activity transgress against conservative sexual norms, they usurped parental authority and preyed on children. People like Voth and Falwell portrayed gays not as harmless queers but as dangerous enemies of the family. As a result, opposing gay rights became part of the larger family values agenda. Christian right leaders portrayed the struggle against gay rights as a contest of authority. In the "traditional" family, heterosexual parents claimed authority over biological children. The literature of the Christian right suggested that sin proliferated when families lost authority. And because gays and lesbians could not produce biological children, they had to infiltrate the homes and families of upstanding Christians. In his 1978 book *The Unhappy Gays*, Tim LaHaye contended that the erosion of parental authority had contributed to countless children's "conversion" to homosexuality. He counseled parents whose son came out of the closet not to kick him out of the house, because doing so would "throw him to the homosexual wolves, who are anxious to prey upon his young body."[20]

LaHaye's characterization reflected two key beliefs about homosexuality common to conservative evangelicals in the late 1970s. First, conservative evangelicals insisted that gays and lesbians were not born that way. Rather, people "became homosexuals" as they indulged sinful thoughts. LaHaye even provided a formula: "a predisposition toward homosexuality + that first homosexual experience * pleasurable and positive homosexual thoughts + more homosexual experiences * more pleasurable thoughts = a homosexual."[21] LaHaye, like Voth and Falwell, assumed everyone had "heterosexual potential" and that homosexuality, like other sins, could be overcome. He even provided an eighteen-step plan for triumphing over homosexuality.[22]

Evangelicals' theology demanded they believe same-sex activity was a choice. Though they admitted some people had stronger homosexual urges than others, Christian right leaders had to view homosexuality as a sin Christians could reject. Otherwise, they compromised beliefs in the possibility of "redemption" from this sin and the goodness of creation. Indeed, a popular bumper sticker in the 1990s reminded people that God created "Adam and Eve," not "Adam and Steve." The creation story of Genesis, in which God created man and woman to live together, served as the template for family life. Conservative evangelicals recognized ways sin wrecked that first family, but they insisted that humans—not God—brought sin into the world. Since they thought of homosexuality as a sin, they insisted God did not create people as gays or lesbians.

Second, conservative evangelicals thought of gays and lesbians as particularly immoral. In a 1979 newsletter, conservative political operative H. Edward Rowe declared, "There is no way that one can begin to describe in decent company the depth of depravity exhibited by homosexuals." Rowe forged ahead anyway, outlining for his decent readers the preponderance of sadism, masochism, pederasty, pedophilia, venereal disease, and suicide among gays.[23] While Rowe went farther than most of his compatriots, conservative evangelical accounts of the "homosexual movement" tended to emphasize the salacious. Most insisted that promiscuity was the norm, and that lifelong monogamy was virtually nonexistent among gays and lesbians. Tracts against gay rights never failed to describe the frequency of casual and even anonymous sex among homosexuals, often portraying gay bathhouses in New York and San Francisco as the modern equivalents of Sodom. Evangelicals (along with many other Americans) in the mid-1980s saw AIDS, which affected a disproportionate number of gay men, as a divine judgment on homosexuals' amoral lifestyles. Conservatives' heavy usage of the term "homosexual"—rather than gays and lesbians—defined people who engaged in same-sex activity according to their sexuality. Though this usage was typical of mainstream Americans in the 1970s (the *New York Times* preferred the term "homosexual" until 1987), it flouted the wishes of gays and lesbians, most of whom did not want to be defined solely according to their sexual behavior. Evangelicals' belief in the depravity of gays and lesbians underlined the importance of keeping them away from impressionable youth. As U.S. Representative William Dannemeyer put it in his widely cited book on homosexuality, *Shadow in the Land*, "we must not allow our children to be the victims of an unnatural appetite that has become obsessive in our society."[24]

Conservative evangelicals repeatedly censured one fringe gay rights group: the North American Man Boy Love Association (NAMBLA), a small, controversial organization dedicated to celebrating intergenerational relationships and abolishing age of consent laws. Founded in Boston in 1978, NAMBLA railed against the "criminal injustice system" that outlawed "benevolent" relationships between men and boys. Not surprisingly, NAMBLA's emergence created a firestorm of criticism, and it was widely shunned by mainstream gay rights groups. For conservative evangelicals, the existence of such a group simply confirmed their fears about homosexuals' designs on young children. In his book *Are Gay Rights Right?*, lawyer Roger Magnuson contended that NAMBLA "is carrying the ideology of the homosexual movement to its natural conclusion. If there is no such thing as perversion and if sex is good . . . then why should children be denied this good?"[25] Other conservative evangelical tracts made similar arguments. They assumed NAMBLA was a chink in the armor—an organization only controversial among gay rights groups because it dared to speak the deepest desires of gays and lesbians aloud.

In this climate of fear, singer Anita Bryant mounted one of the most controversial political campaigns of the 1970s. A popular gospel singer and former Miss Oklahoma, Bryant had traded on her wholesome appeal to market Florida orange juice and settle into a comfortable life in south Florida. But she felt called into political action in January 1977, when her preacher at Northwest Baptist Church in Miami told the congregation about a proposed Dade County ordinance that would eliminate restrictions preventing gays and lesbians from teaching in public schools. Like other evangelicals, Bryant believed homosexuals intended to recruit children to their "lifestyle." The thought of gay teachers was beyond the pale. Bryant stoked fears by focusing on the ability of a gay teacher to influence impressionable young minds, drafting kids into a homosexual lifestyle that stood in stark contrast to their parents' values.

The proposed ordinance came before the Dade County Board of Commissioners on 19 January 1977. Supporters and opponents gathered to testify on the day of the vote; Bryant reported that opponents outnumbered supporters eight-to-one. In a telling sign of the growing co-belligerency of conservative activists, opponents included Baptists, Catholics, and Orthodox Jews; a brief *New York Times* story about the rally indicated surprise at the collaboration of the Miami Archdiocese with Southern Baptists.[26] Members of each religious group insisted homosexuality was immoral and asked the county commissioners to reject the ordinance. But the commissioners voted 5-3 in favor of the ordinance, paving the way for gays and lesbians to have full access to education, employment, and housing opportunities.

Though shocked and disappointed by the vote, Bryant resolved to continue the fight. She and her husband Bob Green incorporated the political action group Save Our Children, Inc., shortly after the vote. Appearances on Jim Bakker's *PTL Club* and Pat Robertson's *700 Club* television shows attracted supporters from around the nation. She described the county ordinance as an "attempt to legitimize homosexuals and their recruitment plan for children." She distributed leaflets that tied gay men to several recent child abuse cases. The media aided Bryant's campaign by disseminating statistics exaggerating gays' propensity for pedophilia. For example, Bryant cited reports suggesting that more than one million boy prostitutes were working in the United States. She leveraged these reports to argue that the nondiscrimination law would abet homosexuals' activities rather than protect their human rights. One of her organization's flyers declared, "THERE IS NO HUMAN RIGHT TO CORRUPT OUR CHILDREN."[27] Both the flyer and the group's name—Save Our Children—suggested the fear that animated the Christian right's opposition to gay rights: evangelicals thought gays and lesbians intended to pervert innocent children.

Voters agreed. During the spring, local volunteers collected over 60,000 signatures—six times the number required by law—for a petition to hold a popular referendum on the ordinance. Two weeks before Dade County residents voted on the measure, 10,000 anti-gay rights activists gathered in Miami for a "God and Decency" rally led by Jerry Falwell. These high profile events demonstrated the growing power of the opposition to gay rights among evangelical Christians, but gay rights activists still thought they had enough support to sustain the new ordinance. They were wrong. By a two-to-one margin, Dade County residents voted in June 1977 to overturn it. Bryant had succeeded in keeping identified gays and lesbians out of the county's schools.[28]

The aftermath of the campaign witnessed triumphal celebrations among the Christian right and an uptick in opposition to gay rights around the country. Bryant rejoiced that "the normal majority" had "voted to repeal an obnoxious assault on our moral values."[29] National media attention had spotlighted conservative Christian activists once again, this time picking up on interdenominational and interracial collaboration in support of socially conservative measures. Bryant reported over 80 percent support from Catholics, Jews, and African Americans in Dade County for repeal of the gay rights ordinance.[30] Save Our Children attempted to continue the momentum by sending her on a national speaking tour, where she encountered newly devoted supporters and equally aggressive protesters. Gay rights groups staged a nationwide boycott of Florida orange juice in protest of Bryant's sponsorship contract, and gay bars got into the act by taking screwdrivers off their menus. Even late night host Johnny Carson paid attention, zinging Bryant almost nightly during the heart of the campaign. On the other side, conservative groups built on her popularity to launch anti-gay rights measures throughout the nation. The Dade County battle, in short, captured the nation's attention and made gay rights yet another flashpoint in the battle between liberals and family values activists.

The name "Save Our Children" was telling. Bryant admitted that scriptural passages prohibiting homosexual behavior motivated her to protest the Dade County ordinance, but she pointed out that many non-evangelicals joined her campaign not because the Bible forbade same-sex behavior but because they feared gays and lesbians teaching their children. In fact, Bryant framed her activities in terms designed to appeal to a broad cross-section of potential voters. The conservative newsmagazine *Human Events* noted that blacks and Latinos overwhelmingly supported the Bryant campaign, suggesting that a campaign to "save" the children held wide appeal.[31] The Dade County battle showed how Christian right leaders had learned to transform "biblical" issues into "pro-family" issues that attracted people from a variety of theological perspectives. Rather than citing biblical passages that referred to same-sex relationships as "abominations" or "shameful," family values crusaders portrayed gays and lesbians as child predators. One did not have to hew to a particular reading of scripture to join the family values movement. Social conservatives—many religious, some not—flooded the precincts in

Florida to reject the Dade County ordinance. The political success of this "silent majority" depended on Christian right leaders lessening the emphasis they gave to an explicitly Christian rationale for fighting gay rights and spotlighting the "anti-children homosexual agenda."[32]

Bryant's carefully cultivated maternal image was crucial in selling the message of Save Our Children. She framed her protest as that of a mother with a "God-given right to be jealous of the moral environment for my children."[33] Like textbook protesters Norma Gabler and Alice Moore, homeschool champion Mary Pride, and ERA opponent Phyllis Schlafly, Bryant portrayed herself as a mother at the end of her rope. She insisted the only reason she was getting involved was to "save" her children, a task she believed God had given to women. This justification allowed her considerable latitude to engage in political activities. For an evangelical subculture always suspicious and frequently hostile toward feminism, Bryant won approval because she insisted her political activities were primarily about "making this a better place to live for my children and other children."[34] As a mother, she could become an activist.

Bryant's commitment to complementarian teachings about women's subservience to men demanded she portray her activism as necessary but not ideal. In an ideal world, a man would lead the charge. Near the outset of the Save Our Children campaign, she sat down with her pastor, "Brother Bill" Chapman, and asked why God would send a woman to oppose gay rights. Chapman reminded her, "Anytime, throughout the Bible, when God's men didn't take their stand . . . He raised up a woman." A few weeks later, Bryant stood before her congregation, calling for volunteers to support the work of Save Our Children. After a few women came forward, she broke down in tears and cried, "Where are the men?" Duly shamed, men stood up. One told Bryant, "Anita, seeing you cry has made me realize I've been neglecting my duty." These stories, drawn from Bryant's autobiography, reflect important realities about gender among conservative evangelicals. Even though she garnered nationwide attention, she maintained women "could go no farther unless the men were not only in union with us, but were leading us."[35] Furthermore, Bryant played directly into feminine stereotypes by breaking down in tears before her congregation. She framed her activism as an unavoidable consequence of men's failure to lead, and she always made sure to underscore her femininity.

The reality, though, was more complex. In a conservative Baptist congregation, Bryant had to pay lip service to complementarianism. But in a family

☐ **YES, ANITA!**

I want to help you bring America back to God and morality. Please send me all issues of your Protect America's Children Newsletter.

Name_____

Address_____

City_____ State_____ Zip_____

Protect America's Children   P.O. Box 40-2608   Miami Beach, Florida 33140

Figure 8. Anita Bryant hoped to use her 1977 success in Dade County to promote morality around the nation. Jerry Falwell's Moral Majority used similar mailers when it launched two years later. Image courtesy of Stonewall Museum & National Archives.

values world, the mother held unique symbolic and rhetorical power. She could exercise righteous indignation on behalf of her children in a way the father could not. Bryant's public displays of vulnerability only added power to her pleas. These displays projected the image of a Christian mother powerless to stop the invidious advances of gays intent on stealing her children. Such displays were crucial to the success of Save Our Children, and they could only come from a woman. Anita Bryant was no accidental leader of the Save Our Children movement. She presented the perfect package of wholesome feminine appeal, maternal image, and rhetorical savvy.

Bryant's leadership of the campaign testified to a chief irony of the family values agenda. Family values crusaders traded on nostalgic images of the traditional family, where dad went to work while mom stayed home and reared children. Drawing in part on Victorian ideas about "separate spheres"—men held sway in public life while women tended to the home—conservative evangelicals felt unsettled by second-wave feminism. But in a feminist world, cultural norms were shifting. The unspoken rules governing men's and women's roles faced significant opposition. Someone had to speak up for traditionalism. More often than not, it was conservative women who did. This was not an accident; men could no longer get away with voicing women's desires without being seen by opponents as paternalistic chauvinists. But women's opposition to liberal initiatives presented a conundrum for feminists. Leaders like Bryant belied the stereotype of a stay-at-home mother, even as that stereotype continued to legitimate her activities outside the home. The ideal family values crusader was a mother who had been provoked by threats to her children. And there were few threats more menacing than gays and lesbians intent on recruiting young kids.

Bryant accentuated her maternal nature—and her naivety about homosexual behavior—in a twenty-five-page interview in the May 1978 issue of *Playboy*. She told interviewer Ken Kelley that she took a stand "because I am first and foremost a mother, and I was standing up for my rights as a mother to protect my children." As befitted the venue, she candidly discussed the sexual aspects of family life, saying that at the "moment of climax . . . there is a oneness between you and your husband and with God." Evangelicals rarely spoke so frankly about sexuality, which made Bryant's naive comments about homosexual activity even more startling. "I agree with the anti-abortion people that the beginning of life is when the male sperm fertilizes the female egg," said Bryant. "To interfere with that in any way—especially the eating of the forbidden fruit, the eating of the sperm—that's why [homosexuality] is such an abomination." (Bryant suggested she had no idea what sodomy was until a gay rights activist sent her a picture of it, and most evangelicals could not fathom such acts.) When Kelley pressed her on whether all sex must be procreative, or whether birth control was abominable, Bryant said no, because "you are not wasting the sperm." Ultimately, Bryant defined acceptable sexual behavior as not only marital but part of family life. Sex that took place outside the family—much less sex that could never produce children—violated her sense of God's rules for acceptable sex. "God created the family to be a picture of perfection," she said.[36] Her opposition to gay rights partly derived from her sense that gays and lesbians grossly defaced such an image.

Bryant's double identity as aggrieved mother and outspoken activist proved hard to sustain. Her activism resulted in the loss of endorsement deals and a proposed television show, even as *Good Housekeeping* readers named Bryant America's "Most Admired Woman" in 1978 and 1979. She spoke in front of audiences of thousands in the wake of the Miami campaign but found her home life disintegrating. She divorced her husband in 1980 and retreated from the limelight. She insisted the choice to step back was hers, but a divorced woman was a pariah in the family values world. By the early 1980s, Bryant was something of a forgotten woman among conservative evangelicals, even as they ascended to greater political heights.[37]

Gay Men and Masculinity

The Bryant campaign signaled the importance of guarding children from "homosexual recruitment," but conservative evangelicals also feared the normalization of same sex behavior would undermine masculinity. The Christian right trotted out a nostalgic image of the traditional American man: husband, father, firm, reserved, strong, faithful. In popular perception, gay men had none of these qualities. Evangelical literature portrayed them as either flamboyant or butch. Neither the "queens" of Stonewall nor the macho man character typified gay men in America, but evangelicals often let those stereotypes stand as representative. The message was clear: gays flaunted traditional masculinity, through either effeminacy or a caricature of manliness. Conservative evangelicals opposing gay rights believed real men embodied strength and exercised reserve—qualities they thought gays lacked.

The rationale for normalizing masculinity came in part from scripture. In his influential book, *Listen, America!*, Jerry Falwell quoted a passage from 1 Corinthians to damn gay men: "Neither the 'effeminate, nor abusers of themselves with mankind . . . shall inherit the kingdom of God.'"[38] Falwell, like most evangelicals, used the King James Version of the Bible. Published originally in the early seventeenth century, the KJV predominated among American Protestants through the mid-twentieth century. Its lyrical language provided the medium through which most Americans encountered scripture before World War II. But after midcentury, more recent and readable translations began to compete with the KJV, as American Christians gravitated toward Bibles with fewer "thees" and "thous." Nonetheless, many conservative evangelicals and fundamentalists prized the KJV precisely for its anachronistic language, which in their minds lent special authority to biblical texts. The KJV retained its status as Americans' favorite translation into the twenty-first century.[39]

The KJV's anachronistic language occasionally rendered passages in ways that obscured their original meanings. In the case of the 1 Corinthians passage, the KJV is the only widely read English translation to use the word "effeminate." Other popular translations use words like "sexually immoral" instead. Biblical scholars have produced a raft of scholarship on the this passage, noting that while "effeminate" is a technically accurate translation of the Greek word "malakos," ancient understandings of effeminacy differed greatly from modern ones. For instance, signs of effeminacy in the ancient world included eating or drinking to excess, wearing aftershave, or enjoying (heterosexual) sex too much. These signs typically indicate the opposite in modern American culture, where we expect "real men" to do all these things. As a result, most twentieth-century translations jettisoned the word effeminacy.[40] The KJV's retention of that word resulted in a translation that is both technically correct and easily misinterpreted. Given the changing cultural assumptions regarding effeminacy, twentieth-century readers like Falwell were apt to get lost in translation.

That slippage in translation gave Falwell a scriptural imprimatur for his observations about homosexuality's threat to American masculinity. "We would not be having the present moral crisis regarding the homosexual movement," wrote Falwell, "if men and women accepted their proper roles as designated by God. God's plan is for men to be manly." That meant that men needed to exercise leadership in their families and "be strong."[41] Same-sex behavior, in this rendering, revealed weakness. True men were family men, and gays, by definition, could not lead traditional families. Christian right materials often portrayed gays as men who shirked their God-given duty to lead families.

As should be clear, conservative evangelicals' censure of same-sex behavior almost always focused on gay men rather than on lesbians. Tim LaHaye, for instance, used the pronoun "he" to describe homosexuals throughout his 1978 book *What Everyone Should Know About Homosexuality*. Law professor Didi Herman suggested that the Christian right's focus on gay men stemmed from its belief in the greater danger of gay men's sexuality. Stories of lesbians recruiting young girls did not appear in the literature of the Christian right; Herman reported that some leaders thought "lesbians posed little threat at all."[42] One wrote, the "seamier side of exploitive sexuality is not as obvious a feature of lesbianism."[43] While Phyllis Schlafly and the STOP ERA movement did decry the "angry lesbians" leading the feminist movement, lesbians often seemed more of an obnoxious sideshow. The predators conservative evangelicals imagined in the gay rights movement were overwhelmingly male.

This focus on gay men also stemmed from conservative evangelicals' fixation on family values. Conservative evangelicals subscribed to the notion that compared to women's desires, men's sexual appetites were greater and harder to discipline. For centuries, the family had tamed male appetites by promoting monogamous, heterosexual marriages. Sexual relationships outside this norm faced public censure. The gay rights movement threatened this arrangement. By challenging the normative "traditional family," gay rights gave men an out. Conservative evangelicals worried that without the social control imposed by home and church, men would flee their responsibilities and family values would disappear. This is why the Christian right could not abide the idea of "sexual preference." Giving men their preferences would lead to ruin. The family provided stability and restraint in a world threatened by men's hard-to-control sexual urges. Moreover, the Christian right viewed the increasing prevalence of homosexuality as the outgrowth of declining families. Most writers in the movement ascribed gay men's inclination to troubled relationships with their fathers; lesbianism occurred "when a girl disidentifies with her mother whom she experiences as weak, pathetic, vulnerable or in some way inadequate."[44] In this model, the decline of the family and rise of same-sex behavior were linked in a feedback loop. Increasing permissiveness sanctioned same-sex relationships, which weakened traditional families, leading to children alienated from their parents and thus more willing to experiment with their sexuality.

And while mothers could help stem the tide of gay rights, the literature of the Christian right clearly focused on the importance of fathers. If men could be compelled to settle down and lead traditional families, conservative evangelicals believed the gay rights movement could be stopped. Evangelical preachers characterized gay rights as a way for gay men to indulge themselves without the repercussions formerly attached to same-sex behavior. The logic of family values was essential to this belief. If families were indeed the strength of civilization, and if strong heterosexual men were the only viable leaders of those families, allowing men to "become homosexuals" without censure would put American culture on a path to ruin. The importance of maintaining the notion that gays chose their sexuality became clear at this point. If God had ordained that men were to lead the family, then gays were making a choice to go against God's plan. The gay rights movement, in this view, was not a civil rights movement. It was an attempt to legitimate anti-family behavior.

For this reason, Christian right materials decried any attempt to frame gay rights as a matter of civil rights. A 1985 newsletter from the American Legislative Exchange Council (ALEC), a conservative lobbying organization, argued, "the homosexual makes the conscious choice to pursue members of his or her own sex. In fact, it is because homosexual influence upon children alters their normal sex role development that minority status should be questioned."[45] ALEC represented the Christian right viewpoint on gays and lesbians' drive for civil rights unusually clearly here. Granting gays minority status, according to ALEC, would offer protection to a group that perverted normal human sexual desires. Furthermore, the legitimation conferred on same-sex behavior would encourage more men to "explore" homosexuality. In the minds of ALEC members, only a return to the social and legal proscription of homosexual behavior common in earlier periods of American history could stop the cycle.

To insist that same-sex behavior was a choice demanded that Christian right leaders grapple with the studies of sexuality produced by biologist Alfred Kinsey. Along with his colleagues, Kinsey published *Sexual Behavior in the Human Male* in 1948 and *Sexual Behavior in the Human Female* five years later. The books generated controversy immediately. The "Kinsey reports" suggested that human sexuality changed over time and even in an individual's lifetime. Kinsey and his colleagues based their claims on extensive interview data, which investigated both desires and behaviors. The first book reported that 10 percent of American males were "more or less exclusively homosexual" for at least a three-year period between ages sixteen and fifty-five. (This statistic probably inspired the widespread but erroneous claim that the Kinsey reports documented a 10 percent incidence of homosexual behavior in all human societies.) Later researchers found that Kinsey's sample bias—his tendency to investigate primarily white Americans (including many prisoners) who were willing to talk candidly about their sex lives—did not explain away his conclusions. In other words, in spite of some methodological problems, the reports demonstrated the wide range and malleability of human sexuality. In particular, Kinsey and his colleagues convincingly demonstrated the prevalence of same-sex behavior.

Conservative evangelicals feared that widespread acceptance of the once-controversial Kinsey reports had led society to the brink of collapse. California Representative William Dannemeyer contended, "the sex laws of the United States have in part been changed because of the philosophical climate created by Alfred Kinsey and his followers." He went on to point out the reports' "severe bias" and weighting in favor of "extravagant and bizarre sexual behavior." As a result, according to Dannemeyer, the Kinsey reports made the following argument: "most men are having homosexual adventures, so how can we possibly outlaw this conduct?"[46] Dannemeyer and his followers believed these "adventures" were both less common and more dangerous (to participants and the broader society) than Kinsey reported. They contended that the gay rights movement had built a legal edifice protecting same-sex behavior on the shoddy foundation of the Kinsey reports.

More broadly, conservative evangelicals thought the true source of morality came from a different set of books. Christian right leader Tim LaHaye reported, "Sexologists . . . refer to [the Kinsey Reports] authoritatively the way I refer to the Bible."[47] Conservative evangelicals viewed the increasing permissibility of same-sex behavior as an attack on scripture. The Bible, according to conservative evangelicals, had served as the unofficial source of American moral legislation since the beginning of the United States. Only very recently had governments permitted un-biblical behavior. As Dannemeyer put it, "things changed . . . profoundly in the 1960s." Before then, people "saw more clearly the importance of traditional family life to the survival of society as a whole."[48] At the beginning of a book-length repudiation of the gay rights movement, he articulated the logic of family values as it related to the gay rights movement: by sanctioning same-sex relationships, America made it possible for men to come out from under their familial obligations. Gay men were a menace because they went against scripture and shirked their responsibilities to lead families.

Yet this logic—and its tenuous connection to scripture—was only part of the reason the Christian right opposed gay rights. Manhood, according to the Christian right, was an endangered virtue in the late 1970s. Conservative leaders penned a number of articles lambasting the perceived weakness of American political leaders. This weakness was dangerous in a Cold War world. An increasingly assertive Soviet menace demanded that American leaders display strength. Gay men's effeminacy, in the minds of conservatives, disqualified them from leadership and made efforts at normalizing "homosexual lifestyles" a threat to national survival. Leaders needed to display confidence and swagger in the face of Soviet aggression. In a 1976 article for *Human Events*, Republican Senator Jesse Helms wrote, "Leadership is something that calls forth the soul in man . . . calls him to exert his abilities beyond the level of compromise."[49] Political conservatives demanded manliness from their leaders—and gays, according to conservative evangelicals, could not provide that.

Indeed, in 1984 Helms ran an aggressive campaign against Democrat Jim Hunt in which Helms and his supporters accentuated both Helms's masculinity and Hunt's connections to gay rights. North Carolina Democrats had approved a gay rights statement in 1983, and Hunt did not repudiate that plank until late in the 1984 Senate campaign. In the meantime, an anti-gay (and pro-Helms) newspaper called *The Landmark* published increasingly fanciful stories about connections between Democrats and gays. The Helms campaign initially stayed above the fray while Hunt fended off allegations that he accepted large donations from gay rights groups and might have had a gay lover. As the campaign heated up, Helms accused Hunt of accepting over $250,000 from "radical homosexual and militant feminist movements."[50] Moreover, in a televised debate, Helms baited Hunt by asking him, "What war did you fight in?" Hunt responded angrily to Helms's remark, but the senator had scored points. Polls in late 1983 had shown Helms twenty points down in the race, but he came back to defeat Hunt in the 1984 election. Helms's campaign demonstrated that opposition to gay rights, combined with appearance of masculine vigor, was a potent political weapon for conservatives in 1980s America.[51]

In a society that rejected gays' political viability, the perception of effeminacy could doom a leader. Jimmy Carter discovered this the hard way. The conservative political magazine *Human Events* ran pictures of the president that portrayed him as pensive and unsure. He projected neither confidence nor strength. And while no reporter accused Carter of same-sex behavior, innuendo ran rampant in conservative newsmagazines. *Human Events* titled a story about Carter's spending policies, "Carter Comes Out of the Closet." Another report, this one on the 1980 Conference on the Family, bore the moniker, "White House Conference Shapes Up as Gay Affair." *Human Events* tarred the president as a sissified liberal controlled by "lesbians, militant feminists, pro-abortionists, and other radicals."[52] Carter, according to political conservatives, appeased the Soviets, flip-flopped on crucial issues, and caved in to social liberals. He was, in short, the antithesis of a leader.

Conservatives celebrated leaders whose moral and political clarity presented a sharp contrast to the president. Editors of *Human Events* tabbed Helms as "a new kind of politician" who "battles crafty liberals" and "is firmly planted on the bedrock of principle."[53] Nicknamed "Senator No," Helms frequently voted against popular legislation, occasionally as the only Senate opponent of a given measure. Conservatives viewed his "lonely votes" as principled stands rather than empty gestures. Manliness required willingness to stand by one's values even when popular wisdom advised compromise. Helms projected moral certitude that won him admirers among conservatives nationwide. Evangelicals felt that men like Helms were rare. In 1982 *Moral Majority Report* published an article that asked, "Where have all the leaders gone?" The article quoted publisher Michael Korda, who contended that "Not so long ago, teachers ran their classes, generals (or sergeants) ran the army, policemen were feared and obeyed, college presidents were respected figures, remote and awesome. . . . America was ruled, in effect, by authority figures."[54] The political developments of the 1970s, including increased regulation and emphasis on diplomacy at home and abroad, had weakened America and produced impotent politicians. Strong political leaders proved so difficult to find that *Human Events* eventually turned to Hollywood to find heroes. In 1977 the magazine published an homage to John Wayne that focused on the movie star's masculinity. The author of the piece called America "John Wayne country" and argued, "As a man, [Wayne] is loathed and demeaned by sanctimonious 'liberals.'"[55] Wayne's take-no-prisoners persona, like Helms's refusal to compromise, resonated among conservative evangelicals who thought their country was suffering under a sissy president.

Of course, another Hollywood star loomed even larger among conservatives in the late 1970s: California's former governor Ronald Reagan. As conservative evangelicals who had voted for Carter in 1976 tired of him, they clamored for a president who paired moral substance with masculine style. Reagan fit the bill. Reagan struck the *Moral Majority Report* as a man "determined to keep his promises," while *Human Events* called him "the man of the hour."[56] The latter magazine also published a column by Reagan in which he speculated about what would happen if the government ran baseball's World Series. "The pitcher for the home team was a woman," Reagan mused, "because the team had to have one female pitcher for every male pitcher. . . . Unfortunately, the female pitcher was hit pretty hard."[57] Reagan used a sports metaphor to drive home his vigorous assault on weak-kneed bureaucracy and nonsensical gender quotas. He presented himself as an aggressive, red-blooded American man. Conservatives loved him for it. His penchant for plain talk and aggressiveness toward communists, feminists, and liberals appealed to conservative Christians worried about the government's overly conciliatory posture. Reagan's masculine vitality endeared him to conservatives. They saw him as a symbol of strength in troubled times.

Reagan stood in a long line of American politicians whose perceived masculinity won favor among conservative voters, but the emergence of gay rights as a movement had changed the nature of this support. Leaders of the Christian right believed "the homosexual movement reached its maximum level of influence on the federal government during the liberal administration of Jimmy Carter."[58] As such, Reagan's persona appealed to conservatives who wanted to roll back such power. The problem was that Reagan's positions on gay rights initiatives were never as clear as conservative voters would have liked. In 1978 Reagan opposed a California initiative that would have made it possible for school districts to fire any teacher who expressed support for homosexual behavior. Jerry Falwell said Reagan had chosen "the political rather than the moral route" and would have to "face the music from Christian voters two years from now."[59] He did not face the music—at least not in the way Falwell prophesied. In fact, Christian voters helped sweep Reagan into the White House in a landslide vote. Once in office, the Reagan administration did not make rolling back the gay rights movement a priority. The president did not reach out to gay rights groups the same way Carter had done, but he refused to answer Christian right calls for strenuous moral opposition to same-sex behavior. When the AIDS crisis emerged during his first term, the Reagan administration budgeted $26.5 million toward research on the disease, winning praise from San Francisco's liberal mayor Dianne Feinstein and censure from Christian right leaders. These leaders grew even more upset with Surgeon General C. Everett Koop, a devout evangelical who marshaled the significant resources of his office to fight AIDS. Evangelicals who saw homosexual activity as sinful—and the AIDS crisis as a mark of God's judgment—felt betrayed by both the president and their one-time hero, Koop.[60]

Even so, Reagan retained the support of evangelicals worried about the erosion of masculinity. Like Helms, Reagan cultivated an image of standing up to noisy liberals. He talked tough toward communists—calling the Soviet Union an "evil empire" in front of the National Association of Evangelicals in 1983—and he presented himself as an unabashed friend of conservative Christians. Although the president had refused to sponsor any notable legislation limiting abortion or opposing gay rights, in 1984 Falwell declared that Reagan merited "nothing less than 'A+'" for his first term grade. (Pressed by a colleague more inclined to give Reagan a B-minus, Falwell admitted, "I graded on a curve."[61]) Long marginalized by Washington, conservative evangelicals relished the attention given them by the president. Reagan had endorsed a constitutional prayer amendment. More important, he kept the White House door open to conservative evangelicals and signaled his intention to govern according to the dictates of his faith. At the 1984 prayer breakfast, Reagan declared, "Without God, democracy cannot and will not long endure."[62] Reagan presented an image of moral clarity, even if his administration's policies left something to be desired.

Furthermore, Reagan hardly embraced gay rights groups. In fact, these groups frequently opposed Reagan on account of the president's rhetorical support for "pro-family" initiatives. Robin Tyler, a gay activist who would in 2008 successfully challenge California's ban on gay marriage, mocked the Reagan administration's commitment to family values. "If the government is so concerned with the protection of the family," asked Tyler, "why do they continue to build nuclear power plants, why do they continue to poison our oceans, why do they continue to rape our land? . . . Why are they trying to make battering of children in schools legal once again?"[63] Such questions made sense among liberals who saw "family values" as capacious issues demanding comprehensive policy solutions. They connected support of families to opposition of war and commitments to sustainability.

By 1984, evangelicals did not share this vision of family values. Conservative evangelicals had painted a particular picture of the "traditional family." Gays and lesbians did not fit in this frame (much less did concerns about war or the environment). The Christian right's success at defining the notion of "family values" represented one of its greatest triumphs. Voters had come to understand the phrase family values to mean standing against liberal reforms that would weaken the roles and responsibilities of mothers, fathers, and children. Just as conservatives saw feminism and abortion rights as a threat to motherhood, they viewed the gay rights movement as an assault on fatherhood. The movement legitimated men's sexual preferences rather than insisting on men's sexual responsibilities. In so doing, it threatened to undermine completely the strength and stability of families.

The Christian right fought the gay rights movement strenuously. The prejudicial language conservative evangelicals used toward gays and lesbians reflected popular culture's disapproval of homosexuality—which had remained on the American Medical Association list of mental disorders into the 1970s—and also reflected the deep threat the gay rights movement represented to conservative evangelicals. The Christian right had staked its political program on the notion that restoring traditional family values was essential to recovering the lost virtue of America. The gay rights movement suggested not only that such family values were oppressive, but also that opposing gay rights was a way of affirming a broader range of family life in contemporary America. As such, it merited unremitting hostility from members of the Christian right, who saw gays as a menace to children and fatherhood.

In subsequent decades, conservative evangelicals' hostility persisted, and the fight against gay marriage became a major issue in the first decade of the new millennium. Evangelical activists credited anti-gay marriage ballot measures in 13 states—all which passed—for swinging the 2004 presidential election to George W. Bush. (Later studies suggested that Bush's incumbency and fear of terrorism drove his reelection.) The tide finally turned in 2008, as more and more states began sanctioning same-sex marriage. But fighting against gay rights—to serve as teachers, to win protection from discrimination, or to marry—has long served as a potent way to rally conservative evangelicals. This issue resonated because the family values movement convinced many evangelicals that gays violated scriptural norms, threatened children, and undermined fatherhood. If America needed family values, evangelicals argued, it could not sanction gay rights.

CHAPTER 7

Military Men

Bobby Welch, president of the Southern Baptist Convention, minced no words in the introduction to his book, *You, the Warrior Leader*. "The Christian life," wrote Welch, "is a war!" A former army captain, Welch believed Christians must prepare themselves for "scratching, biting, ear-ripping-off war." He called Jesus—known elsewhere as the Prince of Peace—a "warrior leader," who "stormed the stronghold of Satan." According to Welch, twenty-first-century believers needed to follow Jesus' lead. Welch lionized men like U.S. army Master Sergeant Tony Pryor, who killed three Al Qaeda fighters during a 2002 raid in Afghanistan. He described Pryor's hand-to-hand combat with insurgents in graphic detail; the book reported that Pryor "broke [an insurgent's] neck and finished him off with a nine-millimeter pistol." But Welch also noted that at home Pryor had a "teddy bear" reputation and once nursed a newborn raccoon with an eyedropper. Such details might seem incidental or even silly, but they illustrated Welch's masculine ideal. The true Christian man understood that spiritual life was a battle. He fought, but he also showed poise, discretion, and discipline. Christian believers, Welch argued, needed to realize that they were at war with Satan. Fighting that battle required aggression as well as control, intensity as well as understanding. In short, it required military discipline.[1]

To evangelicals the use of war as a metaphor for the Christian life made perfect sense. As Christian identity had become increasingly identified with politics, evangelicals perceived themselves as engaged in a struggle for the nation's survival. In 1991, sociologist James Hunter penned the landmark book *Culture Wars*, which claimed American Christians had divided into two camps: orthodox and progressives.[2] Hunter's label stuck. Evangelicals who had engaged in battles over school prayer, textbooks, home schooling, abortion, the ERA, and gay rights knew that they were in a cultural war. They had used military metaphors for decades to describe their efforts at

maintaining morality. Welch and Hunter were voicing language that resonated with evangelicals. They did battle with the world all the time.

Moreover, evangelicals had grown increasingly supportive of the military
itself. During the Vietnam War, mainline Protestant denominations had become increasingly suspicious of the "military industrial complex." Evangelicals stepped into the breach. The Cold War context had engendered
widespread support of the military among evangelicals, who increasingly saw
the army both as a venue for spreading the gospel and as a positive influence
on men's lives. For instance, General William K. Harrison, who in World War
II helped evangelize Japan, found himself something of a "religious celebrity"
on returning to the United States after the war. In particular, Harrison made
a biblical case for the compatibility of soldiering and Christianity that appealed to evangelicals. Harrison wrote, "After considerable study of the Scriptures . . . I became convinced that while I as a Christian should love my enemy
and pray for him, turning the other cheek as necessary, yet the use of force by
communities and government is ordained of God."[3] Once convinced, Harrison never turned back. Indeed, he became something of a double missionary: spreading the gospel within the armed forces and preaching to
evangelicals about the Godliness of the American military. Owing partly to
his efforts, evangelicals came to see the military as a crucial vehicle for
spreading the gospel in a Cold War world where communists blocked access
to many countries. By the time of the Vietnam War, evangelicals had become
some of the military's strongest supporters.

As a result of this relationship, the rhetoric of war and conceptions of masculinity that characterized the armed forces permeated American evangelicalism.
The perceived symbiosis of Christianity and soldiering depended in part on the
family values movement. Just as women had roles to fulfill, men were expected to
be strong, disciplined, and loyal. What better institution to foster those traits than
the military? Evangelicals' support of the military became obvious in two major
controversies during the 1980s and 1990s: the "nuclear freeze" controversy of
1983 and the battle over gays in the military ten years later. The principle of cultural custodianship facilitated mutual admiration between conservative Christians and the military. Evangelicals and soldiers saw their best selves reflected in
one another, and they built an alliance around shared values of discipline, courage, morality, and masculinity. This alliance strengthened as political debates
over nuclear weapons and homosexuality pitted liberal critics against both evangelicals and military. The two groups' similar responses to these challenges am-
plified the connection each group felt with the other.

The nuclear arms debate and the controversy over homosexuals in the military illuminated complexities in the family values movement's gender norms for men. The masculine ideal celebrated by conservatives possessed some "macho" elements, but it was not reckless. Conservatives who fought nuclear weapons reduction did so not because they relished the prospect of World War III but because they believed "peace can best be insured through strength."[4] The strong posture evangelicals advocated necessitated both a powerful nuclear arsenal and the discipline not to use it. This position reflected the understanding of masculinity that prevailed among conservative Christians. Likewise, evangelicals' opposition to gays in the military emerged from a rigid understanding of biblical teachings on gender and sexuality. Gay rights groups had insinuated that homosexuality was a legitimate "alternative lifestyle," a teaching conservative Christians rejected. And when President Bill Clinton attempted to legitimize homosexuality by lifting the ban on gays in the military, he inflamed opposition concerned about "what would happen to one of the last bastions of American traditionalism if its defining social order were tampered with."[5] The issue of admitting homosexuals in the armed forces provided a perfect venue in which evangelicals could defend their masculine ideal.

Cultural Custodianship

A sense of "cultural custodianship," the belief that God appointed them the guardians of America's values, facilitated evangelicals' identification with soldiers. Like soldiers, conservative Protestants saw themselves as uniquely called to defend liberty and morality. Both groups removed themselves from mainstream culture to preserve discipline and hierarchy that "the world" scoffed at. To the military, civilians could not defend themselves because they had neither the tools nor the discipline required for the task. Likewise, evangelicals thought secular culture held neither the belief structure nor the authority to guard against amorality. They thought most Americans were too lazy, too blind, or too indifferent to defend traditional values. Evangelicals had a strong sense of being set apart to defend against threats to virtue. This belief enabled them to see themselves as soldiers of a different sort, drafted by God to fight agents of immorality.

Evangelicals' belief in the divine sanction of government predisposed them to defend the military's legitimacy. Evangelicals frequently cited

Romans 13, which declared, "the powers that be are ordained of God."[6] Both Jesus and Paul commanded followers to pray for rulers and authorities. Evangelicals believed God sanctioned government. Aside from historic peace churches, most of which came from an Anabaptist tradition that shunned political involvement, American evangelicals embraced a position that combined condemnation of the "world" with approval of the state. This disposition helps explain twentieth-century evangelicals' close relationship with the U.S. military. Conservative Protestants almost universally endorsed the American cause in World War II. After the war, leading evangelists became some of the foremost opponents of communism. Oklahoman Billy James Hargis, for example, broadcast a radio sermon called "For God and Against Communism" and made his Christian Crusade organization into an anti-communist propaganda machine.[7] Evangelicals saw no contradiction between condemning the world and supporting the government. They believed God commanded them to do both.

Yet evangelicals had not always endorsed the military. In the nineteenth century, American evangelicals often expressed suspicion of all-male enclaves like the army, worried that soldiering appealed to men's baser instincts and pushed them away from faith. Even in the run-up to World War I, evangelicals showed significant ambivalence about America's war machine. Prior to 1917, conservative Protestants' "degree of patriotism does not seem to have been much different from that of the American public generally." According to historian George Marsden, that posture changed quite abruptly during World War I.[8] Woodrow Wilson's connection of the war effort to making the world "safe for democracy" resonated among evangelicals who saw themselves as cultural custodians. Furthermore, liberal Protestants accused conservatives of a lack of patriotism, especially after the United States entered the war in 1917. In response, evangelicals and fundamentalists became some of the war's fiercest supporters, convinced that the conflagration heralded the apocalypse and that the American military was playing a role in salvation history. Stirred from ambivalence, evangelicals sensed that "the whole moral course of civilization was involved."[9] Their sense of cultural custodianship, alongside provocation from theological rivals, compelled evangelicals to stand firmly behind the American military, a posture they retained throughout the twentieth century.

Regional particularities also played a role in fostering evangelicals' alliance with the military. Evangelicalism's strength in the Sunbelt—a region of the country stretching from the Old South to California—located them in the region where the military was most prominent. A disproportionate number of soldiers, bases, and veterans in the South facilitated a military-friendly culture. "More than any other region," declared the periodical *Southern Exposure*, "the South remains ensnared by the politics, economics, and culture of war. . . . [It] elects the most hawkish politicians to office and supplies 42 percent of the nation's enlistees."[10] And as evangelicals' support of the armed forces grew, the strong influence of evangelicals in the South reinforced the region's military-friendly culture. Believers who thought God had ordained hierarchies to govern life on earth celebrated the military. In it, officers commanded respect, soldiers submitted to discipline, and everyone sacrificed in service of a higher cause. The military provided Christians concerned about a breakdown in social order with an ideal vision of how God wanted society to work.

The South's peculiar religious history made it more likely that evangelicals there would see political involvement as a legitimate task. Unlike northern evangelicals, who held no illusions that they lived in a world friendly to Christianity, white southern Protestants believed that until the 1960s theirs was an "intact" Christian culture.[11] In his condemnation of the civil disobedience of ministers like Martin Luther King, Jr., Jerry Falwell emphasized the importance of "separation" from the world. Political activity hindered ministers' preaching of the gospel, according to this worldview. But in the South, "separation" from worldly affairs was a murky ideal. Southern laws and customs reinforced (white) Christian mores. So when Falwell preached separation, he employed a rationale that resonated among white southern evangelicals. They worried about King's political activity not solely because it might corrupt religion, but also because King threatened to upset the hegemony of white Protestants in the South. Indeed, the civil rights movement challenged the assumptions of white southerners, and the upheaval of the 1960s convinced many of them that God's law no longer governed their land. But they remembered times when Christianity ruled their culture (even if their memories painted the past in rosy hues). They viewed the state as a divinely ordained institution that would reinforce Christian customs. As Jerry Falwell put it in his 1997 autobiography, "Serving the church and letting government take care of itself had been my lifelong policy and the policy of my Christian friends and family."[12] Like other white southerners, Falwell saw no need for political involvement because the political atmosphere surrounding his church supported both his faith and his politics.

During the 1960s and 1970s, however, white southerners like Falwell felt the earth shaking beneath their feet. While the civil rights movement did not require military battle, argued one historian, "it created new social and political orders that one might expect only a military conflict to produce." White southerners, long accustomed to thinking of their black neighbors as inferior, had to grapple with the reality of black equality in the wake of the movement. Most notably, the dawn of the 1970s witnessed widespread school desegregation across the South, as discussed in Chapter 1. (Though the Supreme Court had ruled segregated schools unconstitutional in the 1954 *Brown v. Board* decision, most southern school districts remained segregated until the late 1960s.) While some white southerners resisted by opening all-white private academies, the majority learned how to live in this new order. An observer returning to the South in 1970 after two decades away could observe both "enormous change" and "evident continuity" as a result of the civil rights movement. Whites now went to schools and shared other public spaces with blacks, but they also retained control over politics and the economy. Blacks remained disadvantaged throughout the region. Yet whites sensed that they had give up a lot. As *Newsweek* reporter Karl Fleming put it in a 1970 article, "even the simplest recognition of human dignity of black people has been a painful concession for whites."[13] This recognition proved difficult because for centuries, white southerners had conceived of themselves in a racial hierarchy above blacks. Slavery and Jim Crow did not require every white southerner to persecute blacks, but those arrangements did require that the vast majority of white southerners uphold the legitimacy of racial hierarchy.

The civil rights movement wrought a fundamental challenge to that moral economy, and white southerners coped in various ways. Some resisted and remained unrepentant, while others had embraced the movement early on and championed a new era of racial equality. But the vast majority were neither Klan members nor civil rights activists. They felt uneasy about the changes occasioned by the civil rights movement but knew the old racial order was gone forever. The question confronting them was, what next? And this question carried special import for evangelicals who saw themselves as cultural custodians. As Falwell's comments indicated, white southern evangelicals felt a pressing need to ensure that Christian values governed society. For as long as they could remember, Christian values had been tied up with a system of white supremacy, so ubiquitous as to seem the "southern way of life." By 1970, it was clear to almost everyone that white supremacy could not endure, at least not in its historic form. But white southern evangelicals also worried that the new racial order betokened a breakdown of *all* systems of social order. They could not abide that.

The military provided a model for how to hang onto hierarchy in a desegregated world. In 1948, President Harry Truman had ordered the military to desegregate. Though the process took a few years to implement, the military's efforts at racial integration prefigured and outpaced civilian initiatives. In 1951—before the nation had even heard of Martin Luther King, Jr.—all U.S. army commands were desegregated. This development made the military an unlikely foe for segregationists, who often found racially integrated units of federal troops thwarting their attempts to preserve segregation in public institutions. But as white southerners gradually came to grips with the end of Jim Crow, they saw the military as a model institution. During the last third of the twentieth century, the military resisted movements advocating for female combat soldiers and for lifting its ban on gays and lesbians. The armed forces retained the belief that cultural custodianship demanded clear command structure and discipline. Evangelicals viewed the military with admiration as it modeled the traditional values and social order they hoped to govern the rest of society.

Evangelicals' growing appreciation for the military coincided with the public's growing disillusionment with the Vietnam War, a coincidence that helped conservative Protestants win greater approval among the armed forces. Peace marches and protests against the government raged across the nation. Evangelicals felt that these demonstrations were assaults on America, and they decried the lawlessness that menaced their country. A lead editorial in the *Free Will Baptist* condemning anti-government marches opined that "those who administer the law must be supported, whatever the cost."[14] Given the mood of the nation, sentiments like this seemed in short supply, and evangelicals' support of the troops earned them strong allies among the military. Historian Anne Loveland argued that because "throughout the war [evangelicals] remained as anticommunist, pro-American, and pro-military as when the war began," they "gained respect and influence within the armed forces."[15] Military leaders won prominent billing in conservative Christian periodicals and found themselves lionized by leading ministers.

In the late 1970s, evangelicals also shared military leaders' frustration with politicians. Conservative evangelicals endorsed a view—common among veterans—that failure in Vietnam resulted from a lack of political will rather than from the sub-par performance of the military. The editor of the *Moral Majority Report*, for instance, approvingly quoted President Reagan's evaluation of the military's performance in Vietnam. "Several years ago," said Reagan, "we brought home a group of American fighting men who obeyed their country's call and fought as bravely and well as any Americans in our history. They came home without a victory not because they had been defeated but because they had been denied permission to win."[16] Reagan intimated that cowardice among civilian politicians doomed the war effort; the military remained above blame. Likewise, conservative Protestants viewed the military as an unimpeachable force. Only civilian fecklessness could check the advances of the army. Evangelicals celebrated the legacy of aggressive generals like Douglas MacArthur and George Patton, and they repudiated the spinelessness of contemporary politicians. Jimmy Carter, scoffed the *Moral Majority Report*, thinks the military "is the strongest it has been in eight years."[17] Evangelicals knew otherwise. A combination of misplaced priorities and weak-kneed politicians had imperiled America's once-proud fighting force.

Heartened to find support, leaders in the armed forces began to embrace the conflation of Christian and military values. In the 1950s and 1960s, chaplains had struggled to convince army leaders that military life was compatible with Christian faith. For instance, one chaplain conceded that the army put troops "beyond the restraining influences of his family and the watchful eye of both the church and the community."[18] The chaplain's comments underlined a bias that pervaded American churches: most Christians felt the army spelled trouble for troops' faith. But by the 1980s, prominent military leaders proudly trumpeted the symbiotic relationship between Christianity and the armed forces. General John W. Vessey, chair of the Joint Chiefs of Staff, told a gathering of business and government leaders, "Christianity is like the service. You're in it no matter what comes up, so you must be ready for action today. . . . Self-control, endurance, and trust constitute the code by which you are judged."[19] Like other prominent military leaders, Vessey endorsed the shared identification between Christians and the armed forces. This shared identification depended on the sense that both groups held responsibility for ensuring America's survival.

Partly as a result of this shared identification, evangelicals made up an increasing portion of military chaplains in the years after the Vietnam War. Whereas liberal and mainline Protestants argued for making the chaplaincy civilian, most conservative evangelicals defended the role of chaplains as members of the military. Liberal Protestants worried that the chaplaincy's position in the armed forces had transformed their role, from providing religious counsel to the military to promoting a "military religion."[20] Evangelicals had fewer qualms about the divine sanction of the U.S. military, and they continued to seek out positions as chaplains. By 2005, nearly 60 percent of chaplains identified as evangelical.[21]

In response to the military's endorsement of them, evangelicals crafted a political message that privileged the military's ideals and priorities. Vessey's comment, for example, stressed self-control, endurance, and trust—not mercy or compassion. Likewise, evangelical political leaders celebrated strength and discipline more often than peace and justice. Debates about the budget often illustrated this tendency among leaders of the Christian right. "Liberal politicians," wrote one Moral Majority editorialist, "substitute welfare dollars for national defense in the interests of getting themselves reelected."[22] This comment played on evangelicals' predisposition to favor defense spending over domestic social programs.[23] But it also reflected conservative Christians' increasing identification with military values. They prized strength over softness, endurance over empathy.

The mutual admiration that characterized the relationship between evangelicals and the military depended on a sense of shared identity that Christians had cultivated for decades. Belief in cultural custodianship, alongside a deep-seated pro-military bias, positioned conservative evangelicals to forge a closer alliance with the armed forces when Vietnam worsened other Americans' view of the military. Military leaders appreciated the praise given them and returned the favor by highlighting common values. The alliance of Christians and military brass also depended on a shared dissatisfaction with the tenor of American politics and culture. When the Christian right stepped up its political activism in the late 1970s and early 1980s, its strident defense of the military won it some prominent army supporters. This support, however, included a quid pro quo. When military backers faced a tough political battle in the early 1980s, they called on evangelicals for support.

The Nuclear Arms Debate

For Americans in the early 1980s, the Cold War dominated geopolitics. The Soviet Union had survived for two generations, expanding its influence over Eastern Europe, Africa, and parts of the western hemisphere. Leading politicians treated the Soviets as a persistent rival rather than as a wartime foe. While politicians still wanted to defeat communism, the more pragmatic sensed that the best one could hope was to manage the U.S. relationship with the USSR. To be sure, political speech retained a strong dose of anticommunism, and politicians who seemed overly friendly toward the Soviets faced significant criticism. Yet many politicians had concluded that the Soviet threat would never disappear. The Soviet Union's persistence convinced many Americans to adopt a measured posture toward communism.

The advent of a sustained nuclear arms race in the 1950s encouraged this development. By the late 1960s, both superpowers possessed enough weaponry to annihilate the other (along with much of the rest of the globe).[24] By stockpiling arsenals that would decimate the other nation, the United States and the Soviet Union guaranteed each other's destruction in the event of nuclear war. This bilateral threat acquired the moniker Mutually Assured Destruction (aptly shortened to the acronym MAD). MAD enforced a precarious nuclear truce between the United States and the Soviet Union from the mid-1960s onward. Convinced that defeating the Soviets would require a nuclear attack, which under MAD would result in horrific Soviet retaliation, many American leaders sought to lessen the likelihood of nuclear war, primarily through reducing nuclear weapon stockpiles. During the 1970s, a succession of strategic arms limitation treaties won popular support in the United States Though only one Strategic Arms Limitation Treaty (SALT I) garnered congressional approval, popular support for reduction of nuclear weapons remained strong. The Soviets' ever-improving nuclear arsenal convinced many American politicians that they needed to stop dreaming about ultimate victory and learn to manage their relationship with the Russians.

Ronald Reagan rejected the idea that communism was something Americans had to learn to live with. He called the Soviet Union "an evil force that would extinguish the light we've been tending for 6,000 years" and said communism "is not a normal way of living for human beings." Perhaps most important, Reagan predicted that the United States would defeat the communists. In 1982 he told Americans, "I think we are seeing the beginning cracks, the beginning of the end."[25] Reagan's critics blasted the president as hopelessly naïve, an ignorant idealist. Worse yet, they worried that his policies threatened to jumpstart a nuclear war. By the early 1980s, defense experts, along with most of the American public, believed the Soviets had eliminated the technical and numerical nuclear advantage the United States had enjoyed since the advent of atomic weapons. Political leaders argued that the Soviets no longer cowered behind an inferior nuclear arsenal. Reagan's saber rattling frightened Americans who worried that the Soviets could overwhelm the United States if sufficiently provoked. Those in favor of nuclear arms limitation believed that when Reagan called the USSR an "evil empire," he not only jeopardized hard-won concessions but also increased the likelihood of America's destruction.

With the prospect of nuclear war haunting Americans, the campaign for a "nuclear freeze"—a complete, bilateral moratorium on the development and production of nuclear weapons—had by 1982 become "the flagship issue for the political left."[26] That June, 750,000 demonstrators flooded Times Square in the largest political rally in New York City's history, demanding an end to the production of nuclear weapons. A 1982 World Health Organization report estimated that nuclear war between the United States and the Soviet Union would result in two billion deaths, about half the world's population. In response to this threat, eight states passed resolutions calling for bilateral reduction of weapons stockpiles, and hundreds of national organizations endorsed a nuclear freeze. The groundswell of popular support suggested public unhappiness with Reagan's plans to augment America's nuclear arsenal. Freeze advocates argued that the only response to exponential nuclear proliferation over the past half-century was immediate and total cessation of nuclear weapons production, alongside commitments from both the United States and the Soviet Union to reduce their nuclear stockpiles.

A significant portion of American Christians endorsed nuclear freeze. In 1982, the National Council of Catholic Bishops drafted a pastoral letter that called for a halt to the development and production of all nuclear weapons, advocated a sharp reduction in nuclear arsenals, and endorsed a "global authority" to oversee such efforts. The bishops acknowledged that that the debate over arms limitation was "fraught with complexity, controversy and passion." Yet because "nuclear weapons are among the most pressing moral questions of our age," they thought the subject unavoidable.[27] The bishops believed Christians must oppose all further testing and development of nuclear weapons. Other believers, including some evangelicals, concurred. The editors of *Christianity Today* endorsed Senator Mark Hatfield's plan to initiate "a complete freeze on the development, testing, and deployment of strategic missile systems."[28] A subsequent issue reported that readers largely agreed: 60 percent of evangelicals supported a bilateral freeze, while only 18 percent opposed it.[29]

Evangelical support for nuclear freeze arose in part because Billy Graham repudiated nuclear weapons. Long a bellwether of evangelical viewpoints, Graham surprised many observers in the late 1970s by taking a strong stand in favor of the second Strategic Arms Limitation Treaty (SALT II). Graham's endorsement of SALT II, which Ronald Reagan had described as a "bad treaty," presaged his call for "SALT 10," a comprehensive treaty that would result in "the bilateral, verifiable eradication of all nuclear, biochemical and laser weapons."[30] In his condemnation of nuclear weapons, Graham made clear that their awesome destructive capabilities rendered them unacceptable from a Christian point of view. In an interview with the liberal evangelical periodical *Sojourners*, Graham admitted that through Bible study and prayer, he had come to realize that his earlier support of American military might could not extend to nuclear weapons. "We must," he said "seek the good of the whole human race, and not just the good of any one nation or race." Characteristically, Graham framed his opposition to nuclear weapons in spiritual terms. He said that sin "has permeated everything – the individual, society, creation. That is one reason why the nuclear issue is not just a political issue—it is a moral and spiritual issue as well."[31] Clearly Graham had not abandoned his sense that individual conversion was the overarching solution to the world's problems. But his support for disarmament represented an unexpected shift in Graham's position; *Sojourners* even titled the interview "A Change of Heart." He also sounded familiar liberal complaints about America spending billions on nuclear arms while impoverished people starved around the world. Graham stumped for SALT 10 around the country and beyond.

Graham's repudiation of nuclear weapons conflicted with typical evangelical support of the military, leading some evangelicals to ambivalence. A 1981 *Christianity Today* article lamented that, "in the midst of strident debate" about how to avert nuclear war, "evangelicals have remained strangely silent."[32] Two years later, the magazine reported that evangelicals attending a conference on American defense policy seemed "uninformed . . . on issues related to nuclear arms."[33] Theologically committed to peace—and anxious about the prospect of nuclear war—most evangelicals nonetheless could not bring themselves to echo Billy Graham's full-throated condemnation of nuclear weapons. The specter of nuclear annihilation frightened conservative Christians, but did not transform most of them into advocates for nuclear freeze. As much of the country mobilized against the president, evangelicals appeared caught in the middle, unwilling to endorse either nuclear freeze or military buildup.

Events in 1983 exacerbated tensions between the United States and the Soviet Union, prodding some evangelicals to abandon their commitments to nuclear freeze. In March, President Reagan announced his Strategic Defense

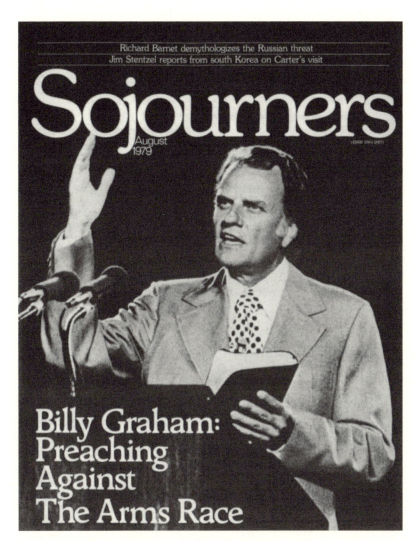

Figure 9. Billy Graham surprised many evangelicals when he began calling for complete nuclear disarmament in the late 1970s. Reprinted with permission from Sojourners, (800) 714-7474, www.sojo.net.

Initiative (SDI), which called for huge investment in a space-based nuclear deterrent. Two weeks later, Reagan referred to the Soviet Union as an "evil empire" in a speech before the National Association of Evangelicals. This language framed the Cold War in cosmic terms designed to appeal to religious believers. For many of those believers, the Soviets confirmed Reagan's characterization when they shot down a Korean airliner in September. The Korean jet had entered Soviet airspace, but it presented no threat to USSR military installations. The attack killed 269 civilians, including Republican Representative Larry McDonald. Leaders of the Christian right contended that the Soviets would carry out more and more such dastardly acts as long as they did not fear American reprisal. They urged evangelicals to support Reagan's pro-military agenda.

Jerry Falwell and Moral Majority, in particular, became some of Reagan's foremost supporters on defense issues. Moral Majority had always endorsed pro-defense policies, and Reagan's language of "peace through strength" became a repeated rallying cry. "There is only one sure formula for peace with freedom and that is through strength," Falwell wrote in an advertisement published in major daily newspapers across the country. "Unless the leaders of this country have military strength at least equal to that available to the Kremlin tyrants, we can in time expect either an attack or nuclear blackmail."[34] The idea of "nuclear blackmail" provided another justification for the president's agenda. Because leaders of the Christian right believed the Soviets were irreversibly committed to world domination, they contended that American might was the only thing preventing a communist takeover of the free world. If the Soviets acquired an overwhelming nuclear advantage, said Falwell, they would certainly impose their atheistic political system on America (and the rest of the world). As such, Moral Majority argued that Christians who hoped to perpetuate religious freedom must support Reagan's plan of military buildup.

Furthermore, evangelical theology, which placed great value on eternal life, predisposed some to regard nuclear war as an acceptable risk. To be sure, no one welcomed the prospect of nuclear annihilation, and many evangelicals, like Billy Graham, considered war with the Soviets something to be avoided at all costs. But others demurred. "War in any form is abominable," said Falwell, "but there is something at least as abominable, and that is life without liberty—life without the freedom to write and speak and pray."[35] Falwell's comment captured an essential reality for conservative Christians: a life without God was not worth living. Even as it endorsed a conditional nuclear freeze, *Christianity Today* noted, "the evangelical is not committed to human physical life as the highest value . . . 100 million deaths may not be too great a price to pay."[36] Language like that came only from those who valued life in the hereafter at least as much as they did life on earth.

Conservative evangelicals' willingness to accept the possibility of nuclear war depended on confidence that God would guard them—a confidence rooted in their beliefs about the end times. Premillennial dispensationalism, the dominant belief among late twentieth-century evangelicals, taught that Christ would "rapture" his followers into heaven before the deadly battle of Armageddon. Some Christians thought this battle would take the form of nuclear holocaust. Those who thought a rain of nuclear weapons would signal the advent of the millennium incorporated a potential World War III into salvation history. For them, nuclear war was not only possible; it was inevitable. The evangelicals who embraced this reasoning figured they would ascend to heaven before the world crumbled. They did not delight in the prospect of nuclear war, but their theological outlook allowed them to face that prospect with more equanimity than most nonbelievers could muster. To say that nuclear weapons threatened God's sovereignty was "blasphemy," according to retired general (and devout Christian) Daniel O. Graham. "When God wants to destroy the world," he said, "He will do it."[37]

To liberal ears, leaders of the Christian right seemed to relish the idea of being part of earth's ultimate destiny. Echoing evangelists throughout American history, Falwell declared, "we are a part of that terminal generation, that last generation, that shall not pass until our Lord comes." This theme has appeared in the sermons of American evangelists since the colonial era, often as a way to convey the importance of conversion. But secular liberals, unaccustomed to such language, expressed alarm at religious conservatives' infatuation with the end of the world. Moreover, they worried that the Christian right's increasing political influence had spread doomsday belief to the White House. Reagan, after all, had speculated, "we may be the generation that sees Armageddon." Because the president held the power to inaugurate World War III, secular commentators feared his belief would become a self-fulfilling prophecy. California state senator James Mills, for instance, wrote that Reagan's "attitudes relative to military spending, and his coolness to all proposals for nuclear disarmament, are consistent with . . . apocalyptic views."[38] In the tense nuclear atmosphere of the early 1980s, conservative Christians' belief in biblical prophecy made them seem comfortable—perhaps even excited—about the prospect of nuclear war.

Leaders of the Christian right, however, embraced Reagan's program because they thought it provided the best prospect of an acceptable peace.
Communists, in the estimation of conservatives, possessed an unquenchable
desire for world domination. "The Soviets negotiate only when it is in their
best interests, [and] they will break their treaties when it suits their need,"
declared one Moral Majority commentator. "The Soviets seek an absolute superiority, not parity."[39] Yet conservatives did not think the Soviets rash or un-
predictable. Leaders of the Christian right, along with the Reagan
administration, thought they could maintain an uneasy truce with the USSR
as long as the United States possessed sufficient deterrent military
capabilities.

As such, conservative evangelical political leaders became some of the
foremost defenders of Reagan's "High Frontier" missile defense system, deri-
sively labeled "Star Wars" by its critics. High Frontier called for the United
States to develop space-based interceptor missiles that could shoot down Soviet intercontinental ballistic missiles (ICBMs). The concept struck many
military analysts as impractical, if not impossible, as it would require a massive outlay in federal spending. Reagan, however, convinced Christian supporters that the High Frontier program would ensure "peace through
strength." Army generals wrote in venues like *Moral Majority Report* to explain how an increase in defense spending would actually lessen the likelihood of war. "The beauty of the High Frontier approach is that we put up a
defensive system which will not kill a single Russian," declared retired General Daniel O. Graham. "The Soviets' missiles would be rendered obsolete by
the high technology in this new defensive strategy."[40] Graham appealed to
conservative Christians' theological commitment to peace, even as he and
others campaigned for pro-defense policies.

Conservatives' belief that peace came only through strength reflected the
importance they attached to firmness in the face of adversity. Reagan had
swept into office in part because he displayed none of the weakness and un-
certainty of his predecessor. He radiated masculinity. Conservative leaders
who thought that liberal sissies had imperiled America rejoiced in Reagan's
strength. For instance, when the editor of *Christian Century* called Reagan "a
'far-right ideologue'" whose anti-Soviet rhetoric imperiled détente, a leader
in the Christian right retorted: "We hope so; that's why he was elected!" The
president, said the Moral Majority, was "firmly committed to deterring the
communist plan for world conquest."[41] Christian conservatives who rallied to
the Republican banner prized leaders who stiffened their spine and fought

Communism. The only appropriate response to Soviet aggression was American strength. And the United States demonstrated that strength by recommitting itself to maintaining a superior nuclear arsenal and investing heavily in missile defense.

The Christian right hinted that those who opposed the president lacked the manliness required for national leadership. One Moral Majority columnist fretted about House Speaker Tip O'Neill, a Democrat, "emasculat[ing] our defense buildup."[42] Falwell labeled anti-nuclear activists "freezeniks." He believed that "loyal members of Congress" would support the president.[43] Another *Moral Majority Report* article lampooned the citizens of Vermont, who in 1982 voted to disarm the United States and the Soviet Union in a series of town meetings. "Vote away nuclear weapons?" the article scoffed. "Vermont can't even vote away black flies in April!"[44] And while Vermont's action occasioned ridicule, evangelicals saw a more insidious threat. "Churchmen have been selling nuclear freeze for 15 years and that's not courage," said General Graham. "Any churchman who falls into the trap that cowardice replaces courage is wrong."[45] Moral Majority worried that liberal ministers had brainwashed countless Christians to see nuclear freeze as a theologically justified position. They fought that perception in part by labeling their foes as disloyal cowards. Leaders in the Christian right impugned "freezeniks" by challenging their masculinity.

This rhetoric struck liberals as careless and even incendiary, yet critics who decried the Christian right's "macho" foreign policy and "warmonger" mentality misunderstood the masculine ideal the movement embraced. Conservative Christians identified discipline as a critical component of masculinity. In the debate over nuclear arms, conservative Christians never viewed their approach as reckless. They wanted to defeat the Soviets by attrition, not with a direct attack. In their estimation, Reagan neither shrank from the threat of nuclear war nor invited it. Most leaders of the Christian right believed the president's strategy was more disciplined than that of his foes. "We need not choose between . . . Arms Control or Armageddon," said General Graham. By supporting Reagan's SDI, "we can defend ourselves and our deterrent forces against nuclear attack . . . [and] drive the possibility of nuclear war back to near zero."[46] The statements of Christian right leaders reflected a desire for peace. They thought that strength, as shown through military might, best inoculated the United States against war.

The tension that wracked the nation in 1982 and 1983 eased as it became apparent that neither the United States nor the Soviet Union planned to launch a preemptive attack, and Reagan's once-unpopular policies won general acceptance. Congress passed only a symbolic nuclear freeze resolution, while it renewed funding for the MX missile program and authorized plans to proceed with the SDI. Aided by an economic recovery that began in late 1983, Reagan overwhelmed Walter Mondale in the 1984 election. Critics of the president's nuclear policies took another hit in 1985, when Reagan met with Soviet premier Mikhail Gorbachev and initiated a series of arms reduction treaties that implicitly commended the president's agenda of "peace through strength."[47] The doomsday scenarios that captivated Americans in 1983 seemed less credible two years later. The nation's political attention shifted elsewhere.

At one of the tensest moments of the Cold War, the Christian right emerged as a stalwart supporter of pro-military policies. Not every evangelical went along Reagan's policies, but the eventual passage of the president's military agenda demonstrated grassroots support, some of which the Christian right helped establish. Christian political leaders, taking their cue from the president, framed the political standoff over military spending as one that pitted tough-minded, pragmatic conservatives against weak-kneed liberals. As it did with debates over textbooks and the ERA, the Christian right portrayed its agenda as a common-sense expression of popular values. These values coincided with those of the military. Moreover, conservative Christian political leaders leveraged the debate over nuclear freeze in order to demonstrate their commitment to the president and to their pro-defense pledge. By the mid-1980s, conservative evangelicals had become some of the military's foremost supporters.

Even so, the horror nuclear weapons evoked made defense of them politically uncomfortable for the Christian right. Polls of evangelicals revealed that most favored an idealistic version of nuclear freeze as well as maintenance of American military superiority.[48] They wanted détente alongside aggressive defense of American interests. Even Jerry Falwell admitted that "none of us feel comfortable in the moral milieu of nuclear weapons"[49] Falwell was not shy about promoting pro-military policies, but as fears of a Russian attack subsided, so did his attention to the defense of nuclear weapons.

The nuclear freeze debate of 1983 provided a good example of the Christian right's growing political savvy. Leaders of the movement, whose statements sounded so doctrinaire to secular ears, proved shrewd and pragmatic. In a 2000 interview, Falwell said, "the general public thinks of me as a 'John the Baptist, confront-the-culture, nuke-the-earth' kind of person." He told the interviewer that he embraced such a characterization because he felt called as a "minister to the media."[50] But he designed his rhetoric to appeal to "common sense" values, many of which drew on popular gendered ideology. In the case of nuclear weapons, Falwell positioned himself and other defenders of military might as the foremost protectors of peace. They—not the "freezeniks"—showed the spine necessary to face down a communist threat. Distracted by his inflammatory rhetoric, liberal critics charged Falwell with warmongering. But they failed to see that his appeal was rooted in a sense that masculine strength—embodied both by the military and by its commander-in-chief—provided the best guarantor of peace in a nuclear age. While nuclear weapons made everyone uncomfortable, the Christian right helped evangelicals see how they could live with the threat.

Family Values and the Threat of Gays in the Military

The Christian right became such a strident defender of Reagan's military buildup in part because the proportion of evangelicals in the military had grown over the course of the twentieth century. Whereas military leaders in the 1950s and 1960s had clashed with evangelical chaplains over issues of proselytization and alcohol regulation, the military leadership of the 1980s included a disproportionate number of evangelicals. Military leaders increasingly identified as evangelicals or at least endorsed evangelical viewpoints. Protestants had consistently comprised approximately 55 percent of the armed forces, but in the second half of the twentieth century, that faction grew more evangelical—like American Protestants generally.[51] As a result, when Reagan spoke about beefing up military spending, the appeal to evangelicals was not simply ideological. Reagan's plan would enlarge an increasingly evangelical army.

The army chief of staff appointed by Reagan in 1983, General John Wickham, made family values a centerpiece of his leadership. Raised as a semi-devout Episcopalian, Wickham redoubled his Christian commitment after a near-death experience in Vietnam. In 1967, Viet Cong and North Vietnamese soldiers attacked Wickham's unit, exploding a rocket next to his tent and shooting him several times. He survived through the night, was evacuated from southeast Asia, and beat long odds to return to active duty (doctors thought he might never walk again). Given a second chance, Wickham decided God wanted him to "make a difference in terms of moral values."[52] On his appointment as Chief of Staff, Wickham immediately commissioned a white paper on army families, and he implemented a Family Action Plan that called on the army to tend soldiers' families in a more comprehensive way. The number of enlisted men with families had grown rapidly since the army became an all-volunteer force in the 1970s, and leadership had dealt with this population in a piecemeal fashion. More broadly, the army had been attempting to improve the ethical lives of soldiers after what many observers saw as moral breakdown in Vietnam. In one sense, then, Wickham's focus on moral values and family responsibility simply furthered efforts that were already underway. But his devotion to evangelical family values came through in some of the policies he pushed. Wickham advocated "caring leadership" among army officers and tried to limit alcohol consumption and smoking. He expressed a desire to purge the army of pornography, as well.

Most notably, Wickham enlisted the support of family values leader James Dobson to implement his army family policy. Introduced to Dobson by Republican congressmen Dan Coats of Indiana and Frank Wolf of Virginia, Wickham commissioned Dobson to produce a version of Focus on the Family's *Where's Dad?* video for the army.[53] The original video featured Dobson preaching at a Focus on the Family seminar about the roles of husband and father as essential to America's survival. Though the army version of *Where's Dad?* excluded the most explicit references to Christianity ("to broaden its appeal to soldiers who are not Christian," according to *Christianity Today*), the underlying message reflected the family values agenda. Dobson said that when he asked God about the biggest need for the nation, God told him that the country needed fathers who led their families and cared for their children. In 1984 the army made plans to screen the movie to all 700,000 of its enlisted men.[54] The soldiers heard an explicitly evangelical message only minimally disguised as secular. Given the difficulties of maintaining an all-volunteer force, the army had turned to evangelicals for support. The evangelical message prioritized family values. Because he endorsed this message, Wickham became a celebrity in evangelical circles, and he constructed a more comprehensive approach to dealing with army families. He also tightened the connection among evangelicals, Republican politicians, and the armed forces. In 1985 Billy Graham's *Decision* magazine ran a story on Wickham titled, "A Soldier Who Cares About Families." The headline just as easily could have read, "An Army That Cares About Family Values."[55]

The increasing alliance of family values crusaders and the U.S. armed forces partly explains why Bill Clinton's 1993 attempt to remove the military's fifty-year-old ban on gays in the military outraged military leadership. In contrast to the debate over nuclear weapons, evangelicals showed no reservations about their stance in this debate. Clinton, said one, "is dead wrong."[56] That sentiment summarized the feelings of conservatives throughout the country. When the young Democratic president made lifting the army's ban on gays one of his first campaigns on taking office, Clinton energized a raft of evangelicals who had not mustered much momentum in the previous year's elections.

That Clinton made lifting the military ban on gays a priority testified to the successes of the gay rights movement. In 1970, most gays and lesbians remained in the closet, and many mainstream Americans still regarded homosexuality as a disease. As discussed in Chapter 6, the American Psychiatric Association removed homosexuality from its list of mental illnesses in 1973, and several states subsequently overturned statutes against sodomy. The emergence of AIDS in the early 1980s created a backlash against gays, but as more became known about the disease—and as heterosexuals began acquiring HIV—many Americans viewed the backlash as a reversion to bigotry. By the early 1990s, gays had successfully lobbied several states to criminalize discrimination on the basis of "sexual orientation." Clinton himself framed his attempt to lift the ban on gays in the military as an effort to "end discrimination."[57] Thanks in large part to an active gay rights lobby, by the early 1990s a large portion of Americans considered homosexuality a normal, biologically determined "alternative lifestyle."

Moreover, by 1993 tolerance of gay and lesbian soldiers seemed to prevail in the military itself. In 1949, a Pentagon memo had declared homosexuals "unsuitable" for military service, formalizing the armed forces' scattershot policies regarding gay troops. That memo, however, ignored the growing number and increasing visibility of gays in the military. Historian Allen Bérubé has argued that lax enforcement of anti-gay policies during World War II enabled gay soldiers to inaugurate a thriving subculture in port cities like New York and San Francisco after the war.[58] In 1957 the military commissioned a secret study to examine the suitability of homosexuals for armed service. The resulting Crittendon Report, which remained confidential for two decades, found no link between homosexuality and poor performance in the military. It recommended lifting the navy ban on "one-time, non-habitual offenders."[59] As a result, some military brass ignored the increasingly obvious reality of a large number of gay troops. The expansion of the military during Vietnam only added to the ranks of gays in the service. Though more than

16,000 troops were discharged for homosexuality between 1980 and 1991, that number was less than 2 percent of involuntary separations. By the early 1990s, gays and lesbians had established a significant presence among the armed forces, in spite of the ban. "Never before," wrote one commentator in 1993, "have gay people served so extensively—and in some cases, so openly—in the United States military."[60]

Clinton thought his attempt to remove restrictions on gays in the military was consistent with both the mood of the American people and the reality of the U.S. military, but he underestimated the backlash his initiative would generate. When he announced his plans to lift the ban, conservative critics protested immediately. At a rally in North Carolina, a civilian suggested that the plan "would wreck military morale and discipline."[61] When Clinton pointed out that closeted gays were already serving—and serving well—in the military, military critics said that he missed the point. "We know we have a certain number of gays performing extremely well, but they're in the closet, and as long as they stay there we're fine," said a navy admiral. "But when they come out of the closet and get proactive, it'll be really nasty."[62] The military knew about gays among the ranks, but it remained important to maintain an official standard of conduct consistent with family values. Because many Americans perceived homosexuality as unnatural and perverted, the armed forces believed they could not offer official sanction or toleration. Military leaders appeared comfortable with the prevailing paradox: gays and lesbians could serve only if they kept their sexuality a secret.

Much of the military's opposition to homosexuality stemmed from Christian objections to the practice. As evangelicals' influence in the military grew after Vietnam, evangelical social teaching won greater acceptance among the armed forces.[63] The increasing acceptance of homosexuality in mainstream American culture did not prevail among evangelicals, and the military followed suit. "Homosexual practice is wrong," wrote one evangelical chaplain. "The texts that address homosexuality are plain in their meaning. The chief sin of Sodom was sodomy."[64] Evangelicals privileged a straightforward reading of certain scriptural passages that made God's will clear. In this case, God condemned homosexuality. No matter how many closeted gays served in the military—and no matter how many "hermeneutical acrobatics" liberal Christians used to support their legitimacy—evangelicals agreed that the Bible prohibited homosexual behaviors.[65] And in an army dedicated to (Christian) virtue, "Do these [homosexual] practices merit the support and endorsement an executive order would bestow upon them?"[66] For evangelicals, the answer was an unequivocal no.

Because of leaders like John Wickham, the military had become an institution evangelicals considered Godly. The military's conservatism helped it win evangelical support, but the alliance went deeper than shared politics. Evangelicals understood the military in the context of family values. In this context, men had a well-defined role to play. They had to be tough leaders who confronted external forces that threatened home and country. Evangelical author Stephen Mansfield captured this ethos when he advocated for a Christian "warrior code" to permeate the U.S. military. According to Mansfield, this code "takes a soldier and makes him a knight. . . . His duties are transformed into holy sacrifices."[67] Mansfield's use of the knight imagery typified rhetoric evangelicals used to describe American soldiers, and it implicitly underscored the framework of family values. Knights protected women from harm, just as family values men guarded their wives and children. It went without saying that gays could never be real men in this framework. Evangelicals railed against Clinton's initiative in large part because it threatened family values.

The controversy over Clinton's attempt to lift the ban on gays in the military resulted in two important consequences for politically active conservative evangelicals. First, it restored credence to the Christian right's claims of persecution. After twelve years of Republican control over the White House, the Christian right had lost its ability to rail against the moral failings of American government. While the movement had thrived as an embattled minority, it struggled to maintain its initial focus and determination when in power. Some leaders left, and many followers appeared shaken by the high profile "telescandals" of the late 1980s.[68] Clinton, however, provided a fresh target, and his plan to admit gays into the military confirmed evangelicals' fears about a Democratic administration. One sociologist called Clinton's attempt to lift the military's ban on gays and lesbians "a bonanza for building organizations and raising money." Leaders of Christian right groups believed "they could not have scripted Bill Clinton's first weeks any better." One of those leaders, anti-abortion activist Randall Terry, said, "Clinton has done us a great favor. This is going to help us mobilize people to take action for the next four years."[69] For his first major policy initiative, the president selected an issue that enraged the Christian right. The movement re-energized its base and played a role in the Republican sweep of the 1994 midterm elections.

Second, the issue of whether gays could serve in the military provided evangelicals with a perfect forum for elucidating their understanding of social order. Throughout the 1970s and 1980s, conservative Protestants increasingly advocated legislating issues of gender and sexuality to reinforce traditional family values. They rejected the ERA, campaigned against abortion, and saw feminism as a misguided quest. But the increasing prominence of women working outside the home—even within conservative Christian circles—made the debate over women's roles increasingly problematic. Some conservatives continued to reject women's participation in traditionally masculine areas of society, but by the 1990s such views appeared less frequently than they had only a decade earlier. Homosexuality, on the other hand, remained beyond the pale. Evangelicals perceived homosexuality as a perverse and willful behavior designed to ignore God's teaching about family values. They endeavored to root it out, not endorse it. Clinton's plan provided an ideal target.

And by locating the debate over gay rights in the context of the military, Clinton only exacerbated evangelical opposition. Over the previous two decades, the Christian right had developed an identification with the military, bound by a shared commitment to defend American virtue. Guardianship required strength, and gays—at least in the minds of conservatives—were effeminate. Their admission into the military would imperil the nation's fighting force and compromise its integrity. "When the issue [of homosexuality] was fused to conservative views on the military and the objections of the nation's military leadership," wrote one columnist, "it attained extraordinary emotional power."[70] Clinton's plan struck at the very heart of evangelicals' sense of social order.

Clinton reacted to the firestorm of criticism by hammering out a compromise that satisfied almost no one. After consulting with military brass, most of whom opposed the president's plan, Clinton managed to persuade Congress to pass a bill that kept in place the military's ban on gays but forbade recruiters from asking prospective soldiers about their sexual orientation. Popularly known as "Don't Ask, Don't Tell," the compromise disappointed gay rights groups. It also infuriated conservatives by giving tacit sanction to gays and lesbians. Meanwhile, soldiers reported that little had changed on the base. "It's not that big of a change, especially not here," said a soldier at Fort Bragg, North Carolina. "You'd be an idiot in this division if you came out and announced you were gay."[71] In short, Don't Ask, Don't Tell was a political failure.

But those few months in the first half of 1993 revealed a lot about the pervasiveness of evangelicals' understanding of family values. Clinton wrongly suspected that his election signaled that Americans were ready to accept homosexuality in the name of tolerance, even if they still thought it abnormal. Conservative evangelicals proved unwilling to see "sexual preference" as a matter of civil rights. The Christian right helped make this a viable position by emphasizing the need for family values to govern society. God had outlined clear guidelines for how humans ought to organize society, and the heterosexual, two-parent family stood at the center of that social order. Moreover, scripture charged men with the leadership and protection of their families and of the broader culture. Sanctioning gays in the military would not only provide official endorsement for an "abomination against God and nature;" it would also "feminize a male club" and "weak[en] . . . a mighty fighting force."[72] Those comments, taken from soldiers opposed to Clinton's plan, reflected the ubiquity of conservative Christians' understanding of gender. That understanding drew both on cultural ideals of masculinity and on the teaching of scripture. And it supported a worldview that saw a gendered hierarchy as a divinely sanctioned means of organizing society.

Military Might and Christian Virtue

Evangelicals' aggressive defense of pro-military policies revealed how their understanding of scriptural teaching, gender, and America entwined. Almost all evangelicals endorsed the role and ethos of the military, in spite of strong critiques of American military culture by both insiders and outsiders.[73] For most conservative Christians, attacks on American militarism rang hollow. "Freedom and peace are precious pearls of great price," declared *Christianity Today*. "But they come only to those who are willing to fight for them."[74] True Christians, in this view, had to fight. And because pro-American sentiment colored all members of the Christian right, few had any patience for positions that impugned the motives of the American military. They equated biblical endorsement of the state with advocacy of the United States, and they saw scriptural sanction of fighting as justification for American military endeavors. Most did not endorse fighting per se, but they saw war as a scripturally sanctioned activity because they viewed the defense of America as defense of a godly way of life.

Military might thus became a sort of Christian virtue among members of the Christian right. To be sure, leaders of the movement maintained public commitments to peace, but they believed peace depended on strength. The

Jesus who sacrificed and died rather than assume an earthly kingdom took a backseat to scriptural endorsements of the state's proper function as enforcer of justice. And in some cases, Jesus himself became a military messiah. For instance, Southern Baptist Convention President Bobby Welch called Jesus a "warrior leader." By the dawn of the twenty-first century, evangelicals read the Bible in such a way as to endorse religious militarism.

This militaristic emphasis was not new, but its ubiquity proved one of the key legacies of the family values movement. The movement had revolutionized conservative evangelicals' political agenda by pointing them away from debates over segregation and toward the defense of a gendered order. In so doing, the Christian right made masculinity not simply a valuable character trait but a scripturally sanctioned ideal to be guarded. Attacks on the American military rallied Christian troops to defend a divinely ordained institution against those who challenged its gendered order. They saw this task as a political necessity, and they coalesced with people and groups across the nation that had found little common cause in earlier decades. The Christian right's focus on the politics of gender enabled a coalition of evangelicals to reshape the American political landscape.

CHAPTER 8

Promise Keepers

As the debate over "Don't Ask, Don't Tell" raged in 1993, some of Clinton's main opponents—including James Dobson—offered their support to a new Christian men's group that intended to promote family values in an apolitical setting: the Promise Keepers (PK). A 1994 *Christian Century* article on the group reported that "political labeling" and "ridicule" of liberals were "amazingly absent" from PK literature. In place of partisan invective, PK featured rhetoric that was "broad rather than narrow."[1] The Promise Keepers promised a new style of evangelicalism for the 1990s—an evangelicalism that would promote faithfulness without catering blindly to the political right.

Founded in 1990 by former college football coach Bill McCartney, Promise Keepers grew out of McCartney's belief that America's moral failings stemmed from a breakdown in men's spiritual lives. His organization called on Christian men to adopt the organization's list of "seven promises," each of which focused on a man's relationship to others. Promise #4, for instance, committed men to "building strong marriages and families through love, protection, and biblical values."[2] This language drew on Christian right rhetoric from the previous decade; conservative evangelicals could easily interpret the coded appeals to right-wing politics. PK was never as apolitical as its leaders claimed.

But PK was also more complex than its critics believed. Two key characteristics deserve scrutiny. First, PK's commitment to conservative gender norms showed the pervasiveness of family values rhetoric. By the 1990s, plenty of white evangelicals believed the primary crisis facing America involved the decline of the family. This notion had taken root after decades of family values politics contended that liberals' primary sin was an assault on families. Second, PK's focus on racial reconciliation—alongside its notably integrated leadership—suggested that family values held the potential for interracial appeal. While critics believed that PK's plan to address racial problems was naïve, the group's message resonated across racial lines. More-over, PK's *New Man* magazine ran several articles in the late 1990s that sug-gested the politics of the group were not as reactionary as liberal critics claimed. A 1996 story featured sympathetic portrayals of illegal immigrants and advised readers to work "to understand the unique plight of those who come to our country as immigrants." One year later the magazine defended interracial marriage and attacked Christian militias that espoused white su-premacy.[3] These articles emerged out of PK's well-publicized commitment to racial reconciliation. While critics noted that early rallies hardly featured the interracial multitude projected by the organization's publicity photos, in-creasing numbers of black men joined the group in the late 1990s, and PK's leadership boasted a significant number of minorities.

But if PK's commitment to interracial cooperation distinguished it from earlier Christian right groups, its views on gender reflected a thoroughgoing conservatism. In a famous passage from *Seven Promises of a Promise Keeper*, African American PK leader Tony Evans told husbands, "I'm urging you to take [your role] back. Unfortunately there can be no compromise. Treat the lady gently and lovingly. But lead!"[4] This oft-cited passage became the focus of most feminist critiques. It obscured some diversity and nuance within the organization. In fact, a 1997 article in *New Man* magazine proclaimed, "Jesus was a feminist."[5] But most Promise Keepers viewed feminism with suspicion. The main thrust of the movement was to establish men as leaders.

PK's ability to hold together conservative views about gender with a com-mitment to racial reconciliation emerged from conservative evangelicals' generation-long effort to make family values the fundamental category in constructing social order. Like other Americans, conservative evangelicals in the 1990s saw the civil rights movement as a heroic moment in the nation's history. Most acknowledged white Christians' complicity in racial discrimi-nation, and they repented and set about trying to redeem their forebears' ra-cial sins. But conservative evangelicals believed the road to true racial reconciliation ran through the transformation of individual lives rather than through systemic changes. They also clung to the notion that God ordained a system of social order on the world. Previous generations had not been wrong to impose hierarchies per se; they had been wrong to organize those hierarchies along racial lines. To evangelicals, the Bible clearly spelled out distinctions in the way men and women should comport themselves—at home, at church, and in the broader society.

Promise Keepers also reflected the complex linkages between conservative religion and conservative politics.[6] Critics painted the group as an offshoot of the Christian right, committed to furthering a Republican social agenda on Capitol Hill. They were partly correct. By staging a million-man march in Washington, PK demonstrated a desire for their understanding of gender and family to shape "pro-moral" legislation. Yet few of the million men at the "Stand in the Gap" rally actively campaigned for Christian right initiatives. Most came for other reasons: fellowship with Christian men, or a search for spiritual renewal. Furthermore, PK excluded elected officials from speaking at "Stand in the Gap," and prohibited distribution of any printed materials other than the Bible. These measures demonstrated the organization's commitment to "avoid even a hint of overt politicking."[7] Looking more closely at PK provides a window onto the growing consensus among conservative evangelicals in the 1990s. Chastened by the excesses and failures of groups like Moral Majority, conservative evangelicals determined to make family values more about spiritual renewal than electoral politics. But the political elements of family values were deeply embedded in the messages mouthed by PK leaders. As a result, the political battles of the 1970s and 1980s became implanted in conservative evangelical spirituality, setting the stage for evangelicals to become more politically homogeneous than ever before.

Promise Keeping and Family Values

Bill McCartney founded Promise Keepers in 1990, when he was at the peak of a thirty-year coaching career. McCartney had coached football since the mid-1960s, working his way through a series of assistant positions before landing the head coaching job at the University of Colorado in 1982. After three years, his teams had produced just seven total victories. But beginning with his first winning campaign in 1985, McCartney amassed an 86–30–4 record over the next ten years, with 9 bowl bids, a slew of national coaching awards in 1989, three conference titles, and an AP national championship in 1990. Colorado had never experienced such a run of football success, and McCartney enjoyed nearly universal acclaim. But after compiling an 11–1 record and a #3 national ranking in the 1994 season, McCartney abruptly retired from coaching at fifty-four.

The reasons for his decision were muddy. Few people anticipated McCartney's decision to leave coaching. After all, he capped his final season with a 41–24 beating of Notre Dame in the Fiesta Bowl and had ten years remaining on a \$350,000-a-year contract. While his work with PK had taken energy and created some distractions—notably in 1992, when he called homosexuality "an abomination against almighty God" while wearing a University of Colorado shirt[8]—McCartney managed to become one of the nation's best football coaches while providing leadership to PK. His celebrity as Colorado's coach was instrumental in drumming up interest for Promise Keepers. McCartney told journalists he was leaving Colorado football to take care of his family. Supporters praised McCartney's willingness to take responsibility for the ways his coaching career had taken a toll on his marriage and his desire to care for his wife of thirty-two years, Lyndi. Cynics wondered if he was trying to avoid scandal, or embarrassed about his unmarried daughter Kristy's bearing two children fathered by two players on McCartney's football teams. A *Sports Illustrated* story published in the weeks after McCartney's final game tried to make sense of his disappearance. Reporters Richard Hoffer and Shelley Smith seemed puzzled. "If you believe him," they wrote, "his retirement is only the logical extension of his religious beliefs, a stew of ideas that combines ultraconservative politics with idealized concepts of marriage." If you didn't believe him, they implied, there was good reason to wonder what was going on underneath the surface. Coaches like McCartney rarely walked away.[9]

If his departure stirred up suspicion in the sports world, it made McCartney a hero among evangelicals. In an article written less than a month after McCartney's retirement, *Christianity Today* reported on the powerful example "Coach" McCartney set for his followers. "He took over a football program that was going nowhere and produced a national championship," wrote reporter Edward Gilbreath. "Yet . . . at the very peak of success, he realized how he was failing to fulfill his roles as a husband and father."[10] This classic evangelical formulation—successful figure realizing spiritual emptiness before turning to God—obscured how deeply the family values agenda had wormed its way into evangelical rhetoric. McCartney realized not simply that he needed to rededicate his life to God; he realized that he needed to do so by becoming a better husband and father. God called men, first and foremost, back to their families.

This call to family values saturated everything Promise Keepers published. Throughout the 1990s, scores of testimonies, devotionals, and study Bibles aimed at helping men recommit themselves to their families poured off PK printing presses. An ad for James Dobson's new book in the September 1997 issue of *New Man* told men to "build your house on a rock." Likewise, Regal Books advertised H. Norman Wright's *What Men Want* to

Promise Keepers by encouraging men to "give your wife the husband she's always wanted." Men who read PK literature or attended PK events were besieged by advertisements encouraging them to get their homes in order. McCartney had taken a bold step by leaving his six-figure job. His example became the model for PK men to follow. Christian men had to focus on their families first, even if it required extraordinary sacrifice.

PK believed recommitting to family values would revive the nation. *New Man* ran a breathless cover story in the November/December 1995 issue that compared PK to famous revivals in American history. After detailing the exploits of famous early American evangelists Jonathan Edwards, George Whitefield, and Charles Finney, writer David Halbrook suggested that a new outpouring of the spirit was on the horizon. "Critics shouldn't mistake the excitement and attendance of stadium events as surface emotionalism," he wrote. "The movement's success" and "the striking nature of Bill McCartney's founding vision are powerful evidence of 'a silent preparation by the Holy Spirit in men's hearts.'" The article concluded with a promise that the Promise Keepers would descend en masse on Washington, D.C., in 1997. The implication was obvious. A third Great Awakening was at hand.[11]

While PK was hardly the first evangelical organization to put itself in the company of Edwards, Whitefield, and Finney, its massive stadium rallies gave some credence to these boasts. McCartney's first mass gathering—later described as "unassuming"—drew 4,200 men to the Colorado basketball stadium in 1991. Three years later, over 300,000 men attended PK rallies around the country, and by 1996 that number had more than tripled to 1,000,000. The 1997 Stand in the Gap rally in Washington drew at least 800,000 men to the National Mall for a single event (PK estimated attendance at one million). In 1994 PK launched a bimonthly magazine, *New Man*, which within two years had 320,000 paid subscribers—one of the most successful launches in Christian publishing history.[12] Supporters did not have to look too hard for signs of spiritual renewal. Men attended PK events in droves and testified about how the movement had changed their lives. Their wives also praised PK's work, as the family values message resulted in renewed emotional engagement among their husbands.[13] Everyone within the movement seemed convinced that God was building a massive revival among American men.

This men's revival did not perfectly resemble the others that had preceded it. A massive revival in 1858 featured thousands of men flocking to noontime prayer services during the week. These services catered to the schedules of white-collar workers in major northern cities, and the revival cultivated a

Figure 10. Nearly one million men gathered for Promise Keepers' 1997 Stand in the Gap rally on the National Mall. Reprinted under Creative Commons 2.0 license, courtesy of Elvert Xavier Barnes Photography, https://www.flickr.com/photos/perspective/24666797/in/set-406831.

new evangelical ideal: the "Christian businessman" who showed his faith by "being diligent in business."[14] By the late nineteenth century, a growing cadre of ministers and politicians worried that the effects of the 1857–58 revival had dissipated, leaving American Christianity increasingly feminized and weak. These "muscular Christians" set about to reinvigorate the faith by linking physical activity with the spiritual life. The YMCA went on a building spurt, and the relatively new sports of football and basketball featured Christian backers who extolled the character-building aspects of physical exertion.[15] In both the businessmen's revival and muscular Christianity, Christian leaders saw spiritual deficiencies among men that needed remediation. The best remediation included a program of spiritual renewal that linked faith to the work men did outside the home. Business conducted with a Christian heart would reform a broken society; social reform undertaken by vigorous muscular Christians would reinvigorate slums in troubled cities.

Promise Keepers, on the other hand, thought the renewal of men's spiritual lives began inside the home. Tony Evans, pastor of Oak Cliff Bible

Fellowship in Dallas, penned the most-quoted passage in PK literature in his contribution to *Seven Promises of a Promise Keeper*:

> The first thing you do is sit down with your wife and say something like this: "Honey, I've made a terrible mistake. I've given you my role. I gave up leading this family, and I forced you to take my place. Now I must reclaim that role." Don't misunderstand what I'm saying here. I'm not suggesting that you ask for your role back, I'm urging you to take it back. . . . Unfortunately, there can be no compromises here. If you're going to lead, you must lead. Be sensitive. Listen. Treat the lady gently and lovingly. But lead![16]

Evans clearly understood men as leaders of the family, and he brooked no compromise that placed women and men on equal footing. Critics harped on the patriarchal instructions. But PK supporters said critics missed the point. Unlike so many other areas of American society—and unlike previous men's revivals—PK was demanding that men reengage with their families. The organization seemed to care less for men's standing in the world and more about what they did in their homes.

Appearances did not completely match reality, of course. The most high profile leaders of Promise Keepers had achieved significant success outside the home. McCartney's football fame earned him credibility in a sports-obsessed subculture, and Evans advertised himself as the man who had taken Oak Cliff Bible Fellowship from ten to nearly 10,000 members in thirty-five years. A 2004 story in PK's *New Man* magazine listed its "Men of Decade," lumping McCartney, Bill Bright, and T. D. Jakes alongside other men who had shaped world history over the previous 10 years: Bill Clinton, George W. Bush, Osama bin Laden, and Pope John Paul II. (Jesus topped the list, even though his earthly ministry did not exactly coincide with the decade in question.[17]) Part of PK's appeal depended on its celebrity leadership.

PK also reflected the continuing dominance of that nineteenth-century ideal, the Christian businessman. The organization's magazine encouraged aspiring men's ministries to "introduce systems thinking" akin to corporate growth strategies.[18] PK literature featured countless anecdotes; harried yet devoted businessmen stood at the center of many of them. While PK lionized soldiers and athletes in its monthly magazine, the organization understood white-collar workers as its central constituency. Articles and devotionals presumed a readership comprised of Christian businessmen.

Yet the organization subtly modified the Christian ideal of manhood into one that was less concerned about men's vocations and more attentive to their wives and families. The various PK guides about how men should lead their families differed. One of the first books endorsed by McCartney after PK's founding was Gary Oliver's *Real Men Have Feelings Too*. Oliver outlined a number of conflict-resolution strategies for marriages and even suggested that couples that reached an impasse should flip a coin rather than defer to the husband's desires. This strategy appeared to conflict with Evans's ideas about how men ought to "take back" leadership in their families. Yet the fuzziness with which PK defined male leadership enabled these seemingly contradictory instructions to coexist in the PK world. Some men undoubtedly heard a validation of their "headship" in the family, while others latched onto PK's call to servant leadership and focused on ways they could assist their wives. The precise notion of leadership PK advocated was unclear, as the organization endorsed competing viewpoints on what "leadership of the family" looked like. But at least one thing was clear: men had to engage with their families, emotionally and spiritually. Material provision was not enough. Men needed to attend to their wives and children.[19]

PK's notion of men's roles in the family testified to both the importance of traditional family values and the subtle flexibility of gender norms in conservative evangelicalism. Like the Christian schools evangelicals opened in the 1960s and 1970s and the political action groups they founded in the 1980s, PK promised to restore old-fashioned family values. The group's insistence on male leadership of the family underlined PK's commitment to conservative gender norms. But the literature also revealed the ways conservative evangelicals were changing with the times. A 1997 *New Man* article by Michael Maudlin asserted, "Modern feminism has Christian roots."[20] A 2003 article about Christian right mainstay James Dobson featured the family guru telling men, "If it comes right down to it, you might have to get another job" in order to fulfill your role as husband and father.[21] One can hardly imagine Phyllis Schlafly locating feminism's origins in Christianity, or Jerry Falwell telling men they needed to change jobs to be more sensitive to family needs. The cultural transformations feminism had wrought over the last third of the twentieth century encouraged PK to abandon hard-edged patriarchy and not to dismiss feminists' claims out of hand. Instead, PK told its members that there were many different ways to be a man, and that not all the changes of the last thirty years were bad.

Yet PK captivated conservative evangelicals because it seemed to stand against a sweeping tide of relativism. In this way, the organization echoed a host of earlier evangelical organizations. Just as Mel and Norma Gabler decried the progressive educational theories of John Dewey, and Anita Bryant fought against progressive impulses to normalize homosexuality, the Promise Keepers argued that liberals had mistaken eternal God-given values for outdated cultural constructs. In a *New Man* essay, right-wing talk show host Michael Medved called it the "height of insanity" to deny that "there's any significant difference between men and women."[22] For the Promise Keepers, gender mattered. Looking closely at their literature reveals ways in which the masculine ideal had shifted over time, but PK never gave up on the notion that men had a certain role to play. The organization located that role in the ways men ought to lead their wives and families—"gently" and "lovingly," in the words of Tony Evans—but firm in their conviction that God had called men to leadership.

The Promise of Racial Reconciliation

PK's insistence on a gendered hierarchy within the family stood alongside a firm and repeated commandment to pursue racial reconciliation. Here PK distanced itself from its conservative evangelical forebears. While most white evangelicals had voiced opposition to racial segregation since the late 1960s, few organizations actively pursued reconciliation. Most conservative evangelical organizations remained racially homogeneous throughout the twentieth century. The increasing proportion of white evangelicals who supported the GOP distanced themselves politically from overwhelmingly Democratic black evangelicals. Most leading civil rights organizations understood Christian schools and conservative assaults on social welfare as a new version of white supremacy, not as the benign support for "family values" white evangelicals trumpeted.

PK's insistence on white repentance for racial sins, and on the racial diversity of its membership, marked a partial departure from white evangelicals' past positions. McCartney spearheaded the push for racial reconciliation. His background in football, which certainly encouraged a focus on masculinity, also put him in contact with more African Americans than the majority of his white evangelical friends. In his contribution to *Seven Promises of a Promise Keeper*, McCartney described the experience of attending a funeral for a former Colorado player at a black church, where he heard a "level of pain [he] hadn't seen or felt before." This experience prompted him to engage with dozens of African American friends, players, and colleagues. They convinced him that white American evangelicals had perpetrated "generational sin" against African Americans. McCartney railed against the individualist mindset that kept white evangelicals from claiming responsibility for their historic racism, arguing that the Bible and other cultures offered a more robust accounting of sin that hardly seemed fair to white Americans. It did not matter, said McCartney, how much white evangelicals individually rejected racism. They still had lots to apologize for.[23]

McCartney's stance signaled a new approach for white western evangelicals. When he founded Promise Keepers in 1990, McCartney's home state, Colorado, boasted a population that was 88 percent white and 4 percent black. Unlike the Christian schools that opened a generation earlier in southern areas rife with racial tension, PK emerged in a climate where racial politics were less immediate. White westerners frequently saw themselves as free from the problems and structures they left back east. The migration of white evangelical Christians to booming areas in the American southwest, which accelerated in the 1930s, had by the 1980s given American evangelicalism a different flavor.[24]

In particular, white evangelicals in the American southwest generally ignored racial strife. Insulated in racially homogeneous suburbs, western evangelicals believed the civil rights movement was a problem elsewhere, that it had little to do with their new settlements. Some California congregations featured notable racial diversity, lending credence to the notion of "color-blind conservatism" for members of those churches. More often, western evangelicals contented themselves that their churches' racial homogeneity was the benign result of settlement patterns. Historians have shown us that mid-twentieth-century suburbanization often proceeded according to racialized policies designed to keep African Americans out of white suburbs, and few minorities experienced this process as benign.[25] But for the white evangelical Christians who brought their faith to the booming suburbs of the southwest, segregation and the civil rights movement were among the many things they thought they had left behind.

This belief fit well with the underlying promise of evangelical Christianity: believe in Jesus, and not only will your sins be forgiven, you will be made into a new creation. White western evangelicals enacted this belief as they developed "Racial Relations Sundays" featuring African American preachers and gospel choirs designed to signal the interracial unity of the body of

Christ. These annual services assuaged Sunbelt evangelicals' racial con-
sciences, even as their churches remained homogeneous. Congregations in
the growing suburbs stressed renewal, in both a spiritual and worldly sense.
Not only had they emerged victorious over sin, they had left the racial anxieties of the old South behind when they moved west. [26]

Because observers saw the political unity of white conservatives in the
Republican Party as a direct outgrowth of national Democrats' support for
civil rights, conservative evangelicals highlighted the atypical African Americans who were joining the Republican Revolution in the 1970s and 1980s.
For instance, conservative white churches frequently welcomed black
preacher E. V. Hill to their pulpits, as Hill joined his white colleagues in
stumping for Ronald Reagan during the 1980 presidential campaign. The political action group Moral Majority spotlighted the work of African American Dr. Mildred Jefferson, who penned vitriolic articles against abortion. The
first black woman to graduate from Harvard Medical School, Jefferson became a conservative celebrity in the 1970s, when she ascended to the presidency of the National Right to Life Committee and launched a pro-life
political action committee. Prominent African Americans like Hill and Jefferson signaled the racial inclusivity the Christian right promoted.

Yet the overwhelming racial homogeneity of the movement was impossible to deny. Hopes for a "colorblind conservatism" belied the reality of white
dominance of both the leadership and the rank-and-file. While groups like
Moral Majority spotlighted prominent black supporters in their periodicals,
there was virtually no attention paid to racial oppression. The civil rights
movement existed as an analogue for the pro-life movement, which drew on
civil rights rhetoric to claim "equal rights" for fetuses and encouraged nonviolent action to protest legalized abortion. But leaders of the religious right
kept their distance from the civil rights movement's calls for systemic reform
to economic and housing policies that favored whites. Having distanced
themselves geographically from the region most commonly associated with
slavery and segregation, conservative white evangelicals in the West could
not see how far they were from a truly colorblind conservatism.

Emerging as he did from that milieu, McCartney was an unlikely champion of racial repentance. The reasons behind his commitment stemmed
both from his personal background and from the ways a family values agenda
had reshaped American evangelicalism. The culture of college football allowed McCartney to observe the racial divide and also to see it break down.
In 1994 he wrote about observing his players while they watched a prizefight

between an African American boxer, Pernell Whitaker, and a Latino, Julio César Chávez. The black players universally pulled for Whitaker; the white players were evenly divided. Although almost every observer thought Whitaker had won the fight, Chávez managed to preserve his undefeated record with a highly controversial split decision among the judges. The Whitaker camp felt disrespected, and McCartney half expected his black players to erupt in protest. Instead, they filed out of the room quietly, seemingly resigned to yet another injustice. The experience convinced McCartney that white society had taught African Americans to expect persecution.[27]

McCartney forged deep and complicated relationships with many of his nonwhite players, most notably the two who fathered his grandchildren: Sal Aunese and Shannon Clavelle. Aunese, a Samoan from San Diego, arrived in Boulder in 1987 and led Colorado's ascent to national prominence, quarterbacking successful seasons in 1987 and 1988. Between the two seasons, he began a relationship with McCartney's nineteen-year-old daughter, Kristy. After a Colorado win in the fall of 1988, Kristy told her parents the shocking news: she was going to have a baby, and her dad's star quarterback was the father. McCartney and his wife Lyndi handled the situation with equanimity, even after Aunese advised Kristy to get an abortion and told the coach he had no intentions of marrying the mother of his child. Aunese even asked for a blood test to establish paternity. The story took a turn from the salacious to the tragic when Aunese was diagnosed with terminal cancer in spring 1989. He would never take another snap for Colorado, and died in the midst of the Buffalos' undefeated 1989 regular season. The team dedicated the season to Aunese's memory. McCartney publicly acknowledged Aunese as the father of his grandson at the funeral in September.

Four years later, Kristy again developed a relationship with one of her father's players, African American defensive end Shannon Clavelle. The McCartneys disapproved. "I had been dating Shannon for a while, which they didn't like," Kristy told *Sports Illustrated*, "but I was a grown woman, 24 years old. They couldn't tell me what to do. When I did tell them I was pregnant, they were hurt and upset, but completely supportive."[28] During this pregnancy, Kristy left Boulder to escape the tabloid glare, and McCartney did some soul searching. Clavelle enjoyed considerable success on the field, making it to the NFL after leaving Colorado. But he found trouble off the field, including an assault charge in December 1994. (Aunese also served time for misdemeanor assault, in 1988.) McCartney's ambition led him to recruit star players with marginal academic records and occasional legal issues, and the intensity of his job kept him away from his family. He admitted to reporters he neglected his own children and spent all his time "with someone else's kids."[29] When his daughter had babies with two of these kids—two that family man McCartney would hardly have chosen as suitable partners for her—McCartney was left to wonder how much he had sacrificed on the altar of football success.

McCartney's fraught relationships with Aunese and Clavelle left him convinced of a couple core principles. First, family values could not be a convenient slogan; Christian men had to contend with the messy realities of everyday life. By all accounts, McCartney supported his daughter emotionally and financially during and after both pregnancies. Perhaps he was doing penance for years of (self-admitted) neglect of his family. But by the mid-1990s McCartney understood commitment to his family as the ultimate requirement of his Christian life. Second, McCartney insisted on the centrality of racial reconciliation to the gospel. It is impossible to gauge the effects of Kristy's interracial relationships on this conviction, as McCartney rarely spoke about them. He did acknowledge that the hundreds of recruiting visits he made to African American players' homes, along with thousands of hours with black players on practice fields and in locker rooms, opened his eyes to the realities of racial injustice. More than most white evangelicals, McCartney spoke about the ways white Americans had perpetuated oppression and inequality. This insistence on white guilt emerged at least in part from McCartney's complicated history with his nonwhite players.

More broadly, McCartney's focus on racial reconciliation emerged from white evangelicals' increasing sensitivity to the ways racial discrimination had poisoned their relationships with African Americans. Both PK leaders like McCartney and the men who attended PK events agreed that Christians needed to pursue racial reconciliation. They understood white Christians as the group responsible for racial oppression, though they commonly identified Satan as the root cause of racism. As McCartney put it, "racism is Satan's stronghold . . . one of his best tools for breeding hatred and undermining the church."[30] This spiritual diagnosis of racism's origins called for a spiritual response: prayer, fasting, and worship. PK leaders insisted that governmental and social programs could not eliminate racism. But they also recognized it as a sin plaguing the church. PK was a new model of western evangelicalism, one that saw through the fiction of a "colorblind conservatism" and understood racial reconciliation as an essential task.[31]

Even so, observers who attended regular PK events in the 1990s reported that race was rarely the main topic of conversation. Ethicist L. Dean Allen joined a PK small group in the mid-1990s. After reading the organization's foundational text, *Seven Promises of a Promise Keeper*, Allen expected an overwhelming focus on racial reconciliation at his group's meetings. But he heard very little about race, and none of the men in his small group said they had joined PK because of its focus on reconciliation. Puzzled, Allen pressed farther. Eventually he discovered most men in the group understood racism as an essential problem. A couple of Promise Keepers told him the leadership had "really gone overboard on reconciliation," but most members believed "they should work to overcome racism because God calls them to the task."[32] Though they felt uneasy talking about race, most Promise Keepers understood they had to deal with it.

When the organization did sponsor events to address racial issues, sports provided a means for overcoming the racial divide. Just as coaching football had connected McCartney to African Americans, the cultural residue of popular sports helped white and black Promise Keepers find common ground. At a 1996 "racial reconciliation breakfast" in Chicago, mixed-race groups of men eyed each other self-consciously before a white attendee broke the silence by saying, "You gotta like those Bulls." This icebreaker dispelled the initial awkwardness and led the men into a robust conversation about sports, family, and job-related issues. One observer noted, "sports appeared to be of more common interest than shared religious beliefs."[33] This focus on sports as a means to bridge the racial divide characterized a number of PK events and publications in the mid-1990s.

Sports also provided a multiracial cast of Christian celebrities that PK could promote. According to *New Man* magazine, the 1997 Super Bowl-winning Packers "had enough born-again bodies to form a church-league flag football team." Similarly, the 1996 World Series champions' "undeniable faith element" made them "Redeemed Yankees" rather than the damned ones of seasons past.[34] These celebrity Christians undoubtedly impressed many rank-and-file members of PK. Their on-field successes exemplified masculine vigor. But as the magazine presented them, Christian athletes faced the same struggles as every man. Testimonials talked of struggles with temptation and of idolizing success. If Christian athletes featured prominently in PK literature for their extraordinary on-field achievements, the organization did its best to present these men's off-field lives as ordinary.

The mark of a dedicated Christian man—athlete or otherwise—remained the same: demonstrable devotion to God and family. NASCAR driver Jeff

Gordon talked of praying with his wife daily. NBA star David Robinson donated millions to a childhood education center.[35] Nearly all PK's athlete stars were married, and most asserted that their sports successes took a backseat to their family life. This formulation seems almost trite today, when nearly every prominent man who retires from public life asserts his need "to spend more time with my family." But that phrase's wide usage is of recent vintage.[36] PK played a role in the acceleration of its popularity. Again, McCartney's retirement provided the example. "The essence of many a Promise Keeper's experience can be found in McCartney's own story of how he allowed work to come between him and his family," declared *Christianity Today*. "Yet, in the midst of all the fanfare, at the very peak of success, he realized how he was failing to fulfill his roles as a husband and father—and chose to do something about it."[37]

If sports stars trotted out the family values formulations that had become de rigueur in evangelicalism by the late 1990s, they also provided something new: racial diversity. A 1998 magazine spread on eight Christian athletes featured four white Americans, two African Americans, an Asian American, and a Latino.[38] By the late 1990s, American sports culture was thoroughly integrated. By reaching into that culture, PK could use evangelical athletes as an example of the racial diversity the organization prized. When *New Man* ran an article endorsing interracial marriage, it began with the story of African American Bobby Meacham, a former New York Yankees shortstop married to a white woman.[39] Evangelicalism gave athletes a common language in which to describe their faith. Athletes gave PK a racially diverse cast of Christian heroes.

Moreover, the stadium rallies that became the hallmark of PK linked the organization to this desegregated sports culture. At rallies, McCartney and other PK leaders called on white evangelicals to beg for repentance and demanded that believers of all races circle together and pray for one another. Racial reconciliation seemed more possible in these settings, where believers gathered for hours or days of intense spiritual experiences. United in a struggle, a multiracial cast fought for victory over "the enemy." The analogue to team sports was obvious, especially since many of these rallies took place in the same stadiums where Promise Keepers watched their favorite Christian athletes play. One reporter described rally attendees spending two days "high fiving Jesus in a football stadium."[40] Another observer linked PK stadium events to massive pep rallies, calling the stadiums in which both took place "powerful environmental determinant[s]."[41] Singing, praying, and confessing to men of other races in these intense moments convinced some participants that the movement was on its way to abolishing racial division. McCartney hoped that 1 January 2000, would "mark the end of racism inside the church of Jesus Christ."[42]

Not surprisingly, PK's reach exceeded its grasp. Although the organization's leadership displayed notable diversity—in 1997 30 percent of PK's 437 employees were minorities—the high water mark of diversity among participants came at the 1996 New York rally, where 25 percent of attendees were black. Rallies in the South featured disappointing racial homogeneity: a Memphis event in 1997 attracted a negligible number of minorities, in a city where minorities constituted a majority of the population.[43] By 1997 it had become apparent to McCartney and other leaders that PK would have to take more drastic measures if the organization wanted to diversify its following.

At a June 1997 PK board meeting, McCartney encouraged the board to eliminate fees for the stadium rallies that had become the organization's calling card. Men paid $60 to attend the two-day rallies. Those fees made up 72 percent of the PK annual budget, which had grown to $117 million by 1997. Though the board included several businessmen who expressed concern about wiping out the main revenue stream entirely, no board member seriously challenged McCartney's plan. According to first-person accounts, McCartney convinced the board that the attendance fee for stadium rallies stood in the way of attracting non-Christians and, especially, minorities.[44] The board ratified his proposal. At Stand in the Gap in October, McCartney announced, "Next year, we're going to have 18 stadium events and 19 arena events, and these events are going to change because there's going to be no admission, no charge. We want you to bring the lost! We want you to bring the lukewarm! God is going to show up."[45]

Yet without the admission fees, Promise Keepers could not meet payroll. The organization laid off its entire 345-person workforce on 31 March 1998, following McCartney's 1997 pledge that PK would become all volunteer if any layoffs were required. Though donations had increased by nearly 150 percent—from $8.6 million in 1996 to over $20 million in 1997—the loss of attendance fee revenue nearly bankrupted PK. The organization hoped the layoffs would be temporary, as leadership sought increased donations to stabilize finances. But as time passed, it became clear it had to undergo reluctant transformation. By the turn of the century, PK continued to rely overwhelmingly on volunteer staff. Gone were the radio spots and most of the stadium rallies. *New Man* continued publication, but in a smaller size. PK would never again attain the nine-digit annual budget or attendance numbers of the mid-1990s.

More to the point, the elimination of attendance fees never produced the diversification McCartney desired. Studies consistently reported that over 85 percent of Promise Keepers were white, before and after the 1997 decision. Most rally attendees came from white nondenominational churches, the Southern Baptist Convention, and the Assemblies of God. Over 90 percent were married.[46] The organization clearly responded to a felt need among this faction of American evangelicals, a need that included a desire to atone for the racial sins of generations past. Yet PK's leadership was unable to translate that desire into a racially diverse following.

Battles over worship styles, politics, history, and memory have divided white and black Christians for centuries. PK did not escape those battles entirely. But its leadership—particularly McCartney—partially did away with the "clean slate" language of evangelicalism that could alienate black Christians. McCartney insisted that white Christians, even those who felt themselves free of racism, still had a lot to apologize for. "Even if you have a clear conscience before God with regard to racism," he wrote, "there is a biblical principle that says we bear some responsibility for the unrepented sins of our forefathers."[47] This was a new message for many white evangelicals, who flocked to PK in hopes of becoming better men. Part of that task, according to PK leaders, involved repenting for the racial sins of generations past.

Yet because PK leadership insisted on the "spiritual" nature of racism—and on a supposedly apolitical message—the organization never made much headway in addressing oppressive racial structures. In 1997 one PK leader admitted that while he had "labored for racial reconciliation" since 1980, he had "come to a standstill" in those efforts.[48] The same could be said for PK as a whole. After 1997, a scaled-down Promise Keepers organization focused on the white evangelicals that made up a majority of supporters. New Man published fewer articles about reconciliation, and more about niche ministries—such as those for hard-core adventure junkies and Confederate re-enactors—that appealed mainly to white evangelicals.[49] McCartney's passion for reconciliation never translated into political solidarity with African American Christians. The promise of racial reconciliation remained elusive, even if PK went further than most ministries in pursuing it.

Model Men

While Promise Keepers won only limited success at racial reconciliation, it codified evangelical masculinity for the family values movement. The movement began by fighting for children and won its greatest political successes by advocating a particular view of women as mothers. But until PK came along, what it meant to be a Christian man eluded precise definition. If conservative evangelicals had defined motherhood as a way of resisting feminism, PK reflected a type of Christian response about manhood in a post-feminist world. Just as Robert Bly's seminal book *Iron John* encapsulated for the secular market the malaise modern men felt, Promise Keepers offered a religious space where, as they put it, men could be men.

By "men being men," PK meant that men needed "a battle to fight, an adventure to live, and a beauty to win." The formulation came from John Eldredge, a late convert to Christianity who articulated this vision of masculinity in bestselling books like *The Sacred Romance* and *Wild at Heart*. Eldredge's tripartite understanding of masculinity illustrated both what evangelicals took for granted—heterosexuality and males' propensity to fight—and what they thought the church lacked: adventure. According Eldredge, viewers found meaning in movies like *Braveheart, Gladiator*, and *The Matrix* because the films showed men who had found their adventure by rebelling against their prescribed roles. "Why do you think we love these movies so much?" he asked. "That's *Christ* there. It's our salvation story. It's built into us!"[50]

Eldredge—and, by extension, Promise Keepers—suggested that the church no longer catered to men's hardwired needs. "The church has overemphasized the feminine virtues," said one supporter. "Hey, I need to cry. But I also need to roar. There's no place for me to roar in church."[51] Men, in this understanding, had needs the contemporary American church made no attempt to fill. One might think that preaching this message and maintaining harmonious ties with local churches required a delicate approach, but Eldredge contended churches welcomed his "Wild at Heart" ministry events. "They love it," said Eldredge, who pointed to a 1,000-person waiting list for his seminars.[52] Although some churches worried that PK promoted suspicion of traditional denominations, the churches that sent men to PK rallies and Eldredge seminars appeared wildly supportive.[53]

Evangelical churches supported Eldredge's work because he articulated the last remaining piece of the family values puzzle. Where school battles had rallied support for parental rights, and fights against abortion and feminism had crystallized a powerful rhetoric of motherhood, PK and related men's ministries articulated a vision of manhood that worked within the larger family values movement. Even as leaders like Eldredge encouraged men to follow their adventurous hearts, he reminded them that their "beauty" at home deserved every ounce of their masculine energy. Men, said Eldredge, "wimp out" by failing to "rescue their wives by not offering them their strength, their protection, their words."[54] The adventures Eldredge advocated did not require sacrificing family to follow one's heart. Quite the opposite: he challenged men to find their adventure in the context of the family.

PK's unusual trajectory—from amazing growth to precipitous decline—makes it tempting to view the organization as something of a blip. It clearly benefited from the particular conditions that had come to characterize conservative white evangelicalism in the 1990s. The message that men needed to tend to their roles as leaders of the family had immediate resonance, not because such a message was self-evident, but because white evangelicals had engaged in a fight for family values for decades. As GOP politicians had leveraged abortion and gay rights to win the overwhelming support of white evangelicals, the men who showed up to Promise Keepers were at some level already committed to the main messages of the ministry. McCartney and other leaders voiced maxims many white evangelical men already believed.

The swift decline of PK, however, deserves further analysis. The organization's budget shrank rapidly following the 1997 decision to eliminate stadium fees, and by 2000 nearly all the giant stadium rallies had disappeared. Where 1.2 million men had crowded into rallies in 1997, only 180,000 attended in 2003.[55] The organization spun this decline as a new era of Promise Keepers, focused more on small discipleship groups and partnering with local ministries and churches. That message had some basis in reality, as PK continued to preach its message of masculine renewal in less flashy venues. A host of men's ministries had sprung up in the wake of PK.[56] Yet the organization's halcyon days of rallies aired live on C-SPAN had come and gone. PK would never again attain the celebrity it enjoyed in the mid-1990s.

While a decision to continue charging attendance fees might have prolonged PK's stay in the spotlight, a shifting political consensus had made the organization somewhat superfluous by the late 1990s. If the organization's growth took place against the political backdrop of an ascendant Democratic president whose family values were frequently suspect, its decline coincided with the ascent of Republican George W. Bush, who would have felt right at home in a Promise Keepers rally. The former owner of baseball's Texas Rangers, Bush used sports metaphors frequently. He talked about his faith in classically evangelical ways: a former alcoholic, he found salvation by giving up drinking and turning his life over to God. In 2003 *New Man* ran a glowing profile of "W" replete with flags, cowboy hats, and comparisons to George Washington. The magazine praised Bush's honoring of the civil rights movement while on a trip to Africa and spoke of his wise approach to following the example of "heroes." Bush's main sins, according to PK, were undisclosed sexual trysts during his drinking days, which he had long since repented and repudiated. His daughters' embarrassing drunken escapades won some mention, as well, but only as an example of how even the most devoted family man could not keep his children under control. The magazine suggested Bush's policies emerged from a combination of healthy impulsiveness and searching prayer, and these policies went unquestioned by *New Man*. The PK version of Bush was as evangelical everyman.[57]

With a man like that ensconced in the White House, Promise Keepers could not sustain the sense of marginalization that gave the organization traction in its early years. To be sure, the loss of revenue was the single most important factor in the decline of PK. Yet Bush's election underlined the pervasiveness of family values in American society. Clinton's charisma carried enough power to win two elections, but as a Democrat married to an outspoken feminist, he fought against the currents of American society in the 1990s. More and more Americans identified as evangelicals, and most of them believed family values supplied personal integrity and would promote national cohesiveness.[58] At the 2000 Democratic National Convention, Al Gore tried to convince voters of his commitment to the family by indulging in a passionate kiss with his wife, Tipper. But on the family values front, he still suffered in comparison to Bush, who eschewed passionate kisses for a mantle of "compassionate conservatism" that fit perfectly with the messages PK had been preaching for a decade.

Like the fires of other revivals, PK's massive stadium rallies burned out. But they burned out in part because the fuel of cultural oppression had become hard to find, especially in the cultures where most white evangelicals lived. What PK had labored to promote—family came first, white Christians needed to repent of past racial sins, and men desired adventure—seemed commonplace in the era of George W. Bush. In 2008, the election of a mixed-race Democrat whose family values seemed beyond reproach caused some consternation in the world of conservative evangelicalism. But even Barack

Obama knew better than to challenge the prominence of family values. "America," said the future president in 2008, "is a country of strong families and strong values."[59] While Obama wanted to change the meaning of family values—to allow for new types of families and to promote different sorts of pro-family policies—his own family had to hew closely to the family values ideal that evangelicals had carved out over several decades. If Obama's election signaled a new era in American politics, he nonetheless revealed the ways that American political life would be grappling with the meaning of family values for years to come.

Epilogue

By touting his commitment to family values, Barack Obama exemplified the potency of the phrase in political rhetoric. Since the 1970s, conservative and liberal politicians had fought one another over who had the right to identify as pro-family. This book has focused on the period during the 1970s, 1980s, and 1990s, when conservative evangelicals won the battle to define family values. But Obama's use of it suggests that battle lines are being redrawn in the new millennium. As Republican congressmen and evangelical preachers proved that their pro-family rhetoric did not always match reality, they watched a Democratic president burnish his image as a family man even as he expressed support for gay marriage and abortion rights.

Indeed, one of the evergreen stories of Republican politics in the new millennium involved the inability of family values crusaders to live up to their ideals. In 2009, affairs took down two Republicans associated with an evangelical-owned house in Washington, D.C.: South Carolina Governor Mark Sanford—who disappeared for six days while pursuing an affair with an Argentinian journalist—and Nevada Senator John Ensign, who had a more typical fling with a female staffer. Indiana Representative Mark Souder, a Republican and family values advocate, resigned in 2010 amid rumors of an extramarital affair. Most infamously, pro-family Idaho senator Larry Craig was charged for lewd conduct when he allegedly solicited sex from a police officer in a Minneapolis airport men's room.

Republican politicians were not the only culprits. Conservative evangelical leaders have created scandals of their own. Colorado preacher Ted Haggard, who also served as president of the National Association of Evangelicals, admitted to soliciting a male prostitute in 2006. Homeschooling advocate Doug Phillips, who distributed gendered homeschooling curricula and touted his own family as a model for the type of family values he promoted, admitted to an affair with a staffer in October 2013. Bill Gothard, whose "Institute in Basic Life Principles" seminar spelled out family values to thousands of evangelicals, stood accused of sexual harassment by at least 34 women in February 2014.

Each of these stories has produced a field day for critics who see the family values movement as a farce. The men at the top have proved unable to live up to their stated ideals, and the political and theological messages they espoused encouraged cover-ups that only made the stories worse. As conservative evangelicals have become more integral to the Republican Party, they have made fidelity to family values essential for political success. Even as family values became more and more central to political messaging, it seemed as if hardly a month went by without the latest story of Republican or evangelical infidelity. To be sure, the advent of the twenty-four-hour news cycle and unregulated online gossip has inundated Americans with stories that never made the front page in years past. And pro-family politicians are not the only ones committing these particular sins. But the family values movement's capture of the Republican Party made its proponents' sexual scandals not just salacious but hypocritical as well.

The plethora of sexual scandals begged the question: had the family values movement gone too far? Ted Haggard certainly thought so; he attributed his scandal to childhood trauma and chastised evangelical leaders who disdained therapy as psychobabble. "It is much more convenient [for evangelicals] to believe that every thought, word, and action is a reflection of our character, our spirituality, and our core," said Haggard. "Everyone is either completely good or bad."[1] Haggard thought otherwise. In his quest for redemption, he had good reason to see the world in shades of gray. But Haggard's embrace of psychotherapy marked a different posture for a high profile evangelical leader. Haggard encouraged evangelicals to nuance their understanding of human behavior and practice empathy rather than judgment.

Meanwhile, at Haggard's former New Life Church, a new model of ministry emerged. Pastor Brady Boyd, recruited to New Life during the height of the Haggard scandal in 2006, encouraged pastoral associates to seek more robust theological training. Whereas evangelical megachurches typically kept training "in house," the new New Life model was to send ministry candidates to academic (if still solidly evangelical) seminaries. As they discovered voices from outside American evangelicalism, some of these younger evangelical pastors saw the late twentieth-century fixation on family values as a mistake. They revamped worship services, eschewing flashy lights for ancient liturgies. The church leadership adopted the fourth-century Nicene Creed as its statement of faith. Watchwords like "hospitality" and "service" edged out old warhorses like "morality."[2]

By the 2010s, a growing group of young evangelicals were questioning their parents' fixation on family values. Reared in a culture that spotlighted sexual propriety as the litmus test for faithful living, some of these younger evangelicals reacted with disgust at the hypocrisy they saw in pro-family politics. In the minds of these young evangelicals, the Bible—still the central authority in evangelical faith—spoke with a far clearer voice on issues of poverty, justice, and care for creation than it did on issues of sexual morality. These young evangelicals launched social justice campaigns that reflected these biblical teachings, few of which fell under the rubric of family values.[3] One went so far as to call the marriage between evangelicalism and the Republican Party "a match made in hell."[4]

But the marriage persisted. Even as journalists heralded their discovery of an evangelical left during the second term of the George W. Bush administration, evangelicals proved reliably Republican at the polls. In 2008 white evangelicals broke heavily for John McCain over Obama; over 80 percent of white evangelicals who attended church weekly voted for the GOP candidate.[5] Surveys reported that although "centrist" evangelicals have soured somewhat on the GOP, conservative and "populist" evangelicals have become even more Republican since 2008. Conservatism has remained central to the movement. Members of the evangelical left have proved far more willing to identify as Democrats (57 percent) than as liberals (22 percent).[6] Poll numbers and survey data tell limited stories, but these figures suggest that white American evangelicals remained decidedly conservative in the early years of the new millennium.

That conservatism should not surprise us, since evangelicalism has always prioritized holding onto the central truths of the faith. Throughout evangelical history, preachers have adopted modern means for spreading the gospel even as they claim to preach an old-time religion. What those preachers have defined as "old-time religion" has changed over time. Late twentieth-century evangelicals discovered a bygone America that had favored family values. By making family values the hallmark of Christian life, these evangelicals established norms that have proved remarkably resilient. Even liberal evangelicals have been reluctant to challenge the primacy of the family. Who wants to be against family values?

The U.S. political alignment has played a role in the perseverance of family values, as well. The Democratic Party's unabashed support of abortion rights—a posture the party hardened in the 1980s—has stopped many evangelicals from leaving the GOP. Pro-life politics comprises the majority of evangelical grassroots activism, and evangelicals inclined toward liberal positions on other issues have not abandoned their opposition to abortion. Furthermore, the political realignment of the white South after the civil rights movement consolidated conservative Protestants in the Republican Party, enabling national coalition-building and fundraising efforts. Conservative evangelicals and politicians built massive networks and institutions dedicated to preserving family values and electing Republican candidates. Even if their messages have grown a bit stale, institutions like Focus on the Family and the Family Research Council have retained large mailing lists and donor rolls. Institutional inertia remains a potent force.

Just as important, family values spoke to evangelicals on issues they held dear. Evangelicals could never compromise on the idea that a loving God had ordered society. The family values agenda articulated a clear statement of that order, laying out lines of authority and expectations for fathers, mothers, and children. In a world that seemed to be shifting beneath their feet, evangelicals found in family values firm ground. It anchored them to a God who created them "male and female." It stabilized authority in a society beset by political crises, crime, war, and sexual revolution. It provided a diagnosis and prognosis for the nation's ills. If we could just return to family values, said the movement's advocates, perhaps we could restore American greatness.

Although Obama's ad showed that a mixed-race Democrat could claim family values, too, his message retained some elements of the agenda described in this book. The ad mentioned Obama's single mother, but it also echoed themes of hard work and heartland morality. He underlined the pervasiveness of family values rhetoric—rhetoric conservative white evangelicals defined in the three decades following the 1960s. Liberals have adopted the language of family values and attempted to redefine it, with mixed results. Since 2008, a number of states have legalized gay marriage. Pop culture increasingly reflects and sanctions the diversity of American family life. But the image of a golden past where fathers, mothers, and children understood their roles and undergirded American prosperity has retained its potency for evangelicals—and for broad swaths of the American electorate. That this golden past was imaginary—"the way we never were," in the words of Stephanie Coontz—made it no less powerful.

Understandings of Christianity and American national character have made this imaginary past central to the present. Evangelicals understood family values as biblical, and they sold them as patriotic. This combination of Christian teaching and conservative politics coalesced in a post-1960s context in which Americans were searching for new ways of ordering society. It spoke to evangelicals' sense that gender mattered, and it reassured conservatives that God had a plan for society. The family values vision these conservative evangelicals defined emerged in the relatively recent past; it drew on Victorian gender norms and industrial era work patterns that circumscribed family life. Yet the family values of late twentieth-century evangelicals seemed timeless. They looked back to a past where God's rules set the agenda for men, women, and children. They created a present where family values dominated political debates and defined the boundaries of Christian life.

NOTES

Introduction

1. James Risen, "Christian Men Hold Huge Rally on D.C. Mall," *Los Angeles Times*, 5 October 1997, A1.

2. Ezekiel 22:30 (KJV). I use the King James Version of the Bible because of its dominance in American culture during the time period of this book (especially among conservative evangelicals and fundamentalists). See Philip Goff, Arthur E. Farnsley, II, and Peter J. Thuesen, "The Bible in American Life," Report for Center for the Study of Religion and American Culture, Indiana University-Purdue University at Indianapolis, 6 March 2014.

3. National Organization for Women, "To Mark Women's Equality Day: Feminists Launch National 'No Surrender' Campaign to Counter Upcoming Promise Keepers' March," 2 August 1997, http://www.now.org.

4. Joe Conason, Alfred Ross, and Lee Cokorinos, "The Promise Keepers Are Coming: The Third Wave of the Religious Right," *The Nation*, 7 October 1996, 11.

5. Ken Abraham, "Ready to Stand in the Gap," *New Man*, October 1997, 29.

6. Bill McCartney, "This Is America's Last Chance," *New Man*, October 1997, 35.

7. Billy Graham Press Conference, 13 August 1963, Los Angeles, Collection 24, box 4, folder 11, Billy Graham Center Archives, Wheaton College, Wheaton, Ill.

8. Oral Memoirs of Morris Chapman, 1998, Texas Collection, Baylor University.

9. On this point, see J. Brooks Flippen, *Jimmy Carter, the Politics of Family, and the Rise of the Christian Right* (Athens: University of Georgia Press, 2011); Robert O. Self, *All in the Family: The Realignment of American Democracy Since the 1960s* (New York: Hill and Wang, 2012).

10. Daniel K. Williams, *God's Own Party: The Making of the Christian Right* (New York: Oxford University Press, 2010), 14.

11. Elaine Tyler May, *Homeward Bound: American Families in the Cold War Era* (New York: Basic, 1988), xvii–xxvi.

12. Ibid., 119–20.

13. Ibid., 133–35.

14. Kevin Michael Kruse, *White Flight: Atlanta and the Making of Modern Conservatism* (Princeton, N.J.: Princeton University Press, 2005), 3–5 and passim; Matthew D. Lassiter, *The Silent Majority: Suburban Politics in the Sunbelt South* (Princeton, N.J.: Princeton University Press, 2006).

15. Harold Lindsell, "Calling the Nation to Christ," Address to National Religious Broadcasters, 28 January 1974, Collection 8, box 24, folder 15, Billy Graham Center Archives.

16. Daniel Patrick Moynihan, *The Negro Family: The Case for National Action* (Office of Policy Planning and Research, U.S. Department of Labor, March 1965); Self, *All in the Family*, 26–36.

17. Jerry Falwell, "Ministers and Marches," Sermon delivered at Thomas Road Baptist Church, Lynchburg, Va., March 15, 1965, Liberty University Archive.

18. Peter A. Stevenson, "Why Christian Education Today?" *Christian School Guide*, November 1968, 3.

19. Rick Perlstein, *Nixonland: The Rise of a President and the Fracturing of America* (New York: Scribner, 2008), 328–45 and passim; Steven P. Miller, *Billy Graham and the Rise of the Republican South* (Philadelphia: University of Pennsylvania Press, 2009), 64–88.

20. "Kazakhstan to Observe Family Day First Time on September 8," *Tengri News*, 6 September 2013.

21. Stephanie Coontz, *The Way We Never Were: American Families and the Nostalgia Trap* (New York: Basic, 1992), 8–14.

22. Self, *All in the Family*, 3–11 and passim.

23. Bethany Moreton, *To Serve God and Wal-Mart: The Making of Christian Free Enterprise* (Cambridge, Mass.: Harvard University Press, 2009), 100–124; Deborah Gray White, "What Women Want: The Paradoxes of Postmodernity as Seen Through Promise Keeper and Million Man March Women," in *Interconnections: Gender and Race in American History*, ed. Carol Faulkner and Alison M. Parker (Rochester, N.Y.: University of Rochester Press, 2012), 229–59.

24. Michelle M. Nickerson, *Mothers of Conservatism: Women and the Postwar Right* (Princeton, N.J.: Princeton University Press, 2012), 69–135.

25. The phrase comes from the title of Lisa McGirr's pathbreaking study, *Suburban Warriors: The Origins of the New American Right* (Princeton, N.J.: Princeton University Press, 2001).

26. On this point, see Self, *All in the Family*, 3–14.

27. Frances FitzGerald, "A Disciplined, Charging Army," *New Yorker*, 18 May 1981.

28. On the relative weakness of theological defenses of segregation, especially by the mid-1960s, see David L. Chappell, *A Stone of Hope: Prophetic Religion and the Death of Jim Crow* (Chapel Hill: University of North Carolina Press, 2004), 105–78. On the shift of evangelicals from theological defense of racism to theological defense of patriarchy, see Paul Harvey, *Freedom's Coming: Religious Culture and the Shaping of the South from the Civil War Through the Civil Rights Era* (Chapel Hill: University of North Carolina Press, 2005), 218–50.

29. Jerry Falwell, *Listen, America!* (Garden City, N.Y.: Doubleday, 1980), 106.

30. Grant Wacker, "Searching for Norman Rockwell: Popular Evangelicalism in Contemporary America," in *The Evangelical Tradition in America*, ed. Leonard I. Sweet (Macon, Ga.: Mercer University Press, 1984), 289–315.

31. See, for instance, Richard Hofstadter, *Anti-Intellectualism in American Life* (New York: Vintage, 1962).

32. Michael Lienesch, *In the Beginning: Fundamentalism, the Scopes Trial, and the Making of the Antievolution Movement* (Chapel Hill: University of North Carolina Press, 2007), 171–97.

33. The strongest articulation of this point is Daniel K. Williams, *God's Own Party: The Making of the Christian Right* (New York: Oxford University Press, 2010), 1–9. See also Darren Dochuk, *From Bible Belt to Sunbelt: Plain-Folk Religion, Grassroots Politics, and the Rise of Evangelical Conservatism* (New York: Norton, 2011), 326–96; William C. Martin, *With God on Our Side: The Rise of the Religious Right in America* (New York: Broadway Books, 1996), 17–46; Matthew Avery Sutton, *American Apocalypse: A History of Modern Evangelicalism* (Cambridge, Mass.: Belknap Press of Harvard University Press, 2014).

34. Herschel H. Hobbs and E. Y. Mullins, *The Axioms of Religion*, rev. ed. (Nashville, Tenn.: Broadman, 1978), 75, 76.

35. This brief survey of competing theological impulses within evangelicalism begs the question: why use the term at all? Indeed, scholars such as D. G. Hart and Donald W. Dayton have called for a moratorium on its use, arguing that the category evangelicalism obscures more than it illuminates. But most other scholars continue to use the term, noting its ubiquity in popular discourse and its dominance as a means of self-identification for conservative Protestants. In his study of evangelist Billy Graham, historian Steven Miller made a persuasive case for using the term

evangelical: "Evangelicalism was an avowed, internalized identity for many of the subjects considered here—including, of course, for Graham." That internalization of evangelical identity means that scholars who avoid the term do so at the risk of obscuring their subjects' self-understanding. I follow those scholars who use the term out of fidelity to evangelicals' own rhetoric, understanding and noting where that rhetoric masked important regional, theological, and denominational differences. Donald W. Dayton, "Some Doubts About the Usefulness of the Category 'Evangelical,'" in *The Variety of American Evangelicalism*, ed. Donald W. Dayton and Robert K. Johnston (Knoxville: University of Tennessee Press, 2001), 245–51; Miller, *Billy Graham and the Rise of the Republican South*, 8; D. G. Hart, *Deconstructing Evangelicalism: Conservative Protestantism in the Age of Billy Graham* (Grand Rapids, Mich.: Baker, 2004).

36. I borrow this term from Peter Goodwin Heltzel, *Jesus and Justice: Evangelicals, Race, and American Politics* (New Haven, Conn.: Yale University Press, 2009), 7–8. On the shifting landscape of American Christianity, see Robert Wuthnow, *The Restructuring of American Religion: Society and Faith Since World War II* (Princeton, N.J.: Princeton University Press, 1988).

37. See the full text at "Chicago Declaration of Evangelical Social Concern," 25 November 1973, www.evangelicalsforsocialaction.org. Good examinations of the Chicago Declaration (and progressive evangelical politics) include Brantley W. Gasaway, *Progressive Evangelicals and the Pursuit of Social Justice* (Chapel Hill: University of North Carolina Press), 47–52; David R. Swartz, *Moral Minority: The Evangelical Left in an Age of Conservatism* (Philadelphia: University of Pennsylvania Press, 2012), 170–84.

38. See, for instance, Heltzel, *Jesus and Justice*; Charles F. Irons, *The Origins of Proslavery Christianity: White and Black Evangelicals in Colonial and Antebellum Virginia* (Chapel Hill: University of North Carolina Press, 2008); Donald G. Mathews, *Religion in the Old South* (Chicago: University of Chicago Press, 1977).

39. Dochuk, *From Bible Belt to Sunbelt*, 285–91.

40. Furthermore, the Christian right self-consciously appropriated rhetoric and strategies from the civil rights movement. See David John Marley, "Riding in the Back of the Bus: The Christian Right's Adoption of Civil Rights Movement Rhetoric," in *The Civil Rights Movement in American Memory*, ed. Renee Christine Romano and Leigh Ford (Athens: University of Georgia Press, 2006); Jon A. Shields, *The Democratic Virtues of the Christian Right* (Princeton, N.J.: Princeton University Press, 2009).

41. Sally K. Gallagher, *Evangelical Identity and Gendered Family Life* (New Brunswick, N.J.: Rutgers University Press, 2003), 129–91; Christian Smith, *Christian America? What Evangelicals Really Want* (Berkeley: University of California Press, 2000).

Chapter 1. Christian Schools

1. Mark Fakkema, "They Have Taken Away My Lord," *Christian School Guide*, September 1962, 1.

2. Paul F. Parsons, *Inside America's Christian Schools* (Macon, Ga.: Mercer University Press, 1987), xiii.

3. Roy Lowrie, "Christian School Growth," *Brethren Missionary Herald*, 15 October 1987, 22, Christian day schools folder, Fundamentalism File, Mack Library, Bob Jones University.

4. See, for instance, Kenneth M. Pierce, "A Case for Moral Absolutes: Christian Schools Go Forth and Multiply," *Time*, 8 June 1981, 54.

5. William C. Martin, *With God on Our Side: The Rise of the Religious Right in America* (New York: Broadway, 1996), 25–46; Ruth Murray Brown, *For a "Christian America": A History of the Religious Right* (Amherst, N.Y.: Prometheus, 2002), 29–80; Randall Balmer, *Thy Kingdom Come: An Evangelical's Lament: How the Religious Right Distorts the Faith and Threatens America* (New York:

Basic, 2006), 1–34; Steven P. Miller, *Billy Graham and the Rise of the Republican South* (Philadelphia: University of Pennsylvania Press, 2009).

6. "Lynchburg Christian Academy Student Handbook," n.d. (probably 1975–77), Liberty University Archive, Pierre Guillermin Library, Lynchburg, Va.

7. Susan D. Rose, *Keeping Them Out of the Hands of Satan: Evangelical Schooling in America* (New York: Routledge, 1988), 38.

8. See, for instance, David Nevin and Robert E. Bills, *The Schools That Fear Built: Segregationist Academies in the South* (Washington, D.C.: Acropolis, 1976).

9. Quoted in ibid., 25.

10. In his analysis of Supreme Court decisions regarding school desegregation, legal scholar Lino Graglia makes a partisan attack against school integration; nonetheless, his book provides valuable legal analysis of relevant Supreme Court decisions. See Lino A. Graglia, *Disaster by Decree: The Supreme Court Decisions on Race and the Schools* (Ithaca, N.Y.: Cornell University Press, 1976), 67–144. For a sustained discussion of *Swann*, see Bernard Schwartz, *Swann's Way: The School Busing Case and the Supreme Court* (New York: Oxford University Press, 1986).

11. Parsons, *Inside America's Christian Schools*, 113–26, 125.

12. This picture can be found on the inside cover of Paul A. Kienel, *What Every Parent Should Know About Christian School Education* (Whittier, Calif.: Association of Christian Schools International, 1987). This volume collected many of the columns Kienel wrote for *Christian School Comment* in 1974–1987.

13. Chris Myers, "White Freedom Schools: Eastern North Carolina and the Rise of 'Segregation Academies' in the South, 1954–1974" (M.A. thesis, University of North Carolina, 2000), 34–35.

14. Crespino concedes that while church schools were hardly progressive on the issue of race, some featured desegregated student bodies and opened in regions where desegregation was not threatening to white parents. "The argument that all private school supporters in Mississippi were carrying on essentially the same fight that had sustained the generation of massive resistance," argues Crespino, "fails to appreciate both the complex social and religious context in which some of those church schools emerged as well as the multiplicity of sources for modern conservative politics in the Deep South." Joseph Crespino, *In Search of Another Country: Mississippi and the Conservative Counterrevolution* (Princeton, N.J.: Princeton University Press, 2007), 237–66, 265. See also Joseph Crespino, "Civil Rights and the Religious Right," in *Rightward Bound: Making America Conservative in the 1970s*, ed. Bruce J. Schulman and Julian E. Zelizer (Cambridge, Mass.: Harvard University Press, 2008), 90–105; Adam Laats, "Forging a Fundamentalist 'One Best System': Struggles over Curriculum and Educational Philosophy for Christian Day Schools, 1970–1989," *History of Education Quarterly* 50, 1 (2010): 60.

15. Quoted in Jerry Falwell, *Falwell: An Autobiography* (Lynchburg, Va.: Liberty House, 1997), 320.

16. "Lynchburg Christian Academy to Be White," *Lynchburg News*, 14 April 1967, quoted in Martin, *With God on Our Side* 70.

17. Falwell claimed to have admitted a black member in 1960 or 1961, but no sources from the time confirmed his memory. See Martin, *With God on Our Side*, 58.

18. Crespino, *In Search of Another Country*, 245.

19. Historian Matthew Lassiter wrote a fascinating account of how Atlanta schools constructed a plan in 1973 that ensured at least a 30 percent minority population at all city schools but stopped short of busing enough black children to create a black majority in schools in white neighborhoods. Moreover, no white students were bused against their will to schools in black neighborhoods. Matthew D. Lassiter, *The Silent Majority: Suburban Politics in the Sunbelt South* (Princeton, N.J.: Princeton University Press, 2006), 94–118.

20. U.S. Census Bureau, Census of Population and Housing, http://www.census.gov/prod/www/abs/decennial/1970.htm.

21. "Five Things We Think You Will Like About Lynchburg Christian Academy," 1975 marketing brochure, Liberty University Archive.

22. "Successful Family Living," *Lynchburg Christian Academy Newsletter* 6, 12, December 1972, Liberty University Archive.

23. *Engel v. Vitale*, 370 U.S. 421 (1962).

24. *Abingdon Township School District v. Schempp*, 374 U.S. 313 (1963).

25. On the fallout from these two decisions, see Warren A. Nord, *Religion and American Education: Rethinking a National Dilemma* (Chapel Hill: University of North Carolina Press, 1995), 114–20; Parsons, *Inside America's Christian Schools*, 160–162.

26. Kienel, *What Every Parent Should Know About Christian School Education*, 108.

27. Tim LaHaye, "Foreword," in *The Philosophy of Christian School Education*, ed. Paul A. Kienel (Whittier, Calif.: Association of Christian Schools International, 1978).

28. Jerry Combee, *History of the World in Christian Perspective*, vol. 1, *Since the Beginning* (Pensacola, Fla.: Beka Book Publications, 1979), 6.

29. A. A. Baker, *The Successful Christian School: Foundational Principles for Starting and Operating a Successful Christian School* (Pensacola, Fla.: Beka Book Publications, 1979), 36.

30. *Lynchburg Christian Academy Newsletter*, October 1972, Liberty University Archive.

31. The term "secular humanism" originated with conservative Catholics in the 1950s; see James Davison Hunter, *Culture Wars: The Struggle to Define America* (New York: Basic, 1991), 202.

32. Katie Hooks, "Private School Growth Creating New Concern," *Durham Morning Herald*, 18 September 1970, B1.

33. "Wake Christian Academy Student Handbook, 1972–73," Wake Christian Academy Archive.

34. *Echoes of Faith*, newsletter of Faith Baptist Church, Ramseur, N.C., July 1968, Wake Christian Academy Archive.

35. "Five Things We Think You Will Like About Lynchburg Christian Academy."

36. Baker, *The Successful Christian School*, 35, 40.

37. "Help Wake Christian Academy Build," n.d., Wake Christian Academy Archive.

38. Jon Barton and John W. Whitehead, *Schools on Fire* (Wheaton, Ill.: Tyndale House, 1980), 25.

39. Baker, *The Successful Christian School*, 87.

40. American Humanist Association, "Humanist Manifesto I," 1933, http://americanhumanist.org/Humanism/Humanist_Manifesto_I (accessed 15 January 2015).

41. James C. Hefley, *Textbooks on Trial: The Informative Report of Mel and Norma Gabler's Ongoing Battle to Oust Objectionable Textbooks from Public Schools—and to Urge Publishers to Produce Better Ones* (Wheaton, Ill.: Victor Books, 1976), 83.

42. Historians Mark Noll, Nathan Hatch, and George Marsden made it clear that the specter of humanism imagined by conservative politicians was more sinister than the actual number of humanists in public education. Conservatives disregarded the relatively small size of the American Humanist Society, which published the Manifesto, and they insisted that the Manifesto served as a creed for public school educators. Secular humanism provided a perfect rhetorical target, and conservatives attacked it with gusto. See Mark A. Noll, Nathan O. Hatch, and George M. Marsden, *The Search for Christian America* (Westchester, Ill.: Crossway, 1983), 127–29.

43. Kienel, *What Every Parent Should Know About Christian School Education*, 108.

44. "Our Nation's Greatest Need Morally Speaking," *Christian School Guide*, May 1965, 4.

45. Quoted in Hefley, *Textbooks on Trial*, 132.

46. "Lynchburg Christian Academy Student Handbook, Jr/Sr High School," n.d., Liberty University Archive.

47. Schools sponsored by Pentecostal churches, for example, were generally less strict in hair and dress codes than schools sponsored by fundamentalist churches. See Parsons, *Inside America's Christian Schools*, 27–30.

48. "Five Things We Think You Will Like About Lynchburg Christian Academy."

49. Bruce Jackson, "Home Education," *AACS Christian School Communicator* 3, 3 (1982), as quoted in Alan Peshkin, *God's Choice: The Total World of a Fundamentalist Christian School* (Chicago: University of Chicago Press, 1986), 127.

50. David L. Hocking, "The Theological Basis for the Philosophy of Christian School Education," in *The Philosophy of Christian School Education*, ed. Kienel, 24.

51. "Lynchburg Baptist College: The Way," student handbook, 1974–75, Liberty University Archive.

52. Baker, *The Successful Christian School*, passim. Historian Grant Wacker connected conservatives' critique of public education with their belief that male leadership was disappearing. Christian academies and colleges developed a "manliness syndrome" to combat the persistent feminization of boys in public schools. See Grant Wacker, "Searching for Norman Rockwell: Popular Evangelicalism in Contemporary America," in *The Evangelical Tradition in America*, ed. Leonard I. Sweet (Macon, Ga.: Mercer University Press, 1984), 305–6.

53. "Our School," student handbook, 1980–81, Wake Christian Academy Archive.

54. Paul A. Kienel, *The Christian School: Why It Is Right for Your Child* (Wheaton, Ill.: Victor, 1974), 114.

55. "Lynchburg Christian Academy Student Handbook, Jr/Sr High School."

56. Ibid.

57. Kienel, *What Every Parent Should Know About Christian School Education*, 9.

58. Baker, *The Successful Christian School*, 36.

59. Frank P. Harrison, "The Battle We Must Not Lose! " *Free Will Baptist* 83, 11 (1968): 3.

60. Jerry Falwell, *Listen, America!* (Garden City, N.Y.: Doubleday, 1980), 29.

61. Baker, *The Successful Christian School*, 36.

62. "Five Things We Think You Will Like About Lynchburg Christian Academy."

63. *The Midweek Message*, weekly newsletter, Greystone Bible Church, Mobile, Ala., 14 May 1969, Wake Christian Academy Archive.

64. "Teaching Children to Live as They Learn," 1968 promotional mailer, Wake Christian Academy Archive.

65. *Lynchburg Christian Academy Newsletter*, March 1973, Liberty University Archive.

66. "Five Things We Think You Will Like About Lynchburg Christian Academy."

67. Kienel, *The Christian School: Why It Is Right for Your Child*, 129.

68. Parsons, *Inside America's Christian Schools*, 153.

69. Accounts of the tour can be found in Jerry Falwell, *Strength for the Journey: An Autobiography* (New York: Simon and Schuster, 1987), 345–46; Martin, *With God on Our Side*, 203–4.

70. "Academy News," n.d., Wake Christian Academy Archive.

71. James Dobson, *Dare to Discipline* (Wheaton, Ill.: Tyndale House, 1970), 105.

72. "Lynchburg Christian Academy: 1971 Loyalty Rally"; "Lynchburg Christian Academy Student Handbook," n.d. (probably 1975–77).

73. Roy Lowrie, Jr., "Your Child and the Christian School," ed. National Association of Christian Schools (Wheaton, Ill.: 1967), 30, collection 91, box 2, folder 18, Billy Graham Center Archives.

74. Connaught Coyne Marshner, *Blackboard Tyranny* (New Rochelle, N.Y.: Arlington House, 1978), 37–38.

75. "Kiddie Lib/International Year of the Child Packet," n.d.; William Carmichael, "Would Your Kid Sue You?," *Spotlight*, 29 January 1979, 8, both in International Year of the Child folder, Fundamentalism File, Mack Library, Bob Jones University

76. Bob Dalton, "'Compelling Interest' vs. Separation of Church and State," *CLA Defender*, 1978, in Christian Day Schools and the State folder, Fundamentalism File, Mack Library, Bob Jones University.

77. Marshner, *Blackboard Tyranny*, 28, 29.

78. Crespino, *In Search of Another Country*, 248.

79. Nevin and Bills, *The Schools That Fear Built*, 11.

80. See the excellent description of the reopening of *Green* in Crespino, *In Search of Another Country*, 252–63.

81. Frank Gaydosh, "The I.R.S. Attack on the Independent Schools," *Remnant Review*, 15 September 1978, 107, in Christian Day Schools and the State Folder.

82. Robert J. Billings, "The IRS Has 'Done It Again!,'" *Christian School Alert*, February 1979, 1, Christian Day Schools and the State Folder.

83. Crespino, *In Search of Another Country*, 254.

84. Weyrich made this comment at a 1990 meeting of scholars and activists discussing the Christian right at the Ethics and Public Policy Center in Washington, D.C. Paul Weyrich, "Comments," in *No Longer Exiles: The Religious New Right in American Politics*, ed. Michael Cromartie (Washington, D.C.: Ethics and Public Policy Center, 1993), 26. Weyrich's admission has convinced some historians that the 1978 IRS decision was the single most important issue in the political mobilization of conservative evangelicals. See Randall Balmer, *Thy Kingdom Come: How the Religious Right Distorts Faith and Threatens America* (New York: Basic, 2007), 13–17.

85. Historian Kim Phillips-Fein proposes a third way to read the 1978 IRS case: as an antigovernment fight "against the tax man." Phillips-Fein connects conservative evangelicals to Republican businessmen and argues that the Christian right's rhetoric about issues of gender and sexuality intermingled with a pro-business ideology that viewed government intervention with disdain. Kim Phillips-Fein, *Invisible Hands: The Making of the Conservative Movement from the New Deal to Reagan* (New York: Norton, 2009), 232–35.

86. Quoted in "Goldwater: Time Has Passed Him," *Moral Majority Report*, 21 September 1981, 6.

87. "Christian Day Schools! Why?" unpublished pamphlet, n.d., in collection 91, box 2, folder 18, Billy Graham Center Archives.

88. Social movement theorists have shown how, as political scientist Michael Lienesch puts it, "political movements . . . are held together with words." See Michael Lienesch, *In the Beginning: Fundamentalism, the Scopes Trial, and the Making of the Antievolution Movement* (Chapel Hill: University of North Carolina Press, 2007), 7. Cf. Robert Wuthnow, *Communities of Discourse: Ideology and Social Structure in the Reformation, the Enlightenment, and European Socialism* (Cambridge, Mass.: Harvard University Press, 1988).

89. Ed Nelson, "Religious Persecution in Nebraska: Christian Schools Under Attack," *Christian School Communicator*, December 1983, 1; Paul Taylor, "Jailings in Nebraska School Case Turn Church-State Separation into Chasm," *Washington Post*, 3 December 1983, A3.

90. Ronald Reagan, Address to National Religious Broadcasters Convention, 30 January 1984, collection 309, box 63, folder 11, Billy Graham Center Archives.

Chapter 2. Textbook Politics

1. "Book Foe Pledges Separate Schools," *New York Times*, 10 November 1974, 53. The most thorough description of the Kanawha County controversy is Catherine Ann Candor, "A History of the Kanawha County Textbook Controversy" (Ed.D. dissertation, Virginia Polytechnic Institute and State University, 1976). The best published source on the controversy is James Moffett, *Storm in the Mountains: A Case Study of Censorship, Conflict, and Consciousness* (Carbondale: Southern Illinois University Press, 1988). Both Candor and Moffett participated in the controversy: Candor was an administrator in the Kanawha County school system, and Moffett directed publication of one of the controversial textbooks.

2. See, e.g., Curtis Seltzer, "A Confusion of Goals," *The Nation*, 2 November 1974, 430–35.

3. Quoted in Ben A. Franklin, "Textbook Dispute Has Many Causes," *New York Times*, 14 October 1974, 31.

4. Howard Phillips, "Uncle Sam's Assault Against the Family," *Human Events*, 19 January 1974, 10. Five years after this article was published, Phillips was instrumental in the founding of Moral Majority, a political action group that placed "pro-family" politics at the top of its agenda.

5. On other postwar conflicts over public education in which evangelicals were prominently involved, see Robert S. Alley, *School Prayer: The Court, the Congress, and the First Amendment* (Amherst, N.Y.: Prometheus, 1994), 146–50, 187–214; Ruth Murray Brown, *For a "Christian America": A History of the Religious Right* (Amherst, N.Y.: Prometheus, 2002), 253–69; Melissa M. Deckman, *School Board Battles: The Christian Right in Local Politics* (Washington, D.C.: Georgetown University Press, 2004), 1–30; Joan DelFattore, *The Fourth R: Conflicts over Religion in America's Public Schools* (New Haven, Conn.: Yale University Press, 2004), 82–143, 178–254; James R. Durham, *Secular Darkness: Religious Right Involvement in Texas Public Education* (New York: Peter Lang, 1995); William C. Martin, *With God on Our Side: The Rise of the Religious Right in America* (New York: Broadway Books, 1996), 100–116.

6. Warren A. Nord, *Religion and American Education: Rethinking a National Dilemma* (Chapel Hill: University of North Carolina Press, 1995), 63–97.

7. Edward J. Larson, *Summer for the Gods: The Scopes Trial and America's Continuing Debate over Science and Religion* (Cambridge, Mass.: Harvard University Press, 1997), 170–224; Michael Lienesch, *In the Beginning: Fundamentalism, the Scopes Trial, and the Making of the Antievolution Movement* (Chapel Hill: University of North Carolina Press, 2007), 59–82, 115–97; George M. Marsden, *Fundamentalism and American Culture*, 2nd ed. (New York: Oxford University Press, 2006), 118–23, 184–95; Michael Kazin, *A Godly Hero: The Life of William Jennings Bryan* (New York: Knopf, 2006), 262–95.

8. James C. Hefley, *Textbooks on Trial: The Informative Report of Mel and Norma Gabler's Ongoing Battle to Oust Objectionable Textbooks from Public Schools—and to Urge Publishers to Produce Better Ones* (Wheaton, Ill.: Victor Books, 1976), 15.

9. William Martin, "The Guardians Who Slumbereth Not," *Texas Monthly*, November 1982, 147.

10. Michelle M. Nickerson, *Mothers of Conservatism: Women and the Postwar Right* (Princeton, N.J.: Princeton University Press, 2012), 70.

11. Quoted in Hefley, *Textbooks on Trial*, 13.

12. A thorough account of the case is James P. Sterba, "Texas Toll of Boys Rises to 27 in Nation's Biggest Slaying Case," *New York Times*, 14 August 1973, 1, 18. At the time, the Houston killings represented the single largest serial murder in the nation's history.

13. Matthew Avery Sutton, *American Apocalypse: A History of Modern Evangelicalism* (Cambridge, Mass.: Belknap Press of Harvard University Press, 2014).

14. *Baltimore Evening Sun*, 24 April 1980, A18, quoted in Frank Edward Piasecki, "Norma and Mel Gabler: The Development and Causes of Their Involvement Concerning the Curricular Appropriateness of School Textbook Content" (Ph.D. dissertation, North Texas State University, 1982), 15.

15. In 1983, Texas changed the rules for adoption hearings, allotting only six minutes for each person wishing to comment on proposed books. Compare this with the eight hours Norma spoke at the 1981 hearings. Nonetheless, by 1983, the Gablers' power had spread far beyond Texas, and in 1985, an Indiana University professor (and critic of the Gablers) conceded that the couple's "influence on textbooks is still immeasurable." Edward B. Jenkinson, "Protecting Holden Caulfield and His Friends from the Censors," *English Journal* 74, 1 (1985): 31.

16. Still headquartered in Longview, the organization remains active. Internet users can access conservative textbook reviews at Educational Research Analysts, http://www.textbookreviews.org/ (accessed 15 February 2010).

17. "Educational Research Analysts—Frequently Asked Questions."

18. Jenkinson, "Protecting Holden Caulfield," 31.

19. Martin, "The Guardians Who Slumbereth Not," 268, 269.

20. Hefley, *Textbooks on Trial*, 14–15.

21. See Robert Wuthnow, *The Restructuring of American Religion: Society and Faith Since World War II* (Princeton, N.J: Princeton University Press, 1988).

22. Andrew Manis, "Protestants: From Denominational Controversialists to Culture Warriors," in *Religion and Public Life in the Southern Crossroads: Showdown States*, ed. William Lindsey and Mark Silk (Walnut Creek, Calif.: AltaMira, 2005), 55. See also Darren Dochuk, *From Bible Belt to Sunbelt: Plain-Folk Religion, Grassroots Politics, and the Rise of Evangelical Conservatism* (New York: Norton, 2011).

23. Quoted in Martin, *With God on Our Side*, 121.

24. Quoted in Jenkinson, "Protecting Holden Caulfield," 31.

25. Hefley, *Textbooks on Trial*, 13.

26. Quotations from Martin, "The Guardians Who Slumbereth Not," 264, 151.

27. Quotes from Hefley, *Textbooks on Trial*, 42, 122.

28. Martin, "The Guardians Who Slumbereth Not," 150.

29. Hefley, *Textbooks on Trial*, 32.

30. Martin, "The Guardians Who Slumbereth Not," 260.

31. Hefley and Smith, "What Should Johnny Read?" 24.

32. Hefley, *Textbooks on Trial*, 178.

33. Ibid.

34. Charles L. Glenn, "Textbook Controversies: A 'Disaster for Public Schools'?" *Phi Delta Kappan* 68 (1987): 454.

35. Martin, "The Guardians Who Slumbereth Not," 260.

36. Ibid., 262.

37. Dale S. Turner, "The Dinosaur Darwin Missed," *Texas Monthly*, November 1981, 148.

38. Hefley, *Textbooks on Trial*, 168.

39. Hefley and Smith, "What Should Johnny Read?" 25.

40. Martin, "The Guardians Who Slumbereth Not," 268.

41. Calvin Trillin, "U.S. Journal: Kanawha County, West Virginia," *New Yorker*, 30 September 1974, 121.

42. Dena Kleiman, "Influential Couple Scrutinize Textbooks for 'Anti-Americanism,'" *New York Times*, 14 July 1981, C4.

43. Russell Shorto, "How Christian Were the Founders?" *New York Times Sunday Magazine*, 14 February 2010.

44. For an account of this story, see Hefley, *Textbooks on Trial*, 158–60.

45. "Book Controversy Generates Heat at Board Meeting," *Charleston Daily Mail*, 24 May 1974; quoted in Candor, "Kanawha County Textbook Controversy," 54–55.

46. Quoted in ibid., 83.

47. Alice Moore, personal e-mail to the author, 11 April 2009.

48. "Shaky Truce Set in Textbook Rift," *New York Times*, 15 September 1974, 32.

49. "Two Book Foes Deny Fueling School Boycott," *Charleston Gazette*, 6 September 1974. Quoted in Candor, "Kanawha County Textbook Controversy." 96.

50. Candor, "Kanawha County Textbook Controversy," 92.

51. Thelma R. Conley, "Scream Silently: One View of the Kanawha County Textbook Controversy," *Journal of Research and Development in Education* 9, 3 (1976): 95.

52. Andrew Gallagher, "Book Foes' Dilemma Seen as Crime vs. Sin," *Charelston Gazette*, 25 September 1974, 2A.

53. Ben A. Franklin, "3 Held in Dispute over Textbooks," *New York Times*, 19 September 1974, 14.

54. For an example of one of these ads, see Elmer Fike, "What Your Children Will Read," *Charleston Daily Mail*, 14 November 1974. Fike, a Charleston businessman, formed an anti-textbook outfit called "The Business and Professional People's Alliance for Better Textbooks," a group whose name signaled distance from the "non-professional" forces in the rural parts of Kanawha County.

55. Trillin, "U.S. Journal," 122.

56. Kay Michael, "Miners Hit in Boycott over Texts," *Charleston Gazette*, 5 September 1974, 1A.

57. On the tension between rank-and-file miners and Miller (a former miner widely respected throughout West Virginia and Pennsylvania), see Paul F. Clark, *The Miners' Fight for Democracy: Arnold Miller and the Reform of the United Mine Workers* (Ithaca: New York State School of Industrial and Labor Relations, Cornell University, 1981), 45–74.

58. Richard Haas and Bob Adams, "Miners Take Over on Text Picketing: School Protest Transformed into Outright Coal Shutdown," *Charleston Daily Mail*, 14 September 1974, 1A.

59. Michael, "Miners Hit in Boycott over Texts," 1A.

60. Moffett, *Storm in the Mountains*, 19.

61. Rick Steelhammer, "County Schools Reopen Today," *Charleston Gazette*, 15 September 1974, 1A.

62. Kay Michael and Rick Steelhammer, "Protest Factions Remain at Odds," *Charleston Gazette*, 22 September 1974, 1A.

63. Rosalie Earle, "Ex-Actor to Explain Texts," *Charleston Gazette*, 10 October 1974, 1A.

64. Ben A. Franklin, "Schools Damaged in Books Protest," *New York Times*, 10 October 1974, 17.

65. "School Is Bombed in Textbook Rift," *New York Times*, 23 October 1974, 30.

66. Candor, "Kanawha County Textbook Controversy," 164.

67. "Education Chief Joins Textbook Controversy," *Human Events*, 14 December 1974, 4.

68. Martin, *With God on Our Side* 143.

69. "Textbook Dispute of 1974 Fades Away," *New York Times*, 23 September 1979, 47.

70. Carl Murburger, "The West Virginia Textbooks," *New York Times*, 24 October 1974, 41.

71. George Hillocks, Jr., "Books and Bombs: Ideological Conflict and the School: A Case Study of the Kanawha County Book Protest," *School Review* 86, 4 (1978): 638.

72. Franklin, "Textbook Dispute Has Many Causes," 31.

73. African Americans made up less than 6 percent of the county's 1970 population. U.S. Census, Census of Population, 1970.

74. James E. Miller, Jr., Robert O'Neal, and Helen M. McDonnell, *Man in Literature: Comparative World Studies in Translation* (Glenview, Ill.: Scott, Foresman, (1970), 8, 30.

75. Botel and Dawkins, *Communicating*, 15.

76. Vitz's study, not surprisingly, won wide acclaim in conservative circles. The National Institute of Education funded his study, rendering his findings somewhat surprising. He discovered a few portrayals of Catholic, Jewish, and Amish religious life, but no books depicted what he termed "contemporary representative Protestantism." And though it was not published until twelve years after the West Virginia controversy, the intervening decade had witnessed textbook publishers becoming increasingly reticent to forward liberal agendas, owing to activists like the Gablers and protests similar to (if not as notorious as) Kanawha. Vitz's study, then, concluded that in spite of the efforts of conservatives, textbooks remained nearly as hostile to Christianity as they had been in 1974. Paul C. Vitz, *Censorship: Evidence of Bias in Our Children's Textbooks* (Ann Arbor, Mich.: Servant Books, 1986), 1.

77. Murburger, "The West Virginia Textbooks," 41.

78. Trillin, "U.S. Journal," 127.

79. Moffett, *Storm in the Mountains*, 60.

80. M. Stanton Evans, "The Parent as Enemy," *Human Events*, 16 November 1974, 1035.

81. June Kirkuff Edwards, "The Textbook Controversy: A Political Confrontation," *Christian Century*, 13 November 1974, 1064.

82. Trillin, "U.S. Journal," 121.

83. See Blair Adams, Joel Stein, and Howard Wheeler, *Who Owns the Children? Public Compulsion, Private Responsibility, and the Dilemma of Ultimate Authority* (Waco, Tex.: Truth Forum, 1983).

84. B. Drummond Ayers, Jr., "School Critics Press Drive for Old Values," *New York Times*, 25 July 1975, 1, 47; Evans, "The Parent as Enemy," 1035.

85. Ayers, "School Critics Press Drive for Old Values," 1.

86. Connaught Coyne Marshner, *Blackboard Tyranny* (New Rochelle, N.Y.: Arlington House, 1978), 37–38.

87. The men led the following churches: Summit Ridge Church of God (Ezra Graley), Cathedral of Prayer (Charles Quigley), Freedom Gospel Mission (Avis Hill), and Leewood Free Will Baptist (Marvin Horan). Barrie Doyle, "West Virginia Uproar: Contesting the Textbooks," *Christianity Today*, 11 October 1974, 44.

88. See Franklin, "Textbook Dispute Has Many Causes," 31.

89. A full list of the stipulations protesters requested can be found in Hefley, *Textbooks on Trial*, 163. Many of the petitioners' demands won approval when the school board passed adoption guidelines for new textbooks in late November.

90. Candor, "Kanawha County Textbook Controversy," 29; Hefley, *Textbooks on Trial*, 162.

91. Priscilla Luther, letter to the editor, *Christianity Today*, 22 November 1974, 24.

92. Quotes from Martin, *With God on Our Side* 141, 142.

93. "Education Chief Joins Textbook Controversy," 4.

94. Hefley, *Textbooks on Trial*, 168.

95. Moffett, *Storm in the Mountains*, 40.

96. Reviews of Presbyterian, Methodist, and Baptist periodicals during the height of the controversy (September–December 1974) revealed no accounts of the West Virginia story, even though major news outlets like the *New York Times*, the *Nation*, and the *New Yorker* published numerous articles on it. *Christianity Today* published two brief news articles on the issue.

Chapter 3: Home Schools

1. James B. Jordan, "Are Christian Schools the Best Answer?" *Biblical Educator*, April 1980, 1–2.

2. Patricia M. Lines, *Estimating the Home Schooled Population* (Washington, D.C.: Department of Education, Office of Educational Research and Improvement, 1991), 1, ED 1.310/2:337903.

3. "Parents' Rights Amendment," *Teaching Home*, December 1985, 21.

4. Generation Joshua, "Generation Joshua: A Brief History," http://www.generationjoshua.org/dnn/About/Media/ABriefHistory/tabid/300/Default.aspx (accessed 14 May 2015).

5. Milton Gaither, *Homeschool: An American History* (New York: Palgrave Macmillan, 2008), 66, 85. Gaither's volume is the best historical treatment of homeschooling available. His blog, *Homeschooling Research Notes*, is also invaluable for anyone studying the homeschooling movement; http://gaither.wordpress.com (accessed 3 June 2010).

6. John Holt, *How Children Fail*, rev. ed. (New York: Delta/Seymour Lawrence, 1982), 85.

7. On Holt, see Gaither, *Homeschool*, 122–28.

8. Jordan, "Are Christian Schools the Best Answer?" 1.

9. Mitchell L. Stevens, *Kingdom of Children: Culture and Controversy in the Homeschooling Movement* (Princeton, N.J.: Princeton University Press, 2001), 36–37.

10. Tim LaHaye, *The Battle for the Public Schools* (Old Tappan, N.J.: Revell, 1983), 80, 81.

11. James Dobson, *The Strong-Willed Child: Birth Through Adolescence* (Wheaton, Ill.: Tyndale House, 1978), 17.

12. Jerry Falwell, *Listen, America!* (Garden City, N.Y.: Doubleday, 1980), 178.

13. On debates over corporal punishment, see John P. Bartkowski, "Spare the Rod . . . , or Spare the Child? Divergent Perspectives on Conservative Protestant Child Discipline," *Review of Religious Research* 37, 2 (1995): 102.

14. James Dobson, *Parenting Isn't for Cowards: The "You Can Do It" Guide for Hassled Parents from America's Best-Loved Family Advocate* (Dallas: Word Publishing, 1987), 92.

15. LaHaye, *The Battle for the Public Schools*, 54.

16. Raymond Moore and Dennis R. Moore, "The Dangers of Early Schooing," *Harper's*, July 1972, 58.

17. Gaither, *Homeschool*, 130–31.

18. Ibid., 128–34.

19. Raymond Moore and Dorothy Moore, "Parents Who Would Be Teachers," *Christian Life*, October 1980, 66.

20. Ellen G. White, *Christ's Object Lessons* (Oakland, Calif.: Pacific Press, 1900), 359.

21. Leading evangelical "cult watcher" Walter Martin labeled Seventh-day Adventism a cult in 1955's *Rise of the Cults* but reversed himself in 1965's *Kingdom of the Cults*.

22. Meg Johnson, "Public School Has Become Public Enemy," *National Educator*, May 1981, 10.

23. Dobson also disagreed with Holt's assessment of public schools: "The degree of student control exercised by school authorities has never been so minimal as it is today in America." James Dobson, *Dare to Discipline* (Wheaton, Ill.: Tyndale House, 1970), 9, 104.

24. Quoted in Gaither, *Homeschool*, 132.

25. James Dobson, "Home Schools: Wave of the Future," *Teaching Home*, June 1983, 9, 20.

26. Dobson, *Dare to Discipline*, 3.

27. Dan Gilgoff, *The Jesus Machine: How James Dobson, Focus on the Family, and Evangelical America Are Winning the Culture War* (New York: St. Martin's, 2007), 20–23, 21.

28. Dobson, *The Strong-Willed Child*, 98.

29. Moore and Moore, "Parents Who Would Be Teachers," 64, 66.

30. Gilgoff, *The Jesus Machine*, 27.

31. Dobson, *The Strong-Willed Child*, 11.

32. Ibid., 24.

33. Matthew Scully, "Right Wing and a Prayer—Still Alive and Kicking," *Washington Times*, 8 November 1989.

34. Gilgoff, *The Jesus Machine*, 31–33.

35. "North Carolina Limits Educational Freedom," *Christian Liberty Report*, September 1983, 1–3. Clipping available in Education—Home Schools—Education of Children folder, Fundamentalism File, Mack Library, Bob Jones University.

36. Sam Allis, "Schooling Kids at Home," *Time*, 22 October 1990, 84–86.

37. A 1987 study found that only 13 percent of subscribers to *Growing Without Schooling* described themselves as "independent/fundamentalist Christian," whereas 34 percent reported no religious affiliation (more than the combined total of "independent/fundamentalist" and "mainline Protestant"). Sonia K. Gustafson, "A Study of Home Schooling: Parental Motivation and Goals," *Home School Researcher* (1988): 6.

38. The Singer ordeal received book-length coverage in David Fleisher and David M. Freedman, *Death of an American: The Killing of John Singer* (New York: Continuum, 1983).

39. "Slain by Officers: Polygamist 'Murdered in Cold Blood,' Mother Says," *Los Angeles Times*, 19 January 1979, A2.

40. *Alarming Cry* (Winter 1982): 1. Clipping available in Education—Home Schools—Education of Children folder, Fundamentalism File, Mack Library, Bob Jones University.

41. Fred Barbash, "Parents Say Schooling at Home a Right, and Judge Agreed," *Washington Post*, 24 March 1980, A2.

42. *Wisconsin v. Yoder*, 406 U.S. 205 (1972).

43. The relevant cases are *Scoma v. Chicago*, 391 F.Supp. 452 (1974); *State v. Riddle*, 285 SE 2d 359 (1981); *Jernigan v. State*, 412 So. 2d 1242 (1982); *Duro v. District Attorney*, 712 F.2d 96 (1983); *State v. Schmidt*, 29 3d 32 (1987); and *State v. Patzer* 382 NW 2d 631 (1986). See also Gaither, *Homeschool*, 176–79.

44. *Pierce v. Society of Sisters*, 268 U.S. 510 (1925).

45. Scott W. Somerville, *The Politics of Survival: Home Schoolers and the Law* (Paeonian Springs, Va.: Home School Legal Defense Association, 2001).

46. See *Scoma v. Board*, 391 F.Supp. 452 (1974); *Hanson v. Cushman*, 490 F.Supp. 109 (1980); *Edgington v. State*, 663 P. 2d 374 (1983); and *Murphy v. State*, 853 F. 2d 1039 (1988). Homeschoolers won one case on Fourteenth Amendment grounds: *Perchemlides v. Frizzle* (1979), an unreported lower-court case with "markedly limited" impact (albeit wide celebration among homeschoolers). Quote in Gaither, *Homeschool*, 177. For more on the *Perchemlides* case, see Richard A. Bumstead, "Educating Your Child at Home: The Perchemlides Case," *Phi Delta Kappan* 61, 2 (1979): 97–100. See also Teri Dobbins Baxter, "Private Oppression: How Laws That Protect Privacy Can Lead to Oppression," *Kansas Law Review* 58 (2010): 415–71.

47. *Mozert v. Hawkins County Bd. of Educ.*, 827 F. 2d 1058 (1987).

48. Michael P. Farris, *Homeschooling and the Law* (Paeonian Springs, Va.: Home School Legal Defense Association, 1990), 54.

49. *Mozert v. Hawkins County Bd. of Educ.*, 827 F. 2d 1058 (1987).

50. For excellent discussions of the *Mozert* case, see Jason Bivins, *The Fracture of Good Order: Christian Antiliberalism and the Challenge to American Politics* (Chapel Hill: University of North Carolina Press, 2003), 100–102; Romand Coles, *Beyond Gated Politics: Reflections for the Possibility of Democracy* (Minneapolis: University of Minnesota Press, 2005), 239–263.

51. Bivins, *The Fracture of Good Order*, 100–103; Gaither, *Homeschool*, 159–61.

52. "National Legal News Update," *Teaching Home*, February/March 1984, 4.

53. Nehemiah 4:17, quoted in Gregg Harris, "Pause & Consder... The Nehemiah Balance," *Teaching Home*, June/July 1986, 20.

54. Michael P. Farris, "Home Schooling and America's Future Freedoms," *Teaching Home*, December 1988/January 1989, 20.

55. Patrick Farenga, "The National Orgainzation Question," *Growing Without Schooling*, August 1989, 2–3.

56. Michael P. Farris, "Legal Issues: Who Speaks for the Movement?," *Teaching Home*, April/May 1989, 17.

57. Gaither, *Homeschool*, 166–67.

58. Raymond Moore and Dorothy Moore, *The Successful Homeschool Family Handbook: A Creative and Stress-Free Approach to Homeschooling* (Nashville, Tenn.: Thomas Nelson, 1994), 18–26, 244, 247.

59. Ibid., 246.

60. A Beka Homeschooling advertisement, *Growing Without Schooling*, August 1989, 25. Clipping available in Education—Home Schools—Education of Children folder, Fundamentalism File, Mack Library, Bob Jones University.

61. Gaither, *Homeschool*, 146.

62. Ibid., 157.

63. CLASS Homeschools, "Worldview: Philosophy of Christian Education," http://www.home schools.org/worldview/philosophyOfChristianEducation.html (accessed 14 May 2015).

64. In spite of these theological differences, most evangelicals were prepared for an imminent apocalypse; see Matthew Avery Sutton, "Was FDR the Antichrist? The Birth of Fundamentalist Antiliberalism in a Global Age," *Journal of American History* 98, 4 (March 1, 2012): 1052–74.

65. Mary E. Hood, "Contemporary Philosophical Influences on the Home Schooling Movement," *Home School Researcher* 7, 1 (1991): 2.

66. For a more detailed account of curricular differences among the three leading conservative evangelical curriculum publishers, see Adam Laats, "Forging a Fundamentalist "One Best System:" Struggles over Curriculum and Educational Philosophy for Christian Day Schools, 1970–1989," *History of Education Quarterly* 50, 1 (2010): 55–83.

67. Mary Pride, *The Way Home: Beyond Feminism, Back to Reality* (Westchester, Ill.: Crossway, 1985), xiii.

68. Gregg Harris, "Leadership Qualities in Home-School Fathers," *Teaching Home*, February/March 1990, 53.

69. For more on contemporary evangelical manhood, see William Bradford Wilcox, *Soft Patriarchs, New Men: How Christianity Shapes Fathers and Husbands* (Chicago: University of Chicago Press, 2004). On fatherhood, see Sally K. Gallagher, *Evangelical Identity and Gendered Family Life* (New Brunswick, N.J.: Rutgers University Press, 2003), 85–104.

70. Falwell, *Listen, America!*, 104.

71. Gaither, *Homeschool*, 201–10.

72. Hanna Rosin, *God's Harvard: A Christian College on a Mission to Save America* (Orlando, Fla.: Harcourt, 2007), 40–53.

73. "Moving into the Land: A Field Report from the 2004 Campaigns," *Home School Court Report*, January/February 2005, 33–34.

74. "Home Schooling Among Black Families on the Rise," *New American*, 6 February 2006.

75. Gaither, *Homeschool*, 201–26.

Chapter 4. Abortion

1. Angela Y. Davis, *Women, Race, and Class* (New York: Random House, 1983), 194–95.

2. Michelle M. Nickerson, *Mothers of Conservatism: Women and the Postwar Right* (Princeton, N.J.: Princeton University Press), 138.

3. Ibid., 136–68.

4. Jimmy Carter, "White House Conference on Families Appointment of Wilbur J. Cohen as Chairman," 14 April 1978, in John T. Woolley and Gerhard Peters, The American Presidency Project, University of California, Santa Barbara, http://www.presidency.ucsb.edu/ws/?pid=30666 (accessed 23 January 2009).

5. "The Anti-Family Conference," *Moral Majority Report*, 14 March 1980, 2.

6. Oral Memoirs of R. Albert Mohler, Jr., Texas Collection, Baylor University, Waco.

7. Jerry Falwell, *If I Should Die Before I Wake* (Nashville, Tenn.: T. Nelson, 1986), 31–32.

8. Jerry Falwell, *Falwell: An Autobiography* (Lynchburg, Va.: Liberty House, 1997), 336.

9. Edward E. Plowman, "Southern Baptists: Unity the Priority," *Christianity Today*, 5 July 1974, 41–42. Before *Roe*, some Protestant denominations even argued for expansion of abortion rights. Southern Baptists, for instance, resolved in 1971 "to work for legislation that will allow the possibility of abortion under such conditions as rape, incest, clear evidence of severe fetal deformity, and carefully ascertained evidence of the likelihood of damage to the emotional, mental, and physical health of the mother." "Resolution on Abortion," Southern Baptist Convention, http://www.sbc .net/resolutions/amResolution.asp?ID=13 (accessed 14 May 2015). That said, the SBC was not nearly as conservative in 1971 as it would become in the 1980s, so this resolution hardly represented a consensus in the denomination.

10. The clearest statement by *Christianity Today* on the *Roe* decision is "Abortion and the Court," *Christianity Today*, 16 February 1973, 32–33. On the varied reactions of other conservative Protestants in the first years after *Roe*, see Daniel K. Williams, *God's Own Party: The Making of the Christian Right* (New York: Oxford University Press, 2010), 113–20.

11. Kristin Luker, *Abortion and the Politics of Motherhood* (Berkeley: University of California Press, 1984), 141. See also William Saletan, *Bearing Right: How Conservatives Won the Abortion War* (Berkeley: University of California Press, 2003).

12. In fact, throughout the 1970s, it was unclear Republicans would champion the pro-life cause. Catholics, a majority of the pro-life coalition for most of the decade, tended to vote Democratic, and some prominent Democrats opposed *Roe*. The pro-life coalition remained almost equally split between Senate Republicans and Democrats until 1979, and a majority of pro-life supporters voted for Carter over Reagan in 1980. See Greg D. Adams, "Abortion: Evidence of an Issue Evolution," *American Journal of Political Science* 41, 3 (1997): 723–30.

13. Luker, *Abortion and the Politics of Motherhood*, 126–37.

14. Donald T. Critchlow, *The Conservative Ascendancy: How the GOP Right Made Political History* (Cambridge, Mass.: Harvard University Press, 2007), 135.

15. Luker, *Abortion and the Politics of Motherhood*, 127–128.

16. Quoted in William C. Martin, *With God on Our Side: The Rise of the Religious Right in America* (New York: Broadway Books, 1996), 193. Martin also discusses the discomfort with which Protestants received Billy Graham's affirmations of John Kennedy, and Brown claims a "lingering anti-Catholic bias" led Protestants to take up the anti-abortion fight surprisingly late.

17. Luker, *Abortion and the Politics of Motherhood*, 144–57.

18. Saletan, *Bearing Right*, 9–56. Like Saletan, I use "pro-life" and "pro-choice" throughout this chapter because partisans chose those names for their respective sides.

19. Jon A. Shields, *The Democratic Virtues of the Christian Right* (Princeton, N.J.: Princeton University Press, 2009), 69.

20. Luker, *Abortion and the Politics of Motherhood*, 11–65.

21. Ibid., 94.

22. L. Nelson Bell, letter to the editor, *Presbyterian Survey*, 1 June 1970, 21–22, clipping in collection 318, box 12, folder 16, Billy Graham Center Archives.

23. Elizabeth Adell Cook, Ted G. Jelen, and Clyde Wilcox, *Between Two Absolutes: Public Opinion and the Politics of Abortion* (Boulder, Colo.: Westview Press, 1992).

24. Quoted in Luker, *Abortion and the Politics of Motherhood*, 97.

25. *Roe v. Wade*, 410 U.S. 113 (1973).

26. Lawrence Van Gelder, "Cardinals Shocked: Reaction Mixed," *New York Times*, 23 January 1973, 81.

27. Quoted in Ziad W. Munson, *The Making of Pro-Life Activists: How Social Movement Mobilization Works* (Chicago: University of Chicago Press, 2008), 84.

28. Luker, *Abortion and the Politics of Motherhood*, 127–33.

29. Pope Paul VI, *Humanae Vitae* [encyclical letter], 1968. American Catholics, to be sure, did not always follow Church teaching. A 1970 study found that 75 percent of married Catholic women in their twenties were using a form of birth control forbidden by the Church. James M. O'Toole, *The Faithful: A History of Catholics in America* (Cambridge, Mass.: Harvard University Press, 2008), 242.

30. Patricia Goodson, "Protestants and Family Planning," *Journal of Religion and Health* 36, 4 (1997): 353–66.

31. Memo from Gordon A. Hanson and Emmett Herndon to PCUS Ministers, 15 February 1971, in Collection 318, box 12, folder 16, Billy Graham Center Archives.

32. Munson, *The Making of Pro-Life Activists*, 85–86.

33. Quoted in William Martin, *A Prophet with Honor: The Billy Graham Story* (New York: Harper, 1991), 275.

34. See advertisement in *National Right to Life News*, July 1975, 7.

35. Francis A. Schaeffer, *A Christian Manifesto* (Westchester, Ill.: Crossway, 1981), 19, 17, 131–32.

36. Francis A. Schaeffer and C. Everett Koop, *Whatever Happened to the Human Race?* (Old Tappan, N.J.: Revell, 1979), 31, 198.

37. Schaeffer, *A Christian Manifesto*, 110. His comment revealed the ways conservative Christians drew on the rhetoric of the civil rights movement. On this point, see David John Marley, "Riding in the Back of the Bus: The Christian Right's Adoption of Civil Rights Movement Rhetoric," in *The Civil Rights Movement in American Memory*, ed. Renee Christine Romano and Leigh Ford (Athens: University of Georgia Press, 2006), 346–62. Cf. Jon A. Shields, *The Democratic Virtues of the Christian Right* (Princeton, N.J.: Princeton University Press, 2009).

38. Oral Memoirs of James T. Draper, Jr., Texas Collection, Baylor University.

39. "6 Questions Asked Most of Christians in Politics," *Moral Majority Report*, 15 May 1980.

40. Jerry Falwell, "Falwell Defends Assault by Bob Jones: Morally Concerned Must Unite Clout," *Moral Majority Report*, 14 July 1980, 4.

41. Falwell's associate Norman Keener recounted this phone call in a letter to Edith Schaeffer dated 24 May 1984, shortly after Francis Schaeffer's death. Francis Schaeffer: letters folder, Liberty University Archive.

42. For a description of the Holiday Inn meeting, see Martin, *With God on Our Side*, 199–200.

43. "Your Invitation to Join the Moral Majority," Moral Majority: Informational Booklets folder, Liberty University Archives.

44. The claim that 30 percent of Moral Majority's budget came from Catholic contributions appeared in Kenneth Baker, "Catholics and Moral Majority," *Moral Majority Report*, 20 April 1981, 14.

45. "Letters from America," *Moral Majority Report*, 1 May 1980, 11.

46. Jerry Falwell, *Strength for the Journey: An Autobiography* (New York: Simon & Schuster, 1987), 335.

47. Catholics' firm opposition to abortion made some of them heroes among evangelicals. Most notably, Lutheran-turned-Catholic Richard John Neuhaus and his periodical *First Things* won widespread acclaim among evangelicals, notably George W. Bush. *Time* even named Neuhaus one of the country's 25 most influential evangelicals in 2004.

48. Falwell, "Falwell Defends Assault by Bob Jones," 4–5. Jones's letter to alumni "preacher boys" was reprinted in its entirety in the same issue of *Moral Majority Report*, 14 July 1980.

49. Falwell, *Strength for the Journey*, 337.

50. "Distinguished Black Physician Opposes Legalized Abortions, Medicine Not 'Social Execution,'" *Moral Majority Report*, 14 March 1980, 4.

51. "Family Manifesto," Moral Majority: Policy Documents, Family Manifesto folder, Liberty University Archive.

52. The advent of birth control presented this question to an earlier generation of mothers, and those who entered the pro-life movement before the late 1970s largely rejected artificial methods of contraception (including condoms, the pill, and intrauterine devices). As the anti-abortion movement grew in the early 1980s, a greater diversity of opinion on the legitimacy of artificial contraception emerged. Luker, *Abortion and the Politics of Motherhood*, 165–68.

53. Ibid., 159–75, 162.

54. Cal Thomas, "It's Do-It-Yourself Abortion Kits," *Moral Majority Report*, May 18, 1981, 4.

55. "Collegians Denounce Abortions," *Moral Majority Report*, April 26, 1982, 16.

56. "Sign This Congressional Petition and STOP ABORTION," *Moral Majority Report*, 18 May 1981, 16.

57. Dennis Hevesi, "Mildred Jefferson, 84, Anti-Abortion Activist, Is Dead," *New York Times*, October 18, 2010.

58. Deryl Edwards, "Jepsen, Laxalt, Smith Say Americans Want to Strengthen Family," *Moral Majority Report*, July 20, 1981, 10.

59. "Judgment Without Justice," *Old-Time Gospel Hour News*, n.d., Liberty University Archive.

60. Almost 1.3 million American women received abortions in 1977, from 193,000 in 1970. Susan B. Hansen, "State Implementation of Supreme Court Decisions: Abortion Rates Since *Roe v. Wade*," *Journal of Politics* 42, 2 (1980): 375.

61. Curtis Young, "Debate: When Does Life Begin?," *Moral Majority Report*, May 18, 1981, 5.

62. Tony Reichhardt, David Cyranoski, and Quirin Schiermeier, "Religion and Science: Studies of Faith," *Nature* 432, 7018 (9 December 2004): 666–69.

63. Adams, "Abortion: Evidence of an Issue Evolution," 723–30.

64. "Carter's Abortion Stand May Woo Right-to-Lifers," *Human Events*, 27 August 1977, 4–5.

65. "Falwell Accuses President of Smear Tactics," *Lynchburg News*, 8 August 1980, A1.

66. Proceedings: 125th Session (1982), Southern Baptist Convention, New Orleans, Baptist Minutes Collection, Archives, Southern Baptist Theological Seminary, Louisville, Kentucky. The SBC underwent a conservative resurgence beginning in 1979, leading to more conservative stances on abortion in official resolutions after the onset of the conservative resurgence.

67. Tim LaHaye, "Pro-Life Movement Faces 'Real Victory,'" *Moral Majority Report*, 16 February 1981, 9; Thomas, "It's Do-It-Yourself Abortion Kits," 4.

68. Luker, *Abortion and the Politics of Motherhood*, 159–61.

Chapter 5. Feminism

1. The text of the resolution can be found at "1st World Conference on Women, Mexico," http://www.choike.org/nuevo_eng/informes/1453.html (accessed 14 May 2015).

2. "Great Changes, New Chances, Tough Choices," *Time*, 5 January 1976.

3. *Christianity Today* conducted a survey of 250 "conservative and liberal" Christians on issues related to women's rights, including ordination, submission, and ERA. The 87 respondents included 23 women. Though such a small sample is far from representative—and the magazine offered no description of its survey methodology—these articles, in the flagship magazine of evangelicalism, indicated that in 1974, the "party line" of conservative Christianity did not necessarily include opposition to ERA. "Editorial: Some Thoughts for the ERA Era," *Christianity Today*, 27 September 1974, 36–38; Cheryl Forbes, "Survey Results: Changing Church Roles for Women?" *Christianity Today*, 27 September 1974, 42–44.

4. Letha Scanzoni and Nancy Hardesty, *All We're Meant to Be: A Biblical Approach to Women's Liberation* (Waco, Tex.: Word, 1974), 60, 205.

5. Alice Mathews, "The Struggle for the Moral High Ground: Christians for Biblical Equality vs. The Council for Biblical Manhood and Womanhood," *Journal of Biblical Equality* 4 (1992): 98, 95.

6. Harold Lindsell, "Egalitarianism and Scriptural Infallibility," *Christianity Today*, 26 March 1976, 45.

7. Carl F. H. Henry, "Reflections on Women's Lib," *Christianity Today*, 3 January 1975, 26.

8. Phyllis Schlafly, "Facing the Future: Family vs. Feminism," *Phyllis Schlafly Report*, April 1990, 1.

9. Beverly LaHaye, Fundraising letter (n.d.), Feminism Folder, Fundamentalism file, Bob Jones University Archive.

10. John R. Rice, *Bobbed Hair, Bossy Wives, and Women Preachers* (Murfreesboro, Tenn.: Sword of the Lord, 2000), 46.

11. Margaret Bendroth, *Fundamentalism and Gender, 1875 to the Present* (New Haven, Conn.: Yale University Press, 1993), 41.

12. Kathleen C. Boone, *The Bible Tells Them So: The Discourse of Protestant Fundamentalism* (Albany: State University of New York Press, 1989), 45–46.

13. Harold Lindsell, *The Battle for the Bible* (Grand Rapids, Mich.: Zondervan, 1976), 20, 21, 24.

14. Donald W. Dayton, "Battle for the Bible: Renewing the Inerrancy Debate," *Christian Century*, 10 November 1976, 976.

15. Harold Lindsell, *The Bible in the Balance* (Grand Rapids, Mich.: Zondervan 1979), 16, 17.

16. Dayton, "Battle for the Bible," 976.

17. Lindsell, *The Bible in the Balance*, 12.

18. Oral Memoirs of Morris Chapman, Texas Collection, Baylor University, Waco. Chapman's memoirs were recorded in 1998 (hereafter Texas Collection)

19. 1 Timothy 2:12, KJV.

20. "1 Timothy 2:13—a Simple, Straightforward Verse That Egalitarians Cannot Explain," *CBMW News*, December 1996, 13.

21. Nancy Hastings Sehested, "We Have This Treasure," sermon given at Women in Ministry Meeting, 1983, reprinted in Walter B. Shurden and Randy Shepley, *Going for the Jugular: A Documentary History of the SBC Holy War* (Macon, Ga.: Mercer, 1996), 82.

22. Tim Bayly, "Where Have All the Fathers Gone?" *Journal of Biblical Manhood and Womanhood* (Spring 1999): 7.

23. Oral Memoirs of R. Albert Mohler, Texas Collection. Mohler's memoirs were recorded for 1997–1999.

24. Quoted in Molly Worthen, "The Reformer: How Al Mohler Transformed a Seminary, Helped Change a Denomination, and Challenges a Secular Culture," *Christianity Today*, 20 October 2010.

25. Oral Memoirs of R. Albert Mohler.

26. For the history and development of this movement, see Pamela Cochran, *Evangelical Feminism: A History* (New York: New York University Press, 2005).

27. Scanzoni and Hardesty, *All We're Meant to Be*, 15.

28. Ibid., 98–105.

29. Ibid., 20.

30. Because individual churches ordain ministers in the SBC, exact ordination statistics are hard to come by. A 1976 article said that before the publication of *All We're Meant to Be*, female SBC pastors numbered in the single digits. Seven years later, an article pegged that number around 200. Sarah Frances Anders, "Women in Ministry: The Distaff of the Church in Action," *Review and Expositor* 80 (1983): 30; C. R. Daley, "Current Trends Among Southern Baptists," *Western Recorder*, 5 August 1976, 2. Both articles cited in Hankins, *Uneasy in Babylon*, 308 n.13. Historian Leon McBeth estimated approximately fifty women had been ordained in SBC churches between 1964 and 1979. Leon McBeth, *Women in Baptist Life* (Nashville: Broadman, 1979), 16.

31. Timothy Weber, "Evangelical Egalitarianism: Where We Are Now," *Journal of Biblical Equality* 1, 1 (1989): 71, 72, 76.

32. Samuel Terrien, *Till the Heart Sings: A Biblical Theology of Manhood and Womanhood* (Philadelphia: Fortress Press, 1985), 194.

33. In her essential study of the charismatic movement Women's Aglow, Marie Griffith has demonstrated the subtle flexibility of the doctrine of submission, showing how evangelical women used it as a method of empowerment. See R. Marie Griffith, *God's Daughters: Evangelical Women and the Power of Submission* (Berkeley: University of California Press, 1997).

34. Scanzoni and Hardesty, *All We're Meant to Be*, 203.

35. Weber, "Evangelical Egalitarianism," 72.

36. Resolution on Racial Reconciliation on the 150th Anniversary of the Southern Baptist Convention (Southern Baptist Convention, 1995), http://www.sbc.net/resolutions/ amResolution. asp?ID=899. See also Hankins, *Uneasy in Babylon*, 240–71.

37. Stephen D. Kovach, "Egalitarians Revamp Doctrine of the Trinity," *CBMW News*, December 1996, 1, 3–5.

38. On this point, see Paul Harvey, *Freedom's Coming: Religious Culture and the Shaping of the South from the Civil War through the Civil Rights Era* (Chapel Hill: University of North Carolina Press, 2005), 246.

39. Oral Memoirs of Dorothy Patterson, Texas Collection.

40. The document took its name from Danvers, Massachusetts, where conservative leaders met to draft and sign the document. The location of that meeting suggests that SBC conservatives were part of a larger movement, but their commitment to complementarianism eventually won them control of the movement's most important institutions.

41. Danvers Statement (1987), http://www.cbmw.org/about/danvers.php.

42. Raymond C. Ortlund, Jr., "Male Female-Equality and Male Headship: Genesis 1–3," in *Recovering Biblical Manhood and Womanhood: A Response to Evangelical Feminism*, ed. John Piper and Wayne Grudem (Wheaton, Ill.: Crossway, 1991), 95.

43. George W. Knight, III, "The Family and the Church: How Should Biblical Manhood and Womanhood Work Out in Practice?" in *Recovering Biblical Manhood and Womanhood*, ed. Piper and Grudem, 345.

44. Southern Baptist Convention, "Comparison of 1925, 1963, and 2000 *Baptist Faith and Message*," 2000, http://www.sbc.net/bfm2000/bfmcomparison.asp (accessed 21 January 2015).

45. Gustav Niehbur, "Southern Baptists Declare Wife Should 'Submit' to Her Husband," *New York Times*, 10 June 1998, A1.

46. "CBMW News Interview: Executive Director, Tim Bayly," *CBMW News*, March 1997, 3.

47. Oral Memoirs of Dorothy Patterson.

48. Susan Foh, *Women and the Word of God: A Response to Biblical Feminism* (Phillipsburg, N.J.: Presbyterian and Reformed Publishing, 1979), 7.

49. Mary Pride, *The Way Home: Beyond Feminism, Back to Reality* (Westchester, Ill.: Crossway, 1985), 92. Pride cited Deuteronomy 6:7: "And thou shalt teach them diligently unto thy children, and shalt talk of them when thou sittest in thine house, and when thou walkest by the way, and when thou liest down, and when thou risest up"; and Deuteronomy 11:19: "Ye shall teach them your children, speaking of them when thou sittest in thine house, and when thou walkest by the way, when thou liest down, and when thou risest up."

50. Ibid., 48, 63.

51. Elizabeth Cady Stanton, *The Woman's Bible, Part II* (New York: European Publishing, 1898), 8.

52. Mary Daly, *Beyond God the Father: Toward a Philosophy of Women's Liberation* (Boston: Beacon, 1973), 70–72.

53. I borrow this phrase from Carol Felsenthal, *The Sweetheart of the Silent Majority: The Biography of Phyllis Schlafly* (Garden City, N.Y.: Doubleday, 1981).

54. "ERA Suffers Defeat," *I Love America: Hotline Report*, September 1980, "I Love America Campaign: Hotline Report" folder, Liberty University Archive.

55. "Conservative Forum," *Human Events*, 7 February 1976, 18.

56. "Ford, Congress Increase Funds for Militant Women's Lobby," *Human Events*, 29 May 1976, 1.

57. Donald T. Critchlow, *Phyllis Schlafly and Grassroots Conservatism: A Woman's Crusade* (Princeton, N.J.: Princeton University Press, 2005), 218.

58. Ibid.

59. Phyllis Schlafly, "Can Federal Bureaucrats Buy Passage of Equal Rights Amendment?" *Human Events*, 15 May 1976, 10.

60. Phyllis Schlafly, "How ERA Would Change Federal Laws," *Moral Majority Report*, January 1982, 9; U.S. Commission on Civil Rights, *Sex Bias in the U.S. Code: A Report of the U.S. Commission on Civil Rights* (Washington, D.C.: Government Printing Office, 1977), iii.

61. Schlafly, "How ERA Would Change Federal Laws," 9.

62. Quoted in Critchlow, *Phyllis Schlafly and Grassroots Conservatism*, 224.

63. Donald G. Mathews and Jane Sherron De Hart, *Sex, Gender, and the Politics of ERA: A State and the Nation* (New York: Oxford University Press, 1990), 43, 36.

64. Phyllis Schlafly, *The Power of the Christian Woman* (Cincinnati: Standard Publishers, 1981), 27, 26.

65. Critchlow, *Phyllis Schlafly and Grassroots Conservatism*, 12.

66. Grant Wacker, "Searching for Norman Rockwell: Popular Evangelicalism in Contemporary America," in *The Evangelical Tradition in America*, ed. Leonard I. Sweet (Macon, Ga.: Mercer University Press, 1984), 311.

67. Stephanie Coontz, *The Way We Never Were: American Families and the Nostalgia Trap* (New York: Basic Books, 1992), 9. See also Elaine Tyler May, *Homeward Bound: American Families in the Cold War Era* (New York: Basic, 1988).

68. "Family Manifesto," Moral Majority: Policy Documents, Family Manifesto folder, Liberty University Archive.

69. Charlie Judd, "Listen America Radio Broadcast," 12 April 1988, transcript in Listen America Radio folder, Liberty University Archive.

70. Rus Walton, "Will Baptists Ever See Through Carter?" *Human Events*, 25 September 1976, 14.

71. Critchlow, *Phyllis Schlafly and Grassroots Conservatism*, 276–81.

72. The most thoughtful and extensive study of the role of evangelicals in the emergence of Sunbelt conservatism is Darren Dochuk, *From Bible Belt to Sunbelt: Plain-Folk Religion, Grassroots Politics, and the Rise of Evangelical Conservatism* (New York: Norton, 2011). Dochuk demonstrates that southern evangelical migrants to southern California were instrumental in establishing grassroots conservatism on the West Coast. In the Old South, conservatives developed a language of "color-blind conservatism" that elided racial divisions and permitted white southerners to appeal more broadly in other regions. On this development, see Matthew D. Lassiter, *The Silent Majority: Suburban Politics in the Sunbelt South* (Princeton, N.J.: Princeton University Press, 2006). Other excellent studies of these phenomena include Kevin Michael Kruse, *White Flight: Atlanta and the Making of Modern Conservatism* (Princeton, N.J.: Princeton University Press, 2005); Lisa McGirr, *Suburban Warriors: The Origins of the New American Right* (Princeton, N.J.: Princeton University Press, 2001); Daniel K. Williams, *God's Own Party: The Making of the Christian Right* (New York: Oxford University Press, 2010).

73. Donald G. Mathews and Jane Sherron De Hart, *Sex, Gender, and the Politics of ERA: A State and the Nation* (New York: Oxford University Press, 1990), 65.

74. "CWA Members Top NOW by 115,000," *Teaching Home*, August/September 1984, 3.

75. Both documents were published by Concerned Women for America in 1979. They are available in the Feminism folder, G. Archer Weniger papers, Fundamentalism File, Mack Library, Bob Jones University.

76. Dee Jepsen, *Women: Beyond Equal Rights* (Waco, Tex.: Word Books, 1984), 65. The statistic came from a study reported in the January 1984 issue of *Glamour* magazine.

77. Ibid., 83.

78. Patrick J. Buchanan, "Buchanan, 'Culture War Speech,' Speech Text," 17 August 1992, http://voicesofdemocracy.umd.edu/buchanan-culture-war-speech-speech-text/ (accessed 21 January 2015).

Chapter 6. Gay Rights

1. James Dobson, *Where's Dad?* (Focus on the Family, n.d.), http://www.youtube.com/watch?v=BbV0p0kh-rc.

2. Edwin Louis Cole, *Maximized Manhood* (New Kensington, Pa.: Whitaker House, 2000), 116.

3. Jerry Falwell, *Listen, America!* (Garden City, N.Y.: Doubleday, 1980), 111.

4. Morrie Ryskind, "What in the World Are We Coming To?" *Human Events*, 3 November 1979, 11.

5. Falwell, *Listen, America!*, 104.

6. Conservative evangelicals, along with most Americans in the 1970s to 1990s, used "homosexuality" to denote a fixed identity. As scholars of gender and sexuality have demonstrated, however, sexual orientation is mutable, and it is a misnomer to define people who engage in same-sex behavior monolithically according to their sexual activity. Throughout the chapter, I use the term homosexual only when quoting or paraphrasing my historical subjects, in order to reflect the understanding of gays and lesbians that predominated during the late twentieth century.

7. Margot Canaday, *The Straight State: Sexuality and Citizenship in Twentieth-Century America* (Princeton, N.J.: Princeton University Press, 2011).

8. Quoted in Didi Herman, *The Antigay Agenda: Orthodox Vision and the Christian Right* (Chicago: University of Chicago Press, 1997), 31.

9. Ibid., 32.

10. For an excellent, concise history of the gay rights movement, see John D'Emilio, "Cycles of Change, Questions of Strategy: The Gay and Lesbian Movement after Fifty Years," in *The Politics of Gay Rights*, ed. Craig A. Rimmerman, Kenneth D. Wald, and Clyde Wilcox (Chicago: University of Chicago Press, 2000), 31–53.

11. Ibid., 35.

12. Ryskind, "What in the World Are We Coming To?" 11.

13. See Philip Jenkins's chapter, "Mainstreaming the Sixties," for analysis of how elements of the 1960s counterculture won official endorsements in the 1970s. Philip Jenkins, *Decade of Nightmares: The End of the Sixties and the Making of Eighties America* (New York: Oxford University Press, 2006), 24–36.

14. David K. Johnson, *The Lavender Scare: The Cold War Persecution of Gays and Lesbians in the Federal Government* (Chicago: University of Chicago Press, 2009).

15. "Falwell Lied About Carter, White House Aide Says," *Lynchburg News*, 7 August 1980, A2.

16. Falwell, *Listen, America!*, 157, 159.

17. Charlie Judd, "Listen America Radio Broadcast," 28 December 1987, T\transcript in Listen America Radio folder, Liberty University Archive.

18. James Dobson and Gary L. Bauer, *Children at Risk: The Battle for the Hearts and Minds of Our Kids* (Dallas: Word Books, 1990), 59–60.

19. Quoted in Falwell, *Listen, America!*, 160.

20. Tim LaHaye, *The Unhappy Gays: What Everyone Should Know About Homosexuality* (Wheaton, Ill.: Tyndale House, 1978), 163. Throughout the book, LaHaye refers to homosexuals as males; he rarely discusses lesbians.

21. Ibid., 91.

22. Ibid., 119–40.

23. H. Edward Rowe, "Homosexuality and the Suicide of Civilizations" (unpublished essay), July 1979, box 145, National Association of Evangelicals collection, Wheaton College Archives.

24. William Dannemeyer, *Shadow in the Land: Homosexuality in America* (San Francisco: Ignatius Press, 1989), 19.

25. Roger J. Magnuson, *Are Gay Rights Right?* (Portland, Ore.: Multnomah, 1990), 13. On NAMBLA's fractious relationship with the mainstream gay rights movement, see Jenkins, *Decade of Nightmares*, 259–61; Benoit Denizet-Lewis, "Boy Crazy," *Boston Magazine*, May 2001.

26. "Bias Against Homosexuals Is Outlawed in Miami," *New York Times*, 19 January 1977, 14.

27. Jenkins, *Decade of Nightmares*, 120–22.

28. For a good account of the campaign, see Daniel K. Williams, *God's Own Party: The Making of the Christian Right* (New York: Oxford University Press, 2010), 146–53. See also "Issues: Gay Rights Showdown in Miami," *Time*, 13 June 1977.

29. Anita Bryant, *Anita Bryant Story: The Survival of our Nation's Families and the Threat of Militant Homosexuality* (Old Tappan, N.J.: Fleming H. Revell, 1977), 125.

30. Ibid., 135.

31. "Will White House Cool It on Counterculture?," *Human Events*, 18 June 1977, 3.

32. On the role of fear—specifically, fear of gays and lesbians—in late twentieth-century evangelicalism and conservative politics, see Jason Bivins, *Religion of Fear: The Politics of Horror in Conservative Evangelicalism* (New York: Oxford University Press, 2008), 216–20; Jenkins, *Decade of Nightmares*, 119–25.

33. Bryant, *Anita Bryant Story*, 24–25.

34. Ibid., 27.

35. Ibid., 57–59.

36. Ken Kelley, "Playboy Interview: Anita Bryant," *Playboy*, May 1978, 78.

37. Williams, *God's Own Party*, 150–51.

38. Falwell, *Listen, America!*, 158; 1 Corinthians 6:9, 10, KJV.

39. Philip Goff, Arthur E. Farnsley, II, and Peter J. Thuesen, *The Bible in American Life*, National Study, Center for the Study of Religion and American Culture, 6 March 2014, http://www.raac.iupui.edu/files/2713/9413/8354/Bible_in_American_Life_Report_March_6_2014.pdf (accessed 21 January 2015).

40. Dale B. Martin, "Arsenokoites and Malakos: Meanings and Consequences," in *Biblical Ethics and Homosexuality: Listening to Scripture*, ed. Robert K. Brawley (Louisville, Ky.: Westminster John Knox, 1996), 117–36.

41. Falwell, *Listen, America!*, 159.

42. Didi Herman, *The Antigay Agenda: Orthodox Vision and the Christian Right* (Chicago: University of Chicago Press, 1997), 94.

43. John W. Drakeford, *A Christian View of Homosexuality* (Nashville, Tenn.: Broadman, 1977), 57.

44. Herman, *The Antigay Agenda*, 95.

45. American Legislative Exchange Council, "The State Factor," May 1985, in National Association of Evangelicals records, box 145, folder 10, Wheaton College Archives.

46. William Dannemeyer, *Shadow in the Land: Homosexuality in America* (San Francisco: Ignatius Press, 1989), 59.

47. Tim LaHaye, *The Unhappy Gays: What Everyone Should Know about Homosexuality* (Wheaton, Ill.: Tyndale House, 1978), 17.

48. Dannemeyer, *Shadow in the Land*, 9.

49. Jesse Helms, "The One Campaign Issue Is Leadership," *Human Events*, 1 May 1976, 21.

50. Quoted in Ernest B. Furgurson, *Hard Right: The Rise of Jesse Helms* (New York: Norton, 1986), 181.

51. See Mab Segrest, "Anatomy of an Election," *Southern Exposure*, September/October 1985, 19–24. See also William D. Snider, *Helms and Hunt: The North Carolina Senate Race, 1984* (Chapel Hill: University of North Carolina Press, 1985), 136–39.

52. "Carter Comes out of the Closet," *Human Events*, 26 June 1976, 8; "Gays Heavily Represented: Administration Stacks Deck on 'Families' Conference," *Human Events*, 24 May 1980, 1; "White House Conference Shapes Up as Gay Affair," *Human Events*, 16 February 1980, 3.

53. M. Stanton Evans, "Sen. Jesse Helms: A New Kind of Politician," *Human Events*, 5 August 1978, 10, 14.

54. Michael Korda, "The Gradual Decline and Total Collapse of Nearly Everyone," *Family*

Weekly Magazine, 29 August 1982, as quoted in Deryl Edwards, "'Strange Vacuum' Covers America," *Moral Majority Report*, September 1982, 11.

55. George Fowler, "The Meaning of an American Man," *Human Events*, 28 May 1977, 8.

56. John Chamberlain, "A President Reagan Would Be a Moral Leader," *Human Events*, 3 November 1979, 9; Deryl Edwards, "Key Posts Please Conservatives," *Moral Majority Report*, 16 March 1981, 3.

57. Ronald Reagan, "If the Gov't. Ran the World Series," *Human Events*, 13 October 1979, 8.

58. Enrique Rueda, *The Homosexual Network: Private Lives and Public Policy* (Old Greenwich, Conn.: Devin Adair, 1982), 396.

59. Williams, *God's Own Party*, 153.

60. Donald T. Critchlow, *The Conservative Ascendancy: How the GOP Right Made Political History* (Cambridge, Mass.: Harvard University Press, 2007), 216–19.

61. William C. Martin, *With God on Our Side: The Rise of the Religious Right in America* (New York: Broadway, 1996), 235.

62. Ibid., 236.

63. Rueda, *The Homosexual Network*, 396.

Chapter 7. Military Men

1. Bobby H. Welch, *You, the Warrior Leader: Applying Military Strategy for Victorious Spiritual Warfare* (Nashville, Tenn.: Broadman & Holman, 2004), 1, 24, 12–19.

2. James Davison Hunter, *Culture Wars: The Struggle to Define America* (New York: Basic, 1991).

3. Anne C. Loveland, *American Evangelicals and the U.S. Military, 1942–1993* (Baton Rouge: Louisiana State University Press, 1996), 47.

4. Jerry Falwell, "An Open Letter from Jerry Falwell on the Nuclear Freeze," *Moral Majority Report*, April 1983, 15.

5. Catherine S. Manegold, "The Odd Place of Homosexuality in the Military," *New York Times*, 18 April 1993, E1.

6. Romans 13:1b, KJV.

7. Robert H. Krapohl and Charles H. Lippy, *The Evangelicals: A Historical, Thematic, and Biographical Guide* (Westport, Conn.: Greenwood, 1999), 134. Krapohl and Lippy note that Christian Crusade became so political that in 1966 it lost its tax-exempt status.

8. George M. Marsden, *Fundamentalism and American Culture*, 2nd ed. (New York: Oxford University Press, 2006), 142.

9. Ibid., 149.

10. Jordan Green and Chris Kromm, "Missiles and Magnolias: The South at War," *Southern Exposure* (Spring & Summer 2002): 15.

11. Samuel S. Hill famously captured the notion of an intact Christian culture in his 1966 treatise *Southern Churches in Crisis*, which examined the failure of white southern churches to address the civil rights movement. White southern Protestantism, wrote Hill, "remained largely sheltered from serious obstacles and challenges until the present decade." Samuel S. Hill, *Southern Churches in Crisis Revisited*, new ed. (Tuscaloosa: University of Alabama Press, 1999), 16.

12. Jerry Falwell, *Falwell: An Autobiography* (Lynchburg, Va.: Liberty House, 1997), 361.

13. Jason Sokol, *There Goes My Everything: White Southerners in the Age of Civil Rights, 1945–1975* (New York: Knopf, 2006), 323, 344, 345.

14. "Editorial: Concerning Civil Disobedience," *Free Will Baptist* 83, 17 (1968): 2.

15. Loveland, *American Evangelicals and the U.S. Military*, 164.

16. Quoted in "America Speaks! [Letters to the Editor]," *Moral Majority Report*, 16 March 1981, 18.

17. G. Russell Evans, "Shall America Be Defended?," *Moral Majority Report*, 15 September 1980, 8.

18. Thomas W. Klewin, "Blest Be the Tie That Binds," *Free Will Baptist* 83, 21 (1968): 5.

19. Quoted in "America's Top Military Officer Calls Christians to 'God's Army,'" *Christianity Today*, 20 April 1984, 37.

20. Harvey Gallagher Cox, *Military Chaplains: From Religious Military to a Military Religion*, ed. Harvey G. Cox, Jr. (New York: American Report, 1971).

21. Jacqueline E. Whitt, *Bringing God to Men: American Military Chaplains and the Vietnam War* (Chapel Hill: University of North Carolina Press, 2014), 215.

22. Evans, "Shall America Be Defended?" 9.

23. Conservative Christian churches often provided many compassion ministries to their members free of charge, supporting those believers who otherwise would rely on governmental assistance. As such, members of these communities saw the state's welfare concerns as unnecessary and viewed defense and foreign policy as the primary task of government. See James M. Ault, *Spirit and Flesh: Life in a Fundamentalist Baptist Church* (New York: Knopf, 2004), 99–100.

24. In 1969, the United States possessed 28,200 nuclear weapons, the Soviet Union 11,000. Both countries also had delivery vehicles capable of reaching the other nation. These arsenals were sufficient to provide "assured destruction capability," in the words of former U.S. defense secretary Robert McNamara. For a detailed chronology of the global development of nuclear weapons and nonproliferation efforts, see Sarah J. Diehl and James Clay Moltz, *Nuclear Weapons and Nonproliferation: A Reference Handbook* (Santa Barbara, Calif.: ABC-CLIO, 2002), 53–158.

25. Richard Reeves, *President Reagan: The Triumph of Imagination* (New York: Simon & Schuster, 2005), 68.

26. Philip Jenkins, *Decade of Nightmares: The End of the Sixties and the Making of Eighties America* (New York: Oxford University Press, 2006), 221.

27. *The Challenge of Peace: God's Promise and Our Response, a Pastoral Letter on War and Peace* (Chicago: National Conference of Catholic Bishops, 1983), vi, vii.

28. "SALT II: The Only Alternative to Annihilation?," *Christianity Today*, 27 March 1981, 15.

29. "Evangelicals Are of Two Minds on Nuclear Weapons Issues," *Christianity Today*, 5 August 1983, 49.

30. Quoted in William C. Martin, *A Prophet with Honor: The Billy Graham Story* (New York: W. Morrow, 1991), 500. SALT 10 did not actually exist; Graham used the moniker to indicate his frustration with incremental weapons reduction. He thought the nuclear threat demanded that nuclear powers leapfrog minor agreements and make an unambiguous commitment to eradicating nuclear weapons.

31. "A Change of Heart," *Sojourners*, August 1979, 12–14.

32. "SALT II: The Only Alternative to Annihilation?" 14.

33. Randy Frame, "Is the Road to Peace Paved with Might or with Meekness?" *Christianity Today*, 15 July 1983, 42.

34. Falwell, "An Open Letter," 15. *Moral Majority Report* reported that the "open letter" ran in the *Washington Post*, *New York Times*, *Detroit Free Press*, *Chicago Tribune*, and *Los Angeles Times*, as well as in several smaller outlets. Moral Majority credited the ad with stalling Congressional plans to push through a nuclear freeze bill in May 1983. See "Nationwide Anti-Freeze Newspaper Ad Campaign Started," *Moral Majority Report*, May 1983, 6.

35. Falwell, "An Open Letter," 15.

36. Kenneth S. Kantzer, "What Shall We Do About the Nuclear Problem?" *Christianity Today*, 21 January 1983, 11.

37. "General Graham: America Can Defend Itself," *Moral Majority Report*, November 1982, 8.

38. Quoted in Grace Halsell, *Prophecy and Politics: Militant Evangelists on the Road to Nuclear War* (Westport, Conn.: Lawrence Hill, 1986), 32, 47, 49.

39. Robert Baldwin, "Peace through Strength," *Moral Majority Report*, April 1983, 3.

40. Roy C. Jones, "Lt. General Daniel Graham Says High Frontier Guaratees Will Protect U.S.," *Moral Majority Report*, December 1983, 14.

41. G. Russell Evans, "Freedom: Endangered Species of the Nuclear Age," *Moral Majority Report*, 24 May 1982, 10.

42. Walter Williams, "Nuclear Weapons Don't Make War Immoral," *Moral Majority Report*, January 1983, 15.

43. Falwell, "An Open Letter," 15.

44. Dave Sims, "A Noble Move? Vermonters 'Disarm,'" *Moral Majority Report*, 26 April 1982, 9.

45. "General Graham: America Can Defend Itself," 8.

46. Daniel O. Graham, "Dense Pack: Intelligence Insult," *Moral Majority Report*, February 1983, 15.

47. For a more detailed account of the tensions of 1983 and Reagan's role in them, see Jenkins, *Decade of Nightmares*, 219–26.

48. See, for instance, "Evangelicals Are of Two Minds on Nuclear Weapons Issues," 48–50.

49. Dinesh D'Souza, "Falwell at Harvard: Hisses and Jeers, and Even a Few 'Amens,'" *Christianity Today*, 17 June 1983, 41.

50. See Edward Gilbreath, "The Jerry We Never Knew," *Christianity Today*, 24 April 2000, 113, 114.

51. Anne C. Loveland, *American Evangelicals and the U.S. Military, 1942–1993* (Baton Rouge: Louisiana State University Press, 1996), 99, 299.

52. Ibid., 277.

53. A partial audio recording of the film is available on Youtube: Dobson, *Where's Dad?*, https://www.youtube.com/watch?v=fdOMsh8TuMw.

54. "All Active-Duty U.S. Soldiers Are Expected to See Dobson Film," *Christianity Today*, October 5, 1984, 100.

55. Loveland, *American Evangelicals and the U.S. Military*, 275–95.

56. Quoted in B. Drummond Ayres, "Even the Thought Is Off-Limits," *New York Times*, 28 January 1993, A16.

57. Quoted in Colonel Ronald D. Ray, "Lifting the Ban on Homosexuals in the Military: The Subversion of a Moral Principle," in *Gays and Lesbians in the Military*, ed. Wilbur J. Scott and Sandra Carson Stanley (New York: de Gruyter, 1994), 88.

58. Allan Bérubé, *Coming Out Under Fire: The History of Gay Men and Women in World War Two* (New York: Free Press, 1990).

59. Timothy Haggerty, "History Repeating Itself: A Historical Overview of Gay Men and Lesbians in the Military before 'Don't Ask, Don't Tell'" in *Don't Ask, Don't Tell: Debating the Gay Ban in the Military*, ed. Aaron Belkin and Geoffrey Bateman (Boulder, Colo.: Lynne Rienner, 2003), 23, 45 n.38.

60. Randy Shilts, *Conduct Unbecoming: Lesbians and Gays in the U.S. Military, Vietnam to the Persian Gulf* (New York: St. Martin's, 1993), 3–4.

61. Eric Schmitt, "A Military Town Makes Its Anti-Gay Feelings Clear," *New York Times*, 25 March 1993, A16.

62. Eric Schmitt, "Joint Chiefs Fighting Clinton Plan to Allow Homosexuals in Military," *New York Times*, 23 January 1993, 10.

63. See Loveland, *American Evangelicals and the U.S. Military*, 165–180.

64. Alexander F. C. Webster, "Homosexuals in Uniform?" *Christianity Today*, 8 February 1993, 23.

65. Some moderate and liberal Christians supported Clinton's initiative. See, for instance, John

Jesse Carey, ed. *The Christian Argument for Gays and Lesbians in the Military: Essays by Mainline Church Leaders* (Lewiston, N.Y.: Mellen, 1993); Christine E. Gudorf, "Homosexual Stereotypes: Gays in the Military," *Christian Century*, 19–26 May 1993, 540–42; James M. Wall, "Gays and the Military: A Matter of Civil Rights," *Christian Century*, 17 February 1993, 163–64.

66. Webster, "Homosexuals in Uniform?" 23.

67. Stephen Mansfield, *The Faith of the American Soldier* (New York: Tarcher/Penguin, 2005), 116.

68. For instance, two of the most prominent leaders of Moral Majority, Cal Thomas and Ed Dobson, left the movement entirely and wrote a book chronicling their disappointments with the Christian right. See Cal Thomas and Ed Dobson, *Blinded by Might: Can the Religious Right Save America?* (Grand Rapids, Mich.: Zondervan, 1999).

69. Quoted in Peter Applebome, "Gay Issue Mobilizes Conservatives against Clinton," *New York Times*, 1 February 1993, A14.

70. Ibid.

71. Quoted in David Margolick, "At Fort Bragg, Reaction to Gay Policy Is Largely Ho-Hum," *New York Times*, 21 July 1993, A14.

72. Quoted in Manegold, "The Odd Place of Homosexuality in the Military," E1; Margolick, "At Fort Bragg, Reaction to Gay Policy Is Largely Ho-Hum."

73. See, for instance, Carey, ed. *The Christian Argument for Gays and Lesbians in the Military*; Jonathan Schell, *The Fate of the Earth* (New York: Knopf, 1982); Ronald J. Sider and Richard K. Taylor, *Nuclear Holocaust and Christian Hope: A Book for Christian Peacemakers* (New York: Paulist, 1982).

74. Kantzer, "What Shall We Do About the Nuclear Problem?" 11.

Chapter 8. Promise Keepers

1. Carl Crawford Schmidt, "Promise Keepers: Message to Men," *Christian Century*, 7 September 1994, 805–6.

2. See the entire list of promises in Jon P. Bloch, "The New and Improved Clint Eastwood: Change and Persistence in Promise Keepers Self-Help Literature," in *Promise Keepers and the New Masculinity: Private Lives and Public Morality*, ed. Rhys H. Williams (Lanham, Md.: Lexington, 2001), 31.

3. Richard Abanes, "The Dark Side of the Militia," *New Man*, March/April 1997, 69–72; Joe Maxwell, "'Til Race Do Us Part?: Interracial Couples Discover a Stronghold of Prejudice in America," *New Man*, January/February 1997, 26–31.

4. Tony Evans, "Spiritual Purity," in *Seven Promises of a Promise Keeper* (Colorado Springs: Focus on the Family, 1994), 79.

5. Michael G. Maudlin, "Why We Need Feminism," *New Man*, November/December 1997, 37.

6. Sara Diamond analyzed the overlap between conservative religion and conservative politics in *Not by Politics Alone*. Like Diamond, I believe, "the realms of the personal and the political do not correlate neatly or predictably." See Sara Diamond, *Not by Politics Alone: The Enduring Influence of the Christian Right* (New York: Guilford, 1998), viii.

7. Jerry Gray, "Critics Try to Divine Organization's Politics," *New York Times*, 5 October 1997, 25.

8. Brittany Anas, "CU-Boulder Employees Express 'Deep Concerns' About Bill McCartney," *Daily Camera*, 29 November 2010.

9. Richard Hoffer and Shelley Smith, "Putting His House in Order: Bill McCartney Quit as Colorado's Coach for a Greater Quest: Healing His Family," *Sports Illustrated*, 16 January 1995.

10. Edward Gilbreath, "Manhood's Great Awakening," *Christianity Today*, 6 February 1995, 26.

11. David Halbrook, "Is This Revival?" *New Man*, December 1995, 24.

12. Steve Rabey, "Where Is the Christian Men's Movement Headed? Burgeoning Promise Keepers Inspires Look-Alikes," *Christianity Today*, 29 April 1996, 60.

13. Deborah Gray White, "What Women Want: The Paradoxes of Postmodernity as Seen through Promise Keeper and Million Man March Women," in *Interconnections: Gender and Race in American History*, ed. Carol Faulkner and Alison M. Parker (Rochester, N.Y.: University of Rochester Press, 2012), 233–40.

14. Kathryn T. Long, *The Revival of 1857–58: Interpreting an American Religious Awakening* (New York: Oxford University Press, 1998), 86. Long's treatment offers a fascinating look at the interplay of men and women at the noontime prayer meetings, mixed-gender spaces that were nonetheless interpreted as "masculine." Another good study of the 1858 revival, by religious studies scholar John Corrigan, reveals the appeals to "heart religion" that occurred during the mid-nineteenth century, even in a self-styled "businessmen's revival." See John Corrigan, *Business of the Heart: Religion and Emotion in the Nineteenth Century* (Berkeley: University of California Press, 2001).

15. The best treatment of muscular Christianity is Clifford Putney, *Muscular Christianity: Manhood and Sports in Protestant America, 1880–1920* (Cambridge, Mass.: Harvard University Press, 2001).

16. Evans, "Spiritual Purity," 79.

17. Stephen Mansfield, "Men of the Decade," *New Man*, August 2004, 26–36. Mel Gibson and Bono also made the cut.

18. Patrick Morley, "Will the Christian Men's Movement Rise Again?" *New Man*, August 2004, 39.

19. Sociologist John P. Bartkowski has written a number of probing explorations of Promise Keepers' ideologies of masculinity. He helpfully divides "instrumental" discourses from "godly" notions of manhood. The former attribute essential characteristics to men that must be sated by certain activities, while the "godly manhood" advocated by some PK authors suggests that men ought to overcome some of their "natural" inclinations to serve their wives and families. See John P. Bartkowski, *The Promise Keepers: Servants, Soldiers, and Godly Men* (New Brunswick, N.J.: Rutgers University Press, 2004); John P. Bartkowski, "Breaking Walls, Raising Fences: Masculinity, Intimacy, and Accountability among the Promise Keepers," in *Promise Keepers and the New Masculinity*, ed. Williams, 33–53.

20. Michael G. Maudlin, "Why We Need Feminism," *New Man*, November/December 1997, 37.

21. John Calhoun, "Bringing Up Boys," *New Man*, June 2003, 19.

22. Bryan Malley, "Why Gay Marriage Will Hurt America," *New Man*, October 2004, 28.

23. Bill McCartney, "A Call to Unity," in *Seven Promises of a Promise Keeper*, 157, 163. McCartney's diagnosis of "generational sin" went farther than most white evangelicals in assigning blame to contemporary white Americans, but he stopped short of prescribing structural or political remedies for racism, preferring instead the typical white evangelical injunctions to pray and to form personal relationships with men of different "denominational and ethnic backgrounds." White evangelicals' unwillingness to endorse structural and political remedies for systemic racism remained a dividing line between them and black evangelicals throughout the twentieth century. See Michael O. Emerson and Christian Smith, *Divided by Faith: Evangelical Religion and the Problem of Race in America* (New York: Oxford University Press, 2000).

24. Darren Dochuk, *From Bible Belt to Sunbelt: Plain-Folk Religion, Grassroots Politics, and the Rise of Evangelical Conservatism* (New York: Norton, 2011).

25. Kevin Michael Kruse, *White Flight: Atlanta and the Making of Modern Conservatism* (Princeton, N.J.: Princeton University Press, 2005); Matthew D. Lassiter, *The Silent Majority: Suburban Politics in the Sunbelt South* (Princeton, N.J.: Princeton University Press, 2006).

26. Dochuk, *From Bible Belt to Sunbelt*, 172–73.

27. McCartney, "A Call to Unity," 159.

28. Hoffer and Smith, "Putting His House in Order."

29. Ibid.

30. McCartney, "A Call to Unity," 161.

31. L. Dean Allen, II, "Promise Keepers and Racism: Frame Resonance as an Indicator of Organizational Vitality," in *Promise Keepers and the New Masculinity*, ed. William, 55–72.

32. Ibid., 64, 67.

33. Billy Hawkins, "Reading a Promise Keepers Event: The Intersection of Race and Religion," in *The Promise Keepers: Essays on Masculinity and Christianity*, ed. Dane C. Claussen (Jefferson, N.C.: McFarland, 2000), 187.

34. Dave Benson, "Born Again Sports," *New Man*, April 1998, 26.

35. Dave Branon, "God's Divine Lineup: Just the Facts on a Few, Famous Born-Again Athletes," *New Man*, April 1998, 30–31.

36. Google's NGram Viewer provides a crude measure of English-language phrases' popularity in the massive database of books indexed by Google. The phrase "more time with my family" began appearing in the late 1950s, but its use spiked in the 1980s and even more in the 1990s. See http://books.google.com/ngrams (accessed 19 June 2013).

37. Gilbreath, "Manhood's Great Awakening," 26.

38. Branon, "God's Divine Lineup," 30–31.

39. Maxwell, "'Til Race Do Us Part?," 26–31.

40. Marci McDonald, "My Wife Told Me To Go: Why Promise Keepers Is Thriving Despite Feminists' Warnings," *Newsweek*, 6 October 1997, 28.

41. James A. Mathisen, "The Strange Decade of the Promise Keepers: The Revealing Story of the Rise and Fall But Continued Existence of Coach Mac's Men's Movement," *Books & Culture* (October 2001): 36.

42. Brian Peterson and Edward Gilbreath, "'We Repent,'" *New Man*, December 1997, 32.

43. Ted Olsen, "Racial Reconciliation Emphasis Intensified," *Christianity Today*, 6 January 1997, 67.

44. Edward E. Plowman, "What Went Wrong?: The Inside Story of Policy Decisions and Economic Conditions That Pushed Promise Keepers to the Brink of Financial Ruin," *World*, 21 March 1998, 13–16.

45. Peterson and Gilbreath, "'We Repent,'" 31.

46. Mathisen, "The Strange Decade of the Promise Keepers," 39.

47. McCartney, "A Call to Unity," 162.

48. Patrick Morley, "An Open Letter to Men of Color," *New Man*, June 1997, 60.

49. Andy Butcher, "Johnny Rev: Chaplain Roger Niedrich Has a Captive Audience at Civil War Re-Enactments and Carries a Bible, Not a Gun," *New Man*, October 2002, 26–28; John Calhoun, "The Wild Man: Author John Eldredge Is on a Quest to Rescue the Untamed Male Heart. Why Are so Many Guys Answering the Call?" *New Man*, October 2002, 16–20.

50. Calhoun, "The Wild Man," 18.

51. Drew Dyck, "State of a Movement: Promise Keepers Has Become Less Visible Today, but the Men's Movement Is Moving Forward in New Ways," *New Man*, August 2007, 35.

52. Calhoun, "The Wild Man," 20.

53. Rabey, "Where Is the Christian Men's Movement Headed?" 49.

54. Calhoun, "The Wild Man," 20.

55. Morley, "Will the Christian Men's Movement Rise Again?" 38–40.

56. Dyck, "State of a Movement," 30–35.

57. Stephen Mansfield, "Don't Fence Him In: Faith Didn't Tame George W. Bush, It Freed Him to Be Out-of-the-Box, Surprising, and, Above All, to Be His Own Man," *New Man*, December 2003, 18–24.

58. On the ways that evangelicalism became the dominant identity in late-twentieth century America, see Steven P. Miller, *The Age of Evangelicalism: America's Born-Again Years* (New York: Oxford University Press, 2014).

59. Jeralyn E. Merritt, "Obama's New Patriotic, Family Values Ad," *Talk Left*, 19 June 2008.

Epilogue

1. Anugrah Kumar, "Ted Haggard Says Suicides of Pastor Isaac Hunter, Others Reflect Flaws in 'Evangelical Culture,'" *Christian Post*, 14 December 2013.

2. Patton Dodd, "New Life After the Fall of Ted Haggard," *ChristianityToday.com*, 22 November 2013.

3. Brian Steensland and Philip Goff, eds., *The New Evangelical Social Engagement* (New York: Oxford University Press, 2014). For analyses of these campaigns, see the essays by Laurel Kearns (environmentalism), Gerardo Marti and Michael O. Emerson (racial justice), and David Swartz (human rights).

4. Tony Jones, *The New Christians: Dispatches from the Emergent Frontier* (San Francisco: Jossey-Bass, 2008), 82.

5. Joseph Liu, "A Post-Election Look at Religious Voters in the 2008 Election," Pew Research Religion and Public Life Project, December 8, 2008.

6. John C. Green, "New and Old Evangelical Public Engagement: A View from the Polls," in *The New Evangelical Social Engagement*, ed. Philip Goff and Brian Steensland (New York: Oxford University Press, 2014), 144–47.

INDEX

ACKNOWLEDGMENTS

In a toast at my sister's wedding, my moderately conservative father approvingly quoted Hillary Clinton's famous statement, "It takes a village to raise a child," before thanking the gathered "village" who helped rear my sister and me. As I've discovered in writing *Family Values*, it also takes a village to produce a book, even though only one name appears on the cover. Fortunately, I have space here to thank the many people—in my several villages—who helped me see this project to completion.

This book took shape during my time at Duke University, where I benefited immeasurably from my work with Grant Wacker. Grant combines a keen historical mind and exacting standards with graciousness, kindness, and generosity. His presence in scores of acknowledgments sections like this one testifies to his boundless generosity. He has left an enormous legacy in the field of American religious history that will last for decades. I am one of many scholars fortunate to count him as a mentor and friend.

At Duke I also benefited from the counsel of Julie Byrne, Curtis Freeman, Joseph Harris, David Steinmetz, and Peter Wood. Forays down the road to the University of North Carolina brought me into contact with Yaakov Ariel, Michael Lienesch, Laurie Maffly-Kipp, Donald Mathews, and Thomas Tweed. At the University of Virginia, Grace Hale and Charles Marsh encouraged me to research Jerry Falwell, which pushed me into the field of religious history and excited me about the study of evangelical conservatism. I was blessed to have such sterling mentors throughout my career.

I also want to thank the archivists and librarians who graciously accommodated almost all my requests: the inter-library loan staff and divinity library staff at Duke University, the librarians at Pacific Lutheran University (especially Lizz Zitron, who helped with a last-minute request), Russell File and Abigail Sattler at Liberty University, Phil Crane at Wake Christian Academy, Ellen Kuniyuki Brown at Baylor University, Jason Fowler at Southern Baptist Theological Seminary, Robert Erickson, Bob Shuster, and Wayne Weber at the Billy Graham Center Archives at Wheaton College, Ryan Bean at the Kautz Family YMCA Archives at the University of Minnesota, and Patrick Robbins at the Bob Jones University Fundamentalism File.

Several groups provided financial support for this project. Thanks to Duke University, the Franklin Humanities Institute, the Southern Studies Seminar at Duke and UNC, the Louisville Institute, the Thompson Writing Program at Duke, and the Provost's Office at Pacific Lutheran University.

This project benefited immeasurably from my close-knit North Carolina writing group, which met in various incarnations from 2005 to 2011. Steve Berry, Elesha Coffman, Brantley Gasaway, Matt Harper, Sarah Ruble, and Jacqueline Whitt read my work carefully and critically, saving me from numerous errors and missteps. They also offered boundless encouragement and moral support. I can only begin to express the depth of my appreciation for their friendship.

In a similar vein, a larger cohort of scholars of American religion read my work at different stages and offered critique and encouragement. I want to thank Jennifer Ayres, Jason Bivins, Anne Blue Wills, Ed Blum, Kate Bowler, Andrew Coates, Andrew Finstuen, Betsy Flowers, Tim Gloege, Michael Hamilton, Paul Harvey, Sonia Hazard, Charles Irons, David King, Jim Lewis, Katie Lofton, Kelly Kennington, Thomas Kidd, Mary Beth Mathews, Jenny McBride, Mandy McMichael, Brendan Pietsch, Tobin Miller Shearer, Josef Sorett, Angela Tarango, Dan Vaca, and David Watt. Some of the material in Chapters 4, 5, and 6 appeared in articles I published in the journal *Church History* and in the edited collection *Southern Masculinity* (University of Georgia Press); I am grateful to the publishers of those volumes for permission to reuse that material.

My editor at the University of Pennsylvania Press, Bob Lockhart, showed enthusiasm about this project from the beginning, and he has made *Family Values* better through his careful readings and constructive suggestions. Bob patiently endured my delays, and he never failed to provide trenchant critique along with encouragement. He is a wonderful editor. Alison Anderson shepherded me through the copyediting of the manuscript, sharpening the prose and saving me from several missteps. Darren Dochuk and Matt Sutton read the entire manuscript and offered suggestions that made this into a much better book. I am grateful to them for their friendship and advice.

My colleagues in the Religion Department at Pacific Lutheran

University—Agnes Choi, Suzanne Crawford-O'Brien, Tony Finitsis, Erik Hammerstrom, Brenda Llewellyn Ihssen, Doug Oakman, Kevin O'Brien, Samuel Torvend, Marit Trelstad, and Michael Zbaraschuk—have provided collegiality, encouragement, and constructive criticism. I am thankful for them daily, as they make my job and my life richer. They also provided thoughtful, helpful responses to the introduction and the sixth chapter of this book during departmental colloquia. Other colleagues and friends at PLU have made the Pacific Northwest feel more like home with each passing year. Thanks, too, to the many wonderful colleagues and friends in the Thompson Writing Program at Duke, especially Gretchen Case, Stephanie Jeffries, and Keith Wilhite, whose emails kept me writing during busy weeks.

Friendships have sustained me throughout the years I have written this book. I'm grateful for the companionship of Griff Gatewood, Evan Gurney, John Inazu, and Will Revere in Durham. John provided valuable feedback on the second chapter of this book. Brendan Pietsch offered incisive commentary on my writing and hilarity in equal measures. Jen Graber helped me survive the first few years of grad school. Tim Wardle accompanied me to many Duke basketball games and taught me a little about the New Testament. Steve Berry, Kate Blanchard, Sarah Ruble, and Kristi Upson-Saia made for wonderful writing company in the bowels of the Duke divinity school library. Brantley Gasaway has been a fabulous conversation partner and dear friend for years; his own work on the evangelical left and his enthusiasm helped me keep moving forward on this book. Kevin O'Brien, Matt Robbins-Ghormley, Jason Skipper, Mike Spivey, and Joel Zylstra have provided encouragement and good conversation during our runs and breakfast meetings around Tacoma. Dawson Bond, Mike O'Neill, and Shane Painter kept me rooted in worlds outside academia. I am thankful for all of you.

My final words of acknowledgment are for my family. My mother and father, Jim and Sally Dowland, inspired a love of learning and have never stopped encouraging me. They asked about my work (only occasionally voicing their concerns about when the book would be done) and helped me think through this material in many ways. My sister and her husband, Megan and Michael Leuzarder, are loyal and loving, and it's been a joy to watch them make the transition to parenthood. Last but not least, my wife Ami has been a constant support. She is a fantastic reader—the introduction to this book has benefited greatly from her advice—as well as a wonderful companion. I'm so lucky to spend each day with such a thoughtful, funny, smart, and caring partner. It's to Ami that I dedicate this book.